FROM MINOR TO MAJOR

Durham's first year in the Championship

FROM MINOR TO MAJOR

Durham's first year in the Championship

Simon Hughes

Hodder & Stoughton
LONDON SYDNEY AUCKLAND

British Library Cataloguing in Publication Data

Hughes, Simon
  From Minor to Major
  I. Title
  796.35806

  ISBN 0-340-58234-0

First published 1992
Copyright © 1992 Simon Hughes

Published by Hodder and Stoughton,
a division of Hodder and Stoughton Ltd,
Mill Road, Dunton Green, Sevenoaks, Kent TN13 2YA.
Editorial Office: 47 Bedford Square, London WC1B 3DP.

Photoset by Rowland Phototypesetting Ltd,
Bury St Edmunds, Suffolk

Printed in Great Britain by Hazells Ltd,
Member of BPCC Ltd, Aylesbury, Bucks.

Contents

Note on the illustrations

The photographs appear in two sections between pages 64 and 65, and between pages 128 and 129.

Many of the pictures were taken by the author, but he and the publishers would like to acknowledge those of Adam Scott (plates 9, 10, 14, 17, 18); Graham Morris (plates 11, 12, 19–25 inc., 30); and Robert Hallam (plate 29).

They would also like to acknowledge the cartoons by Macey, and thank Alec Spark for drawing the map on page 10.

Author's Acknowledgements

To my mother, Erica Hughes, for faithfully typing up the illegible manuscript; to Ion Trewin for his initial encouragement; to John Bright-Holmes for his painstaking and enthusiastic editing; to Robert Hallam, Graham Morris, David Munden, Adam Scott and Jan Traylen for their photographs; to Macey for his cartoons which first appeared in *The Independent*, and to 'Wottack' for all the statistics.

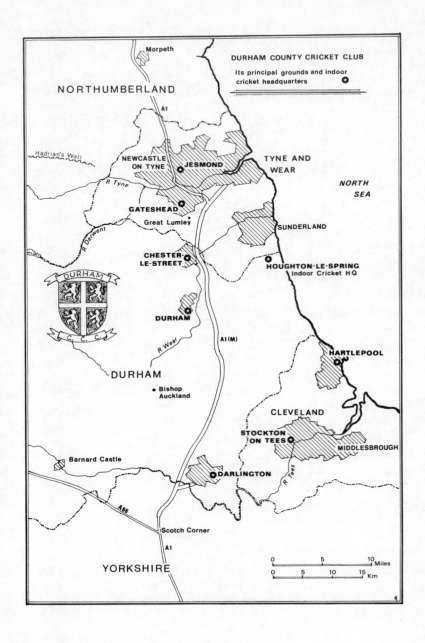

DURHAM COUNTY CRICKET CLUB

Its principal grounds and indoor cricket headquarters ⊗

NORTHUMBERLAND

Morpeth

A1

Hadrian's Wall

NEWCASTLE ON TYNE · JESMOND

R Tyne

TYNE AND WEAR

NORTH SEA

GATESHEAD

Great Lumley

SUNDERLAND

R Derwent

CHESTER-LE-STREET

HOUGHTON-LE-SPRING
Indoor Cricket HQ

DURHAM

DURHAM

R Wear

A1(M)

HARTLEPOOL

Bishop Auckland

CLEVELAND

STOCKTON ON TEES

MIDDLESBROUGH

Barnard Castle

R Tees

DARLINGTON

A66

Scotch Corner

A1

YORKSHIRE

| 0 | 5 | 10 Miles |
| 0 | 5 | 10 | 15 Km |

Chapter 1

Birth of a first-class county

On 19 April 1992, at the dramatic University Racecourse ground, Durham became a major county team. The event, a Sunday League match against Lancashire, was captured live on Sky Television. That day the captain, David Graveney's cricket bag contained:

1 polyarmoured bat, weight 2lb 10oz, slightly used
1 pair lightweight pads with Velcro buckles, new
2 pairs sausage-fingered gloves with built-in sweat bands, new
1 white helmet with metal grill visor
1 thigh pad with fibre inserts, and inside thigh pad
1 plastic box
1 chest pad and arm-guard
1 back corset
3 sweatshirts
Thermal underwear
3 pairs box briefs, 2 jock straps
1 can Ozone-friendly, deep heat spray
1 tube sun block factor 34
1 pair flip-flops
1 wrist strengthener
Sorbothane foot insoles
Three sweaters, 5 shirts with sponsor's logo on collar and chest (2 shortsleeved), 3 pairs of polyester drip-dry trousers
1 pair half-spiked, 1 pair full-spiked Reebok boots, 2 pairs training shoes

Back rub cream, spare spikes, bat tape
1 portable telephone

No wonder he's always prostrate on the physiotherapist's table having to lug that lot about.

Arriving at midday in a two-litre Audi provided by Minories Motors, Graveney wolfed down a salad lunch, signed a few special issue scorecards, then directed the team on to the outfield for limbering-up exercises led by Sheila Job, the club physiotherapist. These included neck rolls, hip swivels, thigh stretches and spine rotations. Then there was fielding practice – high catches, under-arm flicks, shies at the stumps, conducted under the furrowed brow of our Director of Cricket, Geoff Cook. Even Ian Botham put his back into it.

At 1.35 pm Graveney lost the toss and Lancashire's captain, Neil Fairbrother, asked Durham to bat first. Graveney had hoped to be able to send Lancashire in, knowing that their powerful batting line-up was better suited to chasing targets. But his quick pep talk in a cluttered dressing-room worked because Durham, after a slow start, rustled up a daunting 246 in their allotted 40 overs.

It was a pulsating match that went to the wire. The key players performed spectacular deeds. The Australian Dean Jones made a century, Botham took a flying catch, then ran-out Lancashire's last man with nine runs required. There were five balls left unused. I was as relieved as anyone for I was bowling the last over and would have been remembered for ever as the culprit if this momentous first game had been lost.

The last county to be admitted to first-class cricket was Glamorgan – seventy-one years earlier – sensibly delaying their entry until the weather had improved, in May 1921. It was a blissful summer's day as the captain, Norman Riches, walked the half-mile from his dental surgery to the ground, brandishing a long leather bag. In it was:
1 Gray's bat
1 pair skeleton leg-guards
1 pair open-palmed spiked gloves
1 thin vest

2 long-sleeved white shirts
1 woollen jumper
2 pairs cream britches, belted
1 pair calf leather, lace-up boots
1 county cap
1 cravat

The mercury tipped 66°F as Riches knocked up gently on the outfield half an hour before the start, then won the toss and took guard himself against the great Sussex pair of Maurice Tate and Arthur Gilligan. A crowd of around 5,000 in caps and tweed suits (four guineas each), some in shirt sleeves, applauded warmly as Riches and 'Tal' Whittington – the club secretary – put on 38 for the first wicket. After making 16, Riches mishit a ball from the England all-rounder Vallance Jupp, and was caught at mid-off. At lunch an hour later, over a light ale, he could ponder on what he had achieved.

It had not all been plain sailing, of course. At the end of the first world war, Glamorgan cricket was in tatters. Many of the pre-war squad who had appeared in the Minor Counties championship had retired or disappeared. William Edwards, a promising middle-order batsman, had been killed in Palestine. But there was an established fixture list and great enthusiasm from a public keen to watch cricket now that life was reverting to normal.

There were lots of people with time on their hands including two million unemployed (half ex-servicemen) and cricket was a good diversion from the silent cinema, attended by no less than twenty million people a week. Getting about was slow, with a speed limit of 20 mph and, even if you could afford £10 for a flight to Paris, it still took nearly three hours.

But by 1920, a good team had been assembled, though it was never the same from one match to the next. Most players had jobs to attend to, Riches himself had inherited his father's dental practice. But he had always dreamt of playing first-class cricket, and set about staking the county's claim for proper recognition. A 'friendly' against a visiting MCC team was obviously a crucial stepping stone, so a few useful outsiders were hurriedly drafted in. These included Colonel Arthur

O'Bree, reared in Poona, and Willie Gemmill, born in New Caledonia, so neither had much birthright to play for Glamorgan. No-one commented, and MCC were trounced by ten wickets.

Even more important was the backing of the local business community, something that also clinched Durham's election seventy years later. The Cardiff magnate, Sir Sydney Byass, pledged £1,000 over a ten year period, and there were other, smaller sums. The final piece in the jigsaw was the approval from the other first-class counties. Most readily agreed, though one or two had to be offered £200 bait. Finally, in early 1921, MCC gave Glamorgan the nod.

As the jubilant Durham players returned to the temporary refuge of the pavilion, having gained maximum points from their very first competitive match, two proud men were waiting for them. One was Geoff Cook who, as the Director of Cricket, had been saddled with the responsibility of assembling a team from the discarded components of first-class and Minor County cricket. He and the captain, David Graveney, had carefully recruited players with one eye on experience and ability, and another on age. Not too old to be a liability or too young to obstruct the progress of Durham's burgeoning youth. Graveney, the nephew of Tom, was a man universally liked and respected by all cricketers, and no stranger to new challenges having managed the controversial rebel tour of South Africa in 1989. If anyone could knead the various ingredients into a formidable creation, he could. Cook, originally from Middlesbrough, understood the mentality of the north-east and visualised the personalities who would quickly form allegiance in a new environment.

So there was Cook's old Northants opening partner, Wayne Larkins, to set things ablaze at the start of the innings; another ex-international, Paul Parker from Sussex, to solidify the batting effort; proven bowlers with a few wickets still up their sleeve, fringe players previously overshadowed by someone more illustrious. Thinking ahead, Cook had also enlisted the services of a sports psychologist to develop the players'

[14]

mental approach, to try to convert previous failure into future success.

The second man glowing with pride amidst the chaos of discarded pads and sweaters was the Chairman of Durham CCC, Don Robson. In Durham circles he is Mr Big. He owns property, services, sports shops. He is the leader of Durham County Council. He opens doors. He epitomises the Durham ethic that if you want something you don't give up until you get it. (For five hundred years the county of Durham had such independent power it was allowed to print its own money, proof of its strong self-identity.) Robson pleaded the county's case to cricket's hierarchy for two years until they lent him an ear.

He was told that Durham would have to satisfy certain conditions:

1. Provide decent facilities;
2. Guarantee to sustain the considerable expenses of running a first-class county, now around £1 million a year;
3. Undertake development of a brand new ground of international standard.

This last issue was the most contentious. While the site chosen was a large area of common land at Chester-le-Street, seven miles north of Durham, the development would obliterate a row of well-used soccer pitches and local objections had been raised. But Michael Heseltine, then the Secretary for the Environment, declared there was no need for a public enquiry, and the complaints subsided.

It will be a real coup for the area when it is finished in 1995, for Durham will then have a stylish multi-purpose cricket stadium complete with health club, banqueting and conference facilities, and later floodlights. It will cost £8 million but the aim is for it to become England's first modern Test arena which might also stage a match or two in the 1996 World Cup. We shall see.

One sultry March night in Sydney, Australia, South Africa and England were playing a World Cup semi-final that descended

[15]

into farce when a rain interruption and the bizarre bad weather rules meant that the Springboks had to make 22 runs off one ball. I was talking to a delirious South African in the Brewongle stand. 'Which name first springs to mind when you mention county cricket?' I asked. 'Ian Botham,' he replied. 'D'you know who he's playing for this season?' I continued. 'Oh, some team in the West Country.' 'Wrong, Durham.' 'But they're not a professional side,' he said, baffled. 'They are now,' I said.

The most extraordinary thing about Durham's new status is that a set-up so rigidly conservative as English county cricket should allow another club through its closely guarded door. But during a period when the game's administrators were nervously eyeing their bank balances, the north-east of England made them an offer they could not refuse. A successful Minor County side for some years, Durham scooped £1.4 million in sponsorship from sports-mad companies who regard association with a team or celebrated individual as the best exposure for their product. In addition, first-class cricket would immediately become accessible to a new potential audience of five million people.

This is where Ian Botham comes in. The major turnstile attraction in the game, he was disillusioned with travelling from his rural home in North Yorkshire to Worcester, then dragging his heels on to the county treadmill, playing often seven days a week. He needed a break, a new challenge. Durham, aware of the commercial potential of his name in the line-up, negotiated a six-figure contract, the largest in the history of the game.

Aside from the championship of three- and four-day matches, county cricket comprises three major limited-overs competitions. It is something of a five-month endurance test for the twenty or so professionals employed by each county and has been ever since the introduction of the Sunday League in 1969.

CHRONOLOGY

1873:   County Championship starts, comprising Derbyshire, Gloucestershire, Kent, Lancashire, Middlesex, Notts, Surrey, Sussex and Yorkshire.

1891:   Somerset replaces Derbyshire who won only one match in four years.

1895:   Essex, Hampshire, Leicestershire, and Warwickshire join. Derbyshire rejoins. Minor Counties Cricket Association formed, Durham a founder member.

1899:   Worcestershire added to County Championship.

1905:   Northamptonshire joins.

1921:   Glamorgan enters.

1960–62: Counties play 32 three-day championship matches each.

1963:   Gillette Cup introduced (now NatWest Trophy).

1969:   Sunday League begins.

1972:   Introduction of Benson & Hedges Cup.

1977:   Championship reduced to 22 matches per county.

1992:   Durham becomes a first-class county.

Despite the seasonal ordeal, county cricket attracts the best cricketers in the world. Viv Richards is playing out his career with Glamorgan, the 6ft 7in. West Indian demon Curtly Ambrose is pulling on a Northants sweater for the third time in as many years, and the eighteen-year-old Indian maestro Sachin Tendulkar has become Yorkshire's very first overseas player. Where once you looked on several counties as easy prey, these days there are no pushovers.

Botham, meanwhile, would happily admit his pomp is past, he cannot win matches on his own. To compete, Durham had to replace the honest part-timers who had held the fort, though two of them, a supplier of supermarket fittings, Andrew Fothergill, and a 'Portakabin' salesman, John Glendenen, were retained. Fortunately there are always a few old lags on the county circuit tired of their surroundings but with valuable expertise and knowledge to pass on, and Durham swooped. At one stage during the 1991 season almost every cricketer over thirty was rumoured to be a target, and when all the county secretaries met in the autumn to discuss ways of attracting new support, the following exchange took place:

Mike Gear (Durham): 'Well, we're trying to lure more OAP's and disabled people.'

Peter Edwards (Essex): 'Yes, we know about the team, Mike. What about the spectators?'

Another feather in Durham's cap was the recruitment of the dazzling Australian batsman, Dean Jones. He was an irresistible force in his country's charge through the late 1980s, and at the peak of his career. The Australian Board, worried at the debilitating effect an English season would have on one of their most valued players, tried to dissuade him, but he decided to come.

Professional sportsmen are creatures of habit. They moan if they are forced to change in an unfamiliar corner. As a newcomer to the Middlesex dressing-room in 1980, I hung my civvies on an available hook only for them to be forcibly removed by a senior player pulling rank. 'You've got to be someone before you change there, son,' he said. So how would all these new players from varying backgrounds and circumstances blend together? What would they have in common? The answer is rejuvenation. After five or ten years in one place they were being taken for granted. Now they had a role to play and fresh responsibilities.

The salesman, Glendenen, had never played a four-day game before; the fitter, Fothergill, a wicketkeeper, had no idea where to stand to various bowlers; specialist slip fielders had to be identified. I would be opening the attack for the first time in a few years – at my previous club I only touched a new ball when I threw it in from third-man. A pre-season trip to Zimbabwe had helped develop the dressing-room badinage, so prevalent among mature teams. There, players' eccentricities began to be exposed – the worriers, the superstitious, the greedy, the unpunctual. In the unsympathetic realm of professional cricket where you eat, sleep and burp together, every quirk is scrutinised; in a poky pavilion occupied by eleven men for ten hours each day of summer, there are no hiding places.

The focal point of Durham County Cricket Club is the magnificent Racecourse ground which belongs to the university. I know it well, having been an undergraduate there in the early 1980s. The majestic twin towers of Durham Cathedral loom above as a reminder that the university was once exclusively ecclesiastical, and even banned racing from its grounds after 1887.

Cricket has been played on the Racecourse for 149 years, but the contrast between appearing in a professional game here and at Lord's, my illustrious previous home, is substantial. At the Marylebone Cricket Club, spectators are kept firmly behind the fence and women are a sub-species, not allowed in the pavilion except at limited times. My mother was once ordered off the pavilion steps, where she was sheltering from heavy rain, by an MCC steward after a Benson & Hedges final.

At Durham people overflow on to the grass and examine the dusty battle zone between the creases, and children idly flap the tip-up seats or chase each other down the verge. While the Durham Light Infantry beat the Retreat, small boys are able to catch their heroes as they leave and get them to pose for photographs. Meanwhile the energetic Durham ground staff pack up advertising hoardings and portable toilets for transfer to the next home game at one of seven grounds around the county.

At first I had reservations about playing for a new county. When I was contacted the previous October I ummed and ahhed, pondering the travelling and upheaval involved, the effect of another season on fragile knee joints, the damp, insipid northern pitches. But at least I knew from my college days that Durham was not, contrary to popular south-east opinion, a region of slag heaps on the edge of the Arctic Circle where men wore wide ties and tattoos, ate pease pudding for tea and shunned anyone who came from beyond Scotch Corner.

There were three hundred active collieries in County Durham in 1945. Now there are four. The public, blighted by twenty years of unemployment, are sports addicts. Football clubs are supported fanatically despite indifferent league results; everywhere there are impromptu matches on village commons; in summer you can't travel far without encountering a 20-over evening thrash. In fact the Durham Cricket Association boasts 114 affiliated clubs – almost twice as many as Northants or Leicester.

Durham CCC is used to hitting the headlines. In 1973 it became the first Minor County to defeat first-class opposition, beating a strong Yorkshire side in a tense Gillette Cup tie. To prove that was no fluke it happened again in 1986. This time Derbyshire was the victim. These victories gave the county important credibility. Besides that, Durham won the Minor Counties championship nine times outright, and finished top of its section almost every year.

Dynamic overseas all-rounders like Lance Cairns and Wasim Raja took up the cudgels and good crowds were attracted for two-day games played usually on Sundays and Mondays. Many well-known test players, Colin Milburn and Peter Willey for example, had honed their skills in north-east leagues, adding to the region's prowess. The potential for progress was blindingly obvious and a letter was sent to Lord's on 5 March 1989 from the Durham committee, announcing that an application to join the first-class circuit was on its way. The Test and County Cricket Board officially approved the proposal in December 1990.

The extent of regional interest in the new adventure was emphasised by eight-page pull-outs in local newspapers, grounds crawling with TV crews, 5,500 members' subscriptions of £60 each received before the season began. The county has a vast hinterland, stretching from Middlesbrough to Sunderland and from the North Sea coast right across the moors to Cumbria. That, as much as anything, was enough to get the key to the first-class door.

The team's problem, then, will not be luring spectators to the grounds but finding their own way to them. Within a complex network of roads there is every prospect of players being lost en route to one of the less familiar venues – Stockton, Hartlepool or Gateshead Fell. Matches will be flung to the far corners of the county until the new ground is finished, which means that the massed cricket enthusiasts of Tyne, Wear and Tees will not now have a two-hour road journey to see top-class competition.

The advent of Durham County Cricket Club will provide the man in the street with new and exciting summer diversions, the tramelled professional player with fresh aspirations, and local colts with the channels to become thoroughbreds.

Chapter 2

Spring chickens

Wednesday 8 April

My first night of the season in Durham was spent on the floor. The county had managed to acquire two modern flats on a housing estate near Chester-le-Street, but they forgot to furnish them. There was no kettle either, nor any cups. Still, at least it wasn't minus 25° outside, as it was in 1982, the last time I was here in winter.

The team assembled at ten o'clock. Beneath the fanfares of Durham's first official day together – the reporters, the camera crews, the swanky new kit – the bare fact is that we're in a dingy indoor centre on an industrial estate by the A167 trunk road, the sort of location where you would usually find a B&Q. And I don't know where I'm sleeping tonight.

Quickly into action. Geoff Cook, the 'Director', outlines the programme. Warm-ups, stretch tests, strength monitoring, sprint endurance. Oh yes, and a bit of cricket practice. Still in the process of shaking hands and exchanging news we are hustled out of the dressing-room, though Wayne Larkins hangs back to draw on the end of a cigarette.

The bleep test is the worst. Sprinting from one side of the hall to the other between accelerating electronic pulses until you drop. 'Eeee, we're cricketers, not greyhounds,' pleads a voice. Three of the older members – Paul Parker, Andy Fothergill, our wicketkeeper, and I – last longest.

At lunch, of boiled fish and tatties, the Australian Dean

Jones arrives straight from his 27-hour Qantas flight from Melbourne. His memory is tested as he's taken round the team, and given a copy of the *Cricketer's Who's Who*. Then it's on with the pads. 'I just love cricket,' he enthuses. He probably didn't love traipsing round the shops afterwards, though, to buy a cot for his baby.

Meanwhile there are pressmen wanting interviews. We were all asked, of course, why we joined Durham. Here are my reasons: 1. Wanting to be involved at the outset of a new venture – for example, I wrote for *The Independent* in its first week of existence. 2. I spent three years at Durham University and they were the happiest of my life so far. 3. I will have an outlet for my ideas and a chance to influence strategy which I never had in my previous career at Middlesex. They considered me too erratic, mainly because I used to spill full cups of tea into people's bags.

The players pose politely for pictures, repeat themselves to different reporters. 'Where's Botham?' asks one. To be honest the last I heard of him he was on safari in Cape Town. Then it's back to our neat, humble abode to assemble our MFI furniture. Surely the latest signings for the New York Yankees aren't treated like this?

Thursday 9 April

'It's the first Major of the season.' The BBC's Tony Adamson was actually talking about The Masters in Augusta, Georgia, which begins today, but I thought at first he was casting aspersions on the General Election. Apparently there are a record number of candidates – 2,925 – which has only confused the issue more than usual and all the polls are predicting a hung parliament. I won't be influencing the outcome anyway as I'm stuck up a creek without a paddle – that's what it feels like tucked away in the ex-mining village of Great Lumley. I haven't organised a postal vote, but I wouldn't know whom to go for even if I had.

Before positioning ourselves in front of the BBC election

coverage, there was the small matter of some outdoor net practice. How Jones (who has quickly become the Dean of Durham) must have felt coming straight from a Sheffield Shield match at the Melbourne Cricket Ground to bat on a pudding at East Boldon CC surrounded by cows grazing on reclaimed coal slurry, is anyone's guess, but he acquitted himself well as the ball popped and stopped. He has boundless energy, infectious enthusiasm and the quickest turn for two in the business. He immediately emphasised his commitment by requesting a special Durham badge to stick on his helmet.

Eventually went to bed at 1.30 am with the score Blues 67, Reds 102, Yellows 3. Crucially, though, Labour had failed to take many of the marginals and the average swing to them was not enough. Sunderland South – the constituency in which we practised today – was the first result declared (clearly they're better at counting than they are at preparing wickets) and the whole of Co. Durham went for Neil Kinnock.

Friday 10 April

Tories have a majority of twenty, and most of the nation's press fawning around them, I should think. They're not hasselling us today anyway. Gradually players are getting to know each other, though they're treading warily, and there's still the odd accent to decipher. Consider the word 'bun' for instance. Simon Brown (born in Sunderland) pronounces it 'bon'. David Graveney (ex-Glos) 'burrrn'. Paul Parker, a Cambridge University graduate, 'barn'. The squad of twenty-three consists of six players born in Durham, but seventeen from north of Watford Gap. Two have degrees.

I'm the only official Londoner and I've got some work to do to take wickets and suppress my city laissez-faire attitude. It's no good teaching these youngsters bad, casual habits. Added to that, I've got to rediscover my out-swinger if I'm to make an impression as an opening bowler. There's no-one else at this stage. This swing phenomenon has never been adequately explained. There was some theory once aired that it was related

[24]

to wind-speed times, pressure over altitude, but that's got to be claptrap. Chris Old, our part-time bowling coach, can't explain it and he's got a story for everything. 'I sneezed this morning and I've gone in the neck,' he once told the selectors matter-of-factly, and was given the weekend off.

The Director, Geoff Cook, roamed about inspecting, advising, talking on his cellphone, which looked incongruous against a backdrop of Boldon colliery. At the moment he's as placid as his batting used to be (last night at a cricket forum in South Shields he fielded ignorant questions like, 'Eee, why are England allowed to pick all these bloody foreigners?' with dignified patience). If things go awry he looks a potential dummy spitter.

Saturday 11 April

The IRA are at it again – deliberately bombing the North Circular Road so I couldn't get to Chelmsford in time. We were due there for a practice match against Essex, although the manner in which these games are played, you'd hardly call them practice. Essex, last year's county champions, fielded a full team and Durham were severely tested, which was important. It gave the hierarchy a chance to assess everyone under pressure, and if we had won it would have provided an early morale boost. Unfortunately Essex's young batsman Nicholas Knight deposited my slower ball into the crowd in the last over, and that was that.

The players are gradually feeling more comfortable with each other. Nicknames are emerging. There's Chuck (Phil Berry), Chubby (Simon Brown) and Deano (Dean Jones). The latter has fitted in brilliantly, bursts with enthusiasm, cajoles the bowlers and itches to score runs. He has also got to know other players more quickly than I have. It's embarrassing when you're shouting at third-man to move a bit wider and you're not sure of his name.

Gooch got nought but was quite chatty afterwards. 'Got your sponsored thermals ready for Durham?' he said squeakily.

Which is a point. County matches are being played closer to the Arctic than ever before, so I suppose the team has been assembled with one eye on ability and attitude, and another on potential corpulence (for insulation). There is a new rule in first-class matches this year, which forbids batsmen to change their gloves except during official breaks in play. What we, shivering in Durham, would like to know is, does this apply to fieldsmen as well?

Sunday 12 April

Chelmsford again. We didn't compete today. Batting OK, bowling ordinary, fielding lethargic. Graveney pointed out the facts in a blunt post-mortem.

Still, Essex are a pretty good unit, exhibiting the sort of ruthless professionalism that some of our players have not encountered before. Andy Fothergill, for instance, has sold supermarket fixtures and fittings for the last ten years, so is experiencing a new lease of life – 'Wy aye, it's greet,' he trilled, 'and I can still go back to my old job in the winter'. John Glendenen probably won't want to, though. He used to sell Portakabins and I think finds making runs a lot easier, so long as he can tone down his over-confidence. We'll see.

Monday 13 April

The official opening of the domestic season (England's 'A' team v. Champion County at Lord's) was preceded by the usual Radio 4 announcement at 8.30 am: 'There will be gales today, with squally showers. It will feel rather cold.'

We have a day off and, bearing in mind the inclement weather, it seems a good time to select a rugby XV from our assembled ranks. The pack weighs in at 122 stone, but lacks something in terms of mobility.

Have already noticed how Durham evenings are a good deal lighter than in the south, which explains why they can occasionally start a 20-over club match at 7 pm and still get it finished. I don't think we'll be able to discard the long-sleeved sweater up here very often, though.

Tuesday 14 April – Oxford University v. Durham
Three-day first-class friendly match

Today marks our official entry into first-class cricket, with a testing match against Oxford University. (Which reminds me – when I went to take some low-angled photos of the University Boat Race near Barnes Bridge last week, I fell in. If it hadn't been for a group of rescuing students, I'd probably still be there.)

There was substantial media interest. Whenever Patrick Eagar turns up with his bazooka-like lenses, you know there must be something significant going on. David Graveney coaxed us all, minus Botham who was still in the southern hemisphere, out into the chill for looseners and fielding practice.

Then, while everyone groaned at their early-season stiffness, he announced the team, though many of his words were blown out of earshot by a stiff westerly. I was in; then, after twinging a leg muscle in fielding practice, I wasn't. The leg-warmers I had donned – of the type used by the Pakistan army camped up the Khyber Pass – had obviously been inadequate.

At 11 am Graveney lost the toss, which was filmed by Tyne-Tees TV and a posse of national photographers, but the Oxford captain, an Australian, sportingly invited Durham to bat, which was a major relief bearing in mind the hostile weather. 'Does it get any colder than this?' asked Dean Jones, the Australian, huddled in front of the pavilion in three sweaters and a track suit. 'Guess the best way to keep warm is to get out there and smack a ton.' He had a rather long wait though. The Durham openers, Parker and Glendenen, eased the student bowling around and at lunch the score was 119–0. Jones, itching to play his first innings in County Cricket, had to take out his frustration on a large piece of braised steak instead.

Afterwards the heavens opened, and play was called off for the day.

Wednesday, Thursday, 15, 16 April – Oxford University v. Durham
Second and third days

Driving across the Chilterns from London this morning I went through snow and sleet. It was always going to be a day more for perusing the honours boards in the pavilion than for any outdoor activities. The 1899 team included B. J. T. Bosanquet – the man who invented the googly but is more widely known perhaps for having a grandson, Reggie, who read the news on television. C. B. Fry got a blue in 1893. He was an amazing individual who scored Test centuries, held the world long-jump record for twenty-one years, played Association Football for England, never mind gaining a distinction in Classics, and was offered the Throne of Albania. But there were two qualifications: he had to be an English gentleman, and have an income of £10,000 a year. He passed only the first. All related in his autobiography *Life Worth Living*.

Sheila, the physio, took us all to one side after lunch announcing she was going to talk about drugs. 'What, have you got some?' said Chris Scott, our wicketkeeper, enthusiastically. Physios are such a key part of the game these days. Harking back to the early 1980s, we had the partially blind Johnny Miller at Middlesex. He had difficulty recognising people but somehow located even the subtlest injuries. He also had trouble finding his way on to the field, once examining a startled wicketkeeper while an injured player lay prostrate on the ground. Now at Durham we have someone who joins in with everything (except the showers, thankfully) and can read the entrails immediately. Prevention not cure is the motto.

Glendenen and Parker duly completed their centuries. Which reminds me of two silly misquotes in Monday's paper: 'Liverpool Julie completed their victory', and 'Allen scored with a rocket of shit from 25 years'.

Glendenen was the first to three figures and thus becomes the first Durham centurion. He is also the only Durham player who used to sell Portakabins and has a girlfriend called Pam to make a hundred on debut.

The only activity I had all day was a bat on an artificial wicket, where John Wood, our strapping paceman, hit me on the head. Cricket vernacular has various alternatives to describe blows to the cranium – pinned, sconned or crusted are three of the better ones.

At 286–2, we declared, to give the bowlers a run-out in arctic conditions before the five-hour drive to Durham.

Friday 17 April

Good Friday. Press Day. Botham turns up. I arrived by black taxi from the station at 10.30 to see the great man emerge from the pavilion. 'You've got that all the way from London?' was his opening salvo. 'Yep, I'm handing the bill to the club, £223.50 plus a tenner tip,' I replied. 'How was your holiday?' 'Oh, superb. Went to various Game reserves in the Northern Transvaal. I could have stayed, but y'know, duty calls.'

Not for long though – the weather closed in and we retired to the Dun Cow for a few pints of Castle Eden. With Botham and Jones round the table in the dimly lit bar, young players' apprehensions soon disappeared. Jones revealed his knowledge of the deaf and dumb alphabet and a previous job as a prison detective; Botham joked about the World Cup (though he didn't mention walking out of the pre-final dinner), and discussed fishing. 'I've got a lake at my place, but I can hardly catch fish from there. I feed them every day so it wouldn't be difficult. I could virtually scoop them out with my hands.'

It's funny to think that these two were locked in mortal combat at the Sydney Cricket Ground a month ago. Now the mere effect of wearing a yellow cross and blue star on their sweaters has united their cause and encouraged them to trudge round the golf course together. Such is the camaraderie of cricket. Their presence, though, cannot conceal our fragility in bowling. I really think we will struggle to defend even quite large totals and, as the person most likely to have to stem the flow, I feel under pressure.

Photocall very slick, and certainly the best attended I've ever experienced. But then Durham is such a photogenic place. The inevitable Botham press-conference afterwards, with his son Liam at his side. His ambition, he says, is to play in a county side with his son. Certainly fits into a likely script. Botham Act III Scene 5, enter Liam stage left could be the 1996 scenario.

Chicken and leek pie in the Old England, then to bed with the New Geordie Bible at 11.30. A bad pitch is 'a bloody shocker', an idiot is a 'hawa', a flat throw is a 'hoi' or a 'hoss', and spectators 'gurn' rather than grimace when a wicket falls.

Saturday 18 April

Morning net which became like the OK Corral with Botham batting, balls flying everywhere, smote out of sight. The river was within easy range. Brief discussion afterwards about to-morrow's first Sunday League match (v. Lancashire). We hope to bat second, and are all to turn up in our new blazers. No jeans, worse luck. I think a pair of good clean jeans looks as smart as anything. Still, our new gear is good quality, and looks striking. A yellow cross on a blue shield, and the distinctive blue star of Scottish and Newcastle Breweries. I don't much care for their beer, though.

There are long periods of inactivity during cricket seasons, usually filled by benefit matches. It's a bit early for anyone to have a benefit in our set-up, so Phil Bainbridge and I went off to find a golf course. The best we could do was the Roseberry Grange on a bleak hill near Stanley. The Roseberrys' influence is everywhere. Matt Roseberry (father of Mike), one of the six directors of the club, owns half the hotels and pubs in Durham, and Mike has let his luxury house to Dean Jones and family for the summer.

I don't think we'll be going back to the Roseberry Grange though. It's a bit like playing golf on a hilly Wormwood Scrubs.

Sunday 19 April – Durham v. Lancashire
Sunday League match at the Racecourse

Easter Sunday. A glorious day. As a chaser to the main fare, I visited the cathedral for Matins. I have always enjoyed church music; Paul Parker obviously felt the same as he turned up too. Service drab and disappointing after a bright start. Sermon all about tombs, didn't even mention cricket!

At 12 noon the Racecourse ground was already filling up. Marquees emblazoned with the coat-of-arms and 'First-Class Durham', bulging with excited sponsors and ex-players. Long queues buying commemorative scorecards and blocking the Lancashire coach's entry, done-up Rothman's girls giving away cigarettes (eagerly sampled by Larkins), players having to trample in each other's bags to get across the poky changing rooms (the same ones we used ten years earlier for University matches). I felt considerable apprehension but didn't show it. Crucial to make a good start and generate credibility.

A buffet lunch of cold ham and pork helped to settle the butterflies before looseners at 1 pm. David Graveney has sensibly settled on an hour before the start as the time to report. Most county teams are obliged to arrive much earlier, then just sit around doing crosswords or reading porn, which seems a bit pointless. Inevitably the cameras followed our routine but the lenses seemed to point at only one person, which is ironic since his old back doesn't permit him to do half the exercises.

Off the field the Battle of Portaloo had already started. With only six conveniences for a potential 6,000 crowd you needed to know you wanted a pee about half an hour before you actually did. Then Graveney lost the toss, and predictably we were inserted. Lancashire always want to chase a target. So, unfortunately, did we.

There was no team talk; mainly because we couldn't all fit into the dressing-room at the same time. At 2.01 umpires Plews

[31]

and Whitehead strode out, followed by Fairbrother and Lancashire. Then at 2.03, to raucous cheers, Botham and Larkins emerged in white helmets, and 1,000 cameras clicked. When Botham blocked the first ball from Paul Allott, formerly of Durham University, they clicked again. I stood on top of the Sky commentary box where Bob Willis and David Lloyd were already rambling away.

The wicket played deadly slow. Or was Allott just getting old? No, even DeFreitas looked a plodder. It didn't suit Botham who, after one majestic lofted drive, charged Allott and was stumped by a fumbling Hegg. Enter Dean Jones to much anticipation from the picnickers on the bank and the multitude outside the ground on walls and slopes, craning their necks over the temporary sacking fences.

He did not disappoint them. Profiting from the very regularity of the Lancashire attack he made good use of the short boundary, lobbing four sixes on to the bank where students used to lounge. When Parker joined him it became virtually tip-and-run, and Lancashire gave up saving singles. I expected to find two channels either side of the strip that marked their quickstep. Jones brought up his hundred off only 80 balls and punched the air joyfully, before rifling DeFreitas' last ball, a full toss, into mid-wicket's hands. 'Welcome back to the Sunday circus,' the England bowler said glumly as his figures of 8 overs for 53 were read out. 246–4 was a brilliant start.

There was obviously going to be carnage when we fielded, and some of the bowling was nervous. Steve McEwan began with two wides and a beamer, then lured Atherton into a leading edge which I caught out of the sun. The roar was tumultuous. The various Sunderland supporters, decked in the familiar red and white stripes, yelled their approval. Fowler struck a few fours but then I got him in my first over, clinging on to an attempted pull from a ball which kept low. 'Bounced another one out, Yoz,' said Beefy. (I'm surprised they call him Beefy now, Tubby might be better.) The crucial wicket came next ball. Fairbrother sliced McEwan, Botham dived to his right and held a flying catch. (I'll take that 'Tubby' back.) The team was delirious, so were the supporters. Even though

Lancashire had brought a thousand, everyone seemed to be behind us. 52–4.

Watkinson and Speak rebuilt but when both were out they needed 10 runs an over. Then 11, then 12. De Freitas came in at no. 8 to play an astonishing innings: 0, 1, 1, 1, 4, 4, 6, 4, 6, 6, W. 33 off 11 balls. He was gliding Phil Bainbridge's yorker past a non-existent third-man, smiting leg-stump half-volleys from Simon Brown over cover for six. If he'd lasted another four balls, the match would have been over.

22 needed off 2 overs, 2 wickets left. Hegg hit an enormous six, then Allott skied to Parker at long-on, last ball. 10 off 1, 1 wicket left, me bowling. 'Come on, Durham,' people bellowed, many dressed in old-fashioned Sunday best.

I raised my eyes to the heavens in mock despair, having seen this situation rather often before. On one famous occasion, which people often remind me of, Warwickshire needed 10 runs off the last over of the NatWest Final, and Neil Smith hit my slower ball into the Nursery End seats. They've demolished the stand now.

Now my opponent was the Lancashire no. 11, the New Zealander Danny Morrison. We knew we had to keep him on strike, leaving Hegg on hot bricks at the other end. The field closed in, though deep square-leg and long-on were kept out. Fate made me bowl a length ball on leg stump; fate made Morrison push it towards Botham at mid-wicket, and set off. Immortality made Durham's most celebrated acquisition hurtle in, throw under-arm in mid-air and hit the off-stump, with Hegg a foot short. I'll definitely take 'Tubby' back! It was pure, spur-of-the-moment brilliance, and it won the match by 9 runs. 'All part of having a good scriptwriter,' he boasted afterwards.

If we don't win another, we have won the faith of supporters, sponsors and critics and, most importantly, of each other. Even Geoff Cook showed a glimpse of satisfaction. 'Well done, lads,' he said, betraying a slight smile. 'You kept it interesting, though.' Bloody Yorkshiremen.

Stayed at a village pub in High Shincliffe until 4 am surrounded by a throng of our new supporters including three self-ordained as Cody, The Fatman, and The Legion of Doom.

[33]

SCORES: Durham 246 for 4 (Jones 114, Larkins 59); Lancashire 237 (Speak 58, McEwan 3/35, Brown 3/32). Durham won by 9 runs. For full score card, see Appendix.

Tuesday 21 April – Durham v. Glamorgan
Benson & Hedges Cup match at the Racecourse

People like Botham and Viv Richards have this immense aura. Others, I think, feel inadequate in comparison. They are great friends more out of mutual respect than from any emotional bond. They met over early elevenses – the bar at the Racecourse becomes temporarily converted into a dining area for the first few hours of a game.

'Hi ya, Beefy brother, what's 'appenin'?' Richards greeted, complete with diamond stud earring.

'OK, Smokin', OK,' Botham grunted back and slapped him cheerily.

They encountered each other again on the field in front of a fair-sized crowd. Viv urging his team on from mid-wicket – 'Come on now, Watki, donledemoffdehook'; Botham rebuilding Durham's innings from 18–3 after a fine opening spell from Steve Watkin. Botham played very responsibly, keeping his big shots under wraps until much later, the sort of self-denial you thought he wasn't really capable of. Eventually he launched one into orbit, but unfortunately it returned to earth at roughly the same place it had left. Underneath it was, of course, Viv Richards.

Botham's rescue act didn't finish there. Bowling into a draught coming from over the castle, he dismissed Maynard with a regulation half-volley and, five balls later, came a piece of pure inspiration. Richards, plunging his left foot across in familiar fashion, played too early, and the ball lolled up off the leading edge. Bowling at such a leisurely pace doesn't require a follow-through and Botham easily sprang to his right, dived full-length and clutched the ball one-handed an inch from the ground. It was a motion more typical of a seven-stone Russian gymnast than a seventeen-stone northern hulk. The whole

[34]

ground erupted, and Richards trudged off, the only man in the place showing no emotion. I was particularly relieved – I have never enjoyed bowling to either Maynard or Richards, and now that Glamorgan were 8–3 (the other man out was Hugh Morris), I wouldn't have to.

From this position we should have won. Our bowling was tight, but our fielding let us down. Twice John Glendenen dropped Chris Cowdrey – looking incongruous with the Welsh daffodil on his sweater (he is on a one-year contract to play limited-overs matches) – and he fiddled them close to victory with a typical mixture of experience, improvisation and slices of luck. Eventually I got him, but by then they needed 12 off three overs. Colin Metson, the Glamorgan keeper – like me, playing in full view of his old college, St Hild and St Bede – was in at the end to supervise victory.

Had a pint of Castle Eden with him in our old stamping ground, the Dun Cow, afterwards; Botham and Richards said they'd join us but disappeared into a back room of the pavilion, and locked the door. What were they doing? Your guess is as good as mine.

23 April – Reflections

There is something unique about Durham. As if it is in a time warp. The majestic cathedral that Sir Walter Scott described as 'Half church of God, half castle 'gainst the Scot' looms up over the town dwarfing the medieval castle. The Wear flows below Old Elvet bridge beneath which gawky undergraduates slew punts against the tide. In town packs of youths with earrings loiter or play football in the park, out-of-the-way pubs still have lock-ins till all hours. Inside the ground spectators sit quietly dressed in collar and tie, players wear old-fashioned caps. The Director says sunhats are *out*. He's quite a disciplinarian, I reckon.

There is nothing backward about the cricket set-up, though. There are no complaints – from the press, the public, or the players – despite their lack of furniture. It appears that, apart from the usual rigours of the season, there will be no excessive demands on them. Three weeks of pre-season masochism was not deemed necessary, we are required to report only one hour before a match rather than turn up at 9 am idly to complete crosswords, and naughty-boy nets (those detentions the day after a bad performance) are a thing of the past.

It is petty routine that puts players' backs up. We are not at school now and people respond to being treated like adults, none more so than Ian Botham. If he finds the best way to loosen up his back is to wallow in the bath at 10.15 then that's up to him. His mere presence on the field is enough to reassure colleagues and make the opposition jittery. Even his physical size at extra-cover is quite imposing, yet he lacks nothing in mobility – that last ball run-out against Lancs was quicksilver. 'Yeah, Beefy's been practising the under-arm flick at the stumps all week,' Dean Jones told a gullible journalist.

Being in the company of these two great cricketers gives a psychological boost to the rest. It makes us raise our game a degree, not wanting to look inadequate in comparison. Although a Botham congratulatory slap on the back can be a severe experience, it is infinitely preferable to the prospect of playing against him. His bowling seems to have an almost hypnotic effect on opponents, trapping them with ordinary balls, enticing mishits. He will bowl at anyone, knowing that they are likely to be far more nervous than he is. His growling lbw appeal – a mixture of aggression and slight surprise – has won over many a wavering umpire.

The team, a magimix of ingredients, is blending together well. It has to, the dressing-room is minute. It is good to have several strong characters complementing each other, rather than only one. Not the least of these is David Graveney. He may have resembled a traffic cop in the field, getting the speed merchants in the right places – Paul Parker fields long-on at both ends – but he has the confidence and experience to follow an idea through; he is not captaining by committee. When you're in charge, being 6ft 6in. tall is no bad thing, either.

Getting to know team members' habits takes time, of course. Parker likes a rigorous pre-match net, Larkins prefers to rock up at ten past ten for a quiet smoke. Jones fidgets and practises on-drives before going in to bat, Graveney strides up and down nervously wringing his hands. I am perpetually late. The wicketkeeper, Andy Fothergill, is unsure how far back to stand to Botham's bowling. It is immaterial anyway as the ball doesn't pass the bat much.

The supporters are lapping it up. Sunday's atmosphere was reminiscent of a Cup Final, there was pride and credibility at stake, never mind two points. With five and a half thousand members already signed up there was a queue a hundred yards long for commemorative scorecards. Botham was cheered every time he touched the ball, 'Boot, we've coom to see you *all*,' said an elderly member in mitigation. With cricket flung to seven grounds around the county it feels like we're going to see *them*.

Chapter 3

Honeymoon period

Saturday 25 April – Durham v. Leicestershire
First Championship, four-day match at Durham University

If you were anyone in the cricket hierarchy you were here at Durham University today. TCCB, MCC, ICC, they were all sipping g&t's in the marquees, presumably on a freebie. Graveney won an important toss – the wicket looked as if it would turn later.

We played shots that implied we had just spent a week practising in Perth. The guiltiest party was Jones, who drove on the up and lobbed tamely to cover. 'Oh gawd, I can't bat on these puddin's,' he said, drop-kicking his bat into the corner. I have chosen the wrong dressing-room here – Botham and Larkins are smoking like chimneys, Jones has excess frustrated energy, and I'm next to the Pit Bull (alias Darren Blenkiron) who keeps trying to borrow my mobile phone. Which reminds me. I overheard Botham talking on his this morning.

'Hi, it's Ian Botham here, luv. Can you tell me when my car phone will be installed?'

'Certainly, sir, can you tell me how you settle your account?'

'Er, I don't pay the bill, luv, you pay me.'

The pros of being a superstar, though, are somewhat offset by the cons. When he was out for 12, he was forced to remain in the confines of the dressing-room, unable to venture outside because of the number of people who constantly pester him. As he's not the greatest cricket-watcher, he examines every newspaper in an unsuccessful attempt to stave off tedium. He also invents nicknames, and now, inspired by Phil Bainbridge, he calls me Pluto; says I'm on another planet. I do dream a bit, but I'm concentrating really.

We were bowled out for a palpably inadequate 164 – although Botham conjured up two Leicester wickets with the new ball before the close.

Note: Cricket weirdos – the ones in parkas and black training shoes, carrying folding chairs and tupperware – conspicuous by their absence.

Sunday 26 April – Durham v. Leicestershire
Sunday League match at Gateshead Fell

A scratchy ground surrounded by 1930s terraces with nothing much in the way of facilities. In fact only the regulation burger van if you wanted solids. Fortunately the catering for sponsors and players excellent, so heaped a plate with some goodies and hid them under my car till the intended recipients (my parents) had arrived.

Hills attract wind, and Gateshead Fell is no exception. It's not too bad running into a gale to bowl. The worst bit is knowing that the batsman is hitting the ball back with an additional 50 knots. Justin Benson used this scenario to great effect while blasting Leicester to 50–0 off five overs. At which point, Graveney summoned me to bowl – into the wind. I must admit I was a trifle apprehensive – especially having to tack in to bowl off a short run – but after two overs of attempted haymakers, Benson obligingly chipped my slower ball to long-on.

I was immediately withdrawn, and had to bowl my last six overs with Leicester requiring about 9 an over. They alternately lost balls and wickets, until 18 needed off Botham's final over proved too much.

We had the two locals, Glendenen and Fothergill, to thank for making 232 – scampering 8 an over for the last ten overs. It's all happening when Fothergill is at the wicket – false starts, stops, shouts and slices. If he carries on in this stressful vein, he won't live to be forty.

Various wives and girlfriends sat shivering under blankets, but seemed to get on rather well. It's always difficult for them as they are thrown together with nothing in common but their husband's job. Some have had to uproot. Wayne Larkins' Debbie has moved up from Taunton, Dean and Jane Jones have exchanged their 120-year-old farmhouse on the outskirts of Melbourne for Mike Roseberry's brand new Durham town house. David Graveney is staying in the Metro Hotel, and we, in our latter-day hovel in Great Lumley, overlooking Durham's maximum security prison, still haven't got a washing machine, a fridge, or a phone.

We are on top of the Sunday League, though.

Monday/Tuesday 27/28 April – Durham v. Leicestershire Championship match, second and third days

A gruelling two days. The wicket had flattened out (or our bowlers had) and two Leicester players made centuries. We were offered some respite from a fresh westerly by a couple of showers and a sumptuous lunch. Lashings of lasagne and rice salads, boiled new potatoes and fresh rolls. This is what we should always have. Carbohydrates for energy, something tasty and quick to digest, and *hot* – there's nothing worse than slices of processed ham with limp lettuce and strips of spring onion, especially in these arctic conditions.

Impressive century by Ben Smith, a very active back-foot player – unusual for England. 'His middle name's Cutter,' said Tim Boon, and you could see why. After three days the wicket is holding up well, which must be an enormous relief to Tom Flintoff, the groundsman, bearing in mind that he is suddenly having to doctor all these local club wickets with imported Stockton loam to convert them from one-day thrash wickets into four-day belters. We are 4 runs ahead with six wickets standing so will have to fight tomorrow to draw.

Reception tonight at the Durham Light Infantry museum

much better than it sounds. Full of happy, smiling faces and people exclaiming, 'Ee, it's proper champion,' with a team of their own to follow at last. Also some interesting artistic impressions of the new ground at Chester-le-Street (work starts on the square next week). They made it look like somewhere in the Bahamas with palm trees dotted about and people in sombreros and shirt sleeves. Maybe the artist knows something about European climatic progressions that we don't.

Wednesday 29 April – Durham v. Leicestershire
Championship match, final day

That we managed a lead of 141 was due entirely to two people – Parker and Botham. Theirs were markedly different centuries: Parker's measured and limited, full of carefully selected shots and tight singles; Botham's a mixture of watchful defence and outrageous attack. He hit 5 sixes, the best of which was a vast off-drive with that massive full heave of the bat plopping the ball in front of the pavilion, dead centre.

Our tail could not emulate their partnership of 178 and Leicester still had three hours to make the runs, although the wicket was now turning square. We got an early wicket – Boon cutting a Botham long-hop to Jones at gully which caused the catcher to exclaim, 'Blimey, this man's arse is kissed, innit?', but after that there were no more breakthroughs. Batsmen are so much more accomplished against spin these days. They can sweep, cut and shovel, and with today's heavier bats, even a mis-hit clears the inner ring. We were also hampered by a hamstring injury to Graveney which he developed diving awkwardly at mid-off (he used to be a goalkeeper). Even so, Leicester made the necessary runs with some difficulty, and Durham lost its first-ever Championship match. If we had made 40 more on that first day things would have been very different.

SCORES: Durham 164 (Parker 77) and 318 (Parker 117, Botham 105, Millns 5/69); Leicestershire 342 (Boon 110, Smith 100*) and 142 for 3. Leicestershire won by seven wickets.

[41]

Thursday 30 April – Worcestershire v. Durham
Benson & Hedges Cup, at Worcester

Coming straight from the University ground at Durham to New Road, Worcester, makes an interesting comparison. The Durham ground wins – just. The backdrop is more spectacular, and at the moment Worcester Cathedral is covered in scaffolding.

A nerve-wracking day for me – I knew my overs would be saved until Hick and Moody were together. You can't help feeling apprehensive with such responsibility, but I've been bowling with good control, so maybe I shouldn't worry. In the event Phil Bainbridge's wobbly seamers trapped them both, plus two others.

Hick is going through a difficult patch at the moment. Unused to failure or mental fragility, his technique was exposed last summer by Curtly Ambrose and he is still recovering. His batting seems too rigid and coached, lacks touch and flair. At times he looks more like a robotic run-machine than a stylish strokeplayer. Perhaps he needs to relax more.

Tim Curtis was the mainstay of the Worcester innings. He is an old-fashioned cricketer, shunning modern caps and hairstyles. He even has a special deal with a shop in Great Malvern called 'Any Old Flannels' which supplies him with tailor-made cotton shirts and baggy cream cotton trousers with turn-ups. The odour of perspiration on polyester has always been unpleasant anyway.

Inexplicably, Worcester declined from 101–1 to 173 all out. There was considerable ill-discipline in the batting; Curtis will have a hard job controlling this bunch with individualists like Radford who is county cricket's Narcissus. Last year's captain, Phil Neale, doesn't even make it into the eleven.

Paul Parker didn't seem particularly to enjoy captaining (Graveney's hamstring has gone). It made him tense and slightly irascible. There are identification problems too. E.g.:

Me (gesticulating): 'Can I have "Bains" inside the circle?'
Parker: 'I don't think that is "Bains".'
Me: 'Well, whoever it is, then.'

With twelve overs remaining we were in dire straits at 123–6. The thing about playing in a freshly-formed team is that no-one yet knows your individual or collective capabilities. Least of all yourselves. Steve McEwan, a medium-pacer who was never renowned for his batting, lambasted his old employers' bowling past and over cover, and suddenly we were home with four overs to spare. Some of the players, Graveney included, didn't even see his antics – they were banned from the dressing-room for making the remaining batsmen, including me, on edge. It was like a cigarette-testing zone too, with Larkins, Botham and Ian Smith puffing their way through the packets donated by B&H.

Afterwards something happened that I've never heard of before in county cricket. Paul Parker got out his guitar, and we sang along to various old tunes. 'Bye bye, Miss American Pie' was one. Some seemed to know all the words. Have they nothing better to do at home than learn lyrics?

Friday 1 May

Travelled back to London from Worcester on the express via Oxford, the sky alternately glowering and sparkling. Going through Worcestershire and Oxfordshire seems like the most pastoral of journeys. Acres of water meadows, field upon field of brilliant yellow rape, sheep grazing knee deep in lush grass.

Cricketers dread rain around this period of the season. They are just getting into their stride, and the bad weather disrupts it. Worse still, Benson & Hedges games are delayed, then completed on the second day, depriving everyone of much needed time at home, and giving them yet another sleepless night. We were lucky. Eight other teams weren't. Scotland had to hang around this morning to pursue an Essex total of 388.

Saturday 2 May – Combined Universities v. Durham
Benson & Hedges Cup at Fenner's

One of the quotes of the week caught my eye today as we knocked up 271 against Combined Universities at Fenner's.

Chris Sole, goalkeeper of Roehampton Amputees FC: 'Most teams get treated for cuts and bruises at halftime. We have our nuts tightened.' You could take that any way you like.

Trounced the Combined Universities on a patchy wicket. They didn't look as slick a unit as three years ago when they nearly beat a hung-over Middlesex XI at the Parks. It's a good idea drawing the Combined side from all universities – when I was at Durham in the early 1980s, it was exclusively Oxbridge, and consequently much weaker. ('Red-brick' universities provided eight of today's side.)

Food at Fenner's as insipid as ever – the drab salad you dread. Fortunately there was a hamburger stall on the ground, which seemed to give me the energy later to bowl one of my better spells, despite digging a hole almost three inches deep with my front foot. I need all the height I can get.

3, 4 May (Bank Holiday)

Two days off to water the garden, go to parties, sleep in and have dinner with the Middlesex guys who have started to put a few results together.

Obviously John Emburey has needed a firm grip (once round Ramprakash's neck at Cambridge) to get the wayward elements to fall into line under himself and Gatting. And there are injury problems which confound the practice of going to the Algarve for a pre-season week (although that's very pleasant). Norman Cowans, that fine figure of a man, needs a groin operation, Angus Fraser's bowling spells are still rationed, and a puff of wind still occasionally prompts Neil Williams to run up the ladder. Saddest of all, Ricardo Elcock – a delightful teller of ribald stories as well as a spitting image of Buddha – has been forced to retire. He was a superb bowler when fit. The sort of fast, fiery out-swing that would have won him Test caps if his body could have stood up to propelling it. He hopes to train as an airline pilot, following in the footsteps of someone else with little respect for a batsman's well-being – Colin Croft.

Why do so many young bowlers get injured?

Answers: 1) Being forced to play too much cricket too young. 2) Covered wickets and concrete indoor nets which are very hard to land on. 3) Over-zealous fielding requirements (i.e. diving, instead of sticking out a size-11 boot). 4) Poor diet. 5) Low pain threshold encouraged by sophisticated diagnostic equipment which can spot an eyelash out of place.

The low pain threshold argument is particularly significant as twenty-one-year-olds hobble off with supposed shin stress-fractures. This probably results from bruising from standing up and walking around all day which they've scarcely done before. (On an average day bowling 20 overs with a 15-pace run-up you can cover about 12 miles.) But bowling is a painful business – landing on the edge of other bowlers' footmarks, pinging the first one down after two hours' rest, stopping a vicious straight-drive with your instep – you have to be mentally and physically tough. No amount of net practice prepares you for that, whatever Fred Trueman might say.

The University of Western Australia recently published a survey of bone and joint injuries after studying 24 specially selected fast bowlers in Perth, aged between sixteen and eighteen. At the time of the study only two 'had completely normal spinal images and no pain'. Both the bowlers who were injury free had side-on actions; the rest propelled the ball with a swivel of the upper body while their feet and hips pointed towards the batsman.

Bowlers should look after their feet better. I remember John Lever telling me that, while he watched me peeling off a pair of odd boots held together with tape. I've had two knee operations since. So often you find these kids wearing heavy plastic boots with nothing inside to cushion the blow of landing on com-pressed soil. It's a teeth-rattling experience, and that's just letting go of the ball. What happens if it comes whistling back at you? In the case of a batsman like Graeme Hick it is worth practising the horizontal ducking motion for use in the follow-through! In the summer of 1990 when balls were like oranges and bats like blunderbusses the best place to be was on the physio's table. That's when I advocated a new law to be brought in regarding intimidatory batting. It never was, though; instead we bowlers are directed more and more to bowl at the middle of the bat. Short runs on Sunday, balls fractionally off line called wide, now this year we are only allowed one bouncer per over per batsman. 'You cad, sir, pitch it up!' seems to be the motto. It's a dog's life.

Tuesday 5 May – Durham v. Derbyshire
Benson & Hedges Cup at Jesmond

Our worst fears were realised when Paul Parker and I got lost on the way to Jesmond. This was hardly surprising since Newcastle is a maze of roads and the ground is tiny. (The story goes that, in a festival game there, Botham once struck a six which disappeared through the window of an upstairs flat and damaged a TV set on which an elderly gentleman was watching the game.) Despite Jesmond's being in Northumberland, the attraction of big crowds to international festival matches there over the years was a significant factor in Durham's promotion.

Considering this was such an important match (we had to win to qualify for the quarter-finals), our preparation was amazingly relaxed. Maybe this cost us the game. Maybe not. But in this part of the world, 'nets' are what blue-rinsed old ladies put round their hair.

Playing against Derbyshire is rather like competing with the United Nations. West Indians, Danes, Australians, South Africans – but it was a Pom and erstwhile pilot, Johnny Morris (known predictably as 'Animal'), who turned the game. Morris was dropped by Andy Fothergill behind the wicket on 6 and made 121. It prompted such harsh headlines the next day as 'Andy's not so handy' and 'Fothergill's folly lets in Derby', but it was fairly crucial.

Just to make matters worse, Andy's opposite number, Karl Krikken, who walks like a farmer in heavy mud, took two blinding catches and we declined from 142–2 to 180–7. He stood halfway back to the boundary for Bishop and Malcolm which always looks alarming if you're side on to the wicket. But

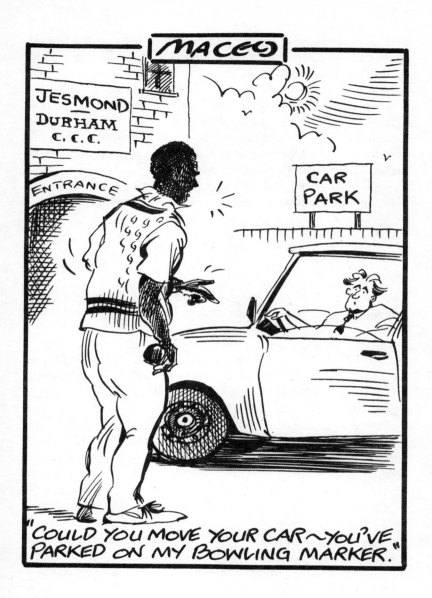

neither bowler had his radar working on this occasion (Bishop could barely fit in his run-up, the boundaries were so short) and it was that doughty campaigner, Ole Mortensen, who turned the game.

After the match Krikken was awarded his county cap. It is perhaps the highlight of a player's career – getting public recognition from your peers and a pay rise! Which reminds me of how I was awarded mine. A letter arrived in my university pigeon hole on 12 December 1981. On a small piece of note-paper was scrawled: 'Dear Simon, Just clearing up a few letters before going to India tomorrow. This note is to ask you if I'd told you you'd got your cap. Did I? I hope so. And hearty congratulations.

'Yours, Mike (Brearley).'

Thursday, Friday 7, 8 May – Kent v. Durham
Championship match, first two days at Canterbury

Lying on the ground doing looseners this morning, I looked up at a clear blue sky and drooled for the day when I could do that on a cricket ground knowing I didn't have to bowl in an hour. I love the game, but fast bowling is physically and mentally hard, especially in this team. I can see myself having to bowl a lot of overs at crucial times. So far my suspect knees haven't buckled.

At lunch after a storming start Kent, on a previously used wicket, were 112–1. By tea they were 230–6. Simon Brown, nicknamed Chubby after the bawdy north-east comedian Chubby Brown, had located a testing line and was swinging the ball in to Kent's discomfort. I meanwhile was chugging in from the other end, beating the bat, and failing to take wickets. I seem to have lost the knack for the moment – Ian Botham asked if maybe I'd been sleeping with a nun.

It was an excellent team effort, though, and that's what counts. Brown finished with 7–105, and that after having been dispatched viciously into the car park by Trevor Ward early on. The pitch, it has to be said, was substandard. Some of the umpiring was questionable too.

Botham claimed some of the credit for Brown's bowling, having last night lured him and six others to a plush Italian establishment near the cathedral where we consumed nine bottles of Barolo and twenty-four flaming sambuchas. I accidentally set the whole table on fire with one.

It brings back great memories for me, this ground. As a schoolboy I used to come here with my father for the festival and watch the great Kent team of the 1970s. Luckhurst, Asif Iqbal and Cowdrey were my heroes – I plucked up courage to ask for Colin's autograph once. It was the only one I ever had, in contrast to today's fanatics who stagger to grounds borne down with heavy albums full of photos and cuttings which they want players to sign. I have never understood the fascination for autographs, and my feelings were reinforced at Uxbridge in my first year with Middlesex. I was walking off the field with the then England captain, Mike Brearley, when a small boy rushed up to him demanding an autograph. He duly signed, then the boy pushed the book and pencil doubtfully at me. I wrote my name which he read, then, moving away a yard or two, rubbed out.

We had to battle against a keen Kent attack and were looking like conceding a deficit of 60 when I joined David Graveney. Somehow we accumulated 49 runs, punctuated by regular air shots, and Graveney's neurosis about the sightscreen. At one point he even insisted that one of our own players desist from sleeping on the balcony as the principle of it was distracting him.

Having got within 5 runs of Kent's score, I aimed a wild slog at Ellison, missed, and our innings ended. I'm glad my father wasn't here to see that!

Saturday 9 May – Kent v. Durham.
Third day

Rained all day, much appreciated by Botham who looked extremely happy. Watched Cup Final in Kent dressing-room. Liverpool 2, Sunderland 0. This means we will probably have a lot of depressed Geordies at our Sunday League match tomorrow, particularly as most London barmen may have refused to serve them after the Cup Final.

BSkyB have just dropped the bombshell of their deal to cover next winter's Premier League exclusively. In a statement announcing their deal with the BBC, Sky have promised to make their coverage more interesting by lingering on players' bodies. 'Bums not balls' is their motto, according to the *Observer*. If they intend introducing this into their cricket coverage, they'll need special wide-angled lenses.

Sunday 10 May – Kent v. Durham
Sunday League match at Canterbury

A great chance of a duel between me and my old friend Graham Cowdrey was dashed by rain. He is having problems with his eyes at the moment which I hope for his sake are resolved. He was badly affected when his father left his mother in the late 1970s and doesn't need a physical problem to exacerbate his bouts of self-doubt. Being a committed follower of the Irish musician Van Morrison, whose philosophy changes almost as often as the price of petrol, is probably not much help.

Evening meal at local Thai establishment with Botham, Parker and Graveney. Botham may be God's gift with bat and ball and he would have to be in my side for the forthcoming one-day internationals, but his effect on team members' coffers is not so beneficial. Keenly patronising the higher-class eating establishments, Botham is happy to part with forty-odd quid for a meal, which means that some of the younger Durham players, on salaries of less than £10,000, take it in turns to dine out with the great man, then make do with the peanuts on the bar the other evenings.

Monday 11 May – Kent v. Durham
Fourth day

Anti-climactic end to an intriguing game. Carl Hooper cracked a blistering century (after I'd got him out with a no-ball – my

[50]

father would go spare if he found out about that) but Kent batted on too long. There was no chance of our getting 260 to win especially after Jones got out early. He has found the slower, seaming wickets, the sloping grounds, the cold weather, his room-mate (me), in fact almost everything, hard to come to terms with, but still says he's enjoying it. It's 'clear-the-dressing-room' time when he gets out, and Sheila, the physio, closes her ears. But he soon calms down.

Spent a fascinating post-tea session watching Alan Knott coaching our keepers. Knotty still has that touch of eccentricity with his upturned collars, country trilby, and thin voice dishing out compliments. His coaching techniques are not altogether conventional either. At one point he was in the showers throwing balls for Fothergill to pop out of a cubicle and catch one-handed. Later he took Chris Scott into the very smart indoor centre at Canterbury, to test out his ability to take half-volleys as a batsman flailed away, deliberately missing them. It was a tricky session but he encouraged constantly.

'Did you ever practise like this?' I asked. 'Oooh, no,' he replied wistfully. 'Couldn't get anyone to do it.' He seemed to advocate simplicity and a minimum of movement standing up. I suppose this is what he himself did, although all that fidgeting and exercise between balls made you think otherwise. 'And if you drop one, forget it, it's gone. Concentrate on catching the next.' A good line in positive thinking, except that he says things in a rather convoluted way.

Reflections on the first month

Geoff Cook deserves to take most of the credit for assembling such a contented and competitive team. True we are still in the honeymoon period of our existence, but there's no doubt it's going to be a fun year. Ian Botham has already declared he's having the best time on the county circuit since his early days at Somerset, and Wayne Larkins backs him up: 'After twenty-two years walking through the same gates every day, taking the field with this bunch is a breath of fresh air,' he said.

[51]

My sentiments are exactly the same. Everyone seems to mix in well, there is a good team spirit. No-one is in it just for their own gratification. Dean Jones is constantly egging us on, Phil Bainbridge is a captain's dream, laughing, playing cameos, breaking stubborn partnerships. And the captain, David Graveney, has a perpetual smile despite pressure from the local media to explain every move and from the board of directors to cut down on expenses. He strokes a furrowed brow as he fathoms the best way of squeezing fifteen people and their kit into five cars for the journey to Cardiff. It is complicated by the fact that we have had three days off and are all reappearing from different directions.

A captain's job is never done. There are disgruntled players complaining about their accommodation, others (me) wanting to travel by train, those out of form to be told they are not in the team. Too often these days individuals discover they are not selected only when they read the printed scorecards at the ground, although this pales into insignificance against the fate of a Yorkshire friend of mine who learned he had been sacked only when he happened to read the newspaper wrapped round his fish and chips.

One of the hardest jobs so far has been restoring self-belief to the wicketkeeper, Chris Scott. He missed a catch in his first game, the Leicester match, and has been inconsolable ever since. 'I was terrified of letting this great opportunity slip,' he said, contemplating the nine years he spent in the shadow of Bruce French at Notts, 'and now my worst fears have been realised.' He has been dropped, but really it is his own fault. Wicketkeepers are invaluable cheer-leaders – constantly at the centre of the action – and a great source of encouragement to the bowlers and fielders, particularly if the chips are down. Mind you, I used to think Paul Downton went a bit too far at Middlesex with his exclamations of 'Come on, boys, want it, feel it!' as we strived to bowl out a side.

Nevertheless, Scott's head was in his hands for most of the match and he wouldn't utter a word, despite the fact that his glove work was slick and his skill offers the bowlers a hint of reassurance that Andy Fothergill doesn't always provide. The

Darlington man makes up for it with sheer ebullience, though, realising that at the age of thirty he is getting a chance that should have passed him by. Vocally, he is a great bonus to the team; technically, he has some work to do. But it's a long season and it won't do either of them any harm to share the job for a while.

No-one, of course, can share Botham's role. His all-round contribution has been quite outstanding, not only on the field but in other more unlikely ways. One day he took Dean Jones aside for a twenty-minute master-class on bat grip – gratefully received by the Australian who, like most of his compatriots, has the utmost respect for him. The next day he was arranging a trip for six of the players to the luxurious St Pierre Country Club near Chepstow where he is an honorary member. Two nights, bed and breakfast, and a couple of rounds of championship golf (with buggies) came to £22 a head, extraordinary value.

It has been a novel experience emerging on to the field to be confronted by a posse of photographers, but all the lenses are focused on one object – the man in the iridescent blue sunglasses gallumphing on to the field. I assume he gets paid a good whack for wearing them, as he does for all the Nike sportswear that keeps turning up in dressing-rooms. He says he receives so many gimmies he throws a lot of it away after a couple of wearings. Someone ought to direct him to the nearest War-on-Want depot.

He contributes to the relaxed atmosphere too, rolling up in jeans, which is frowned on by Ayatollah Cook but approved by everyone else. His presence has injected fun and enjoyment into the mundanity of the county treadmill, which Graveney also promotes. An immensely understanding and tolerant individual, Graveney seems at last to have found a team he is happy in, and has relinquished his almost apologetic nature on the field. When he took guard you felt he was almost mumbling, 'Don't worry, I won't keep you long,' to the close-fielders, but now he is batting with solid commitment and bowling incisive spells. Mind you, he's not one of the fastest runners the game has ever seen, and, aware of this, he resorts to a despairing dive if ever

[53]

the ball is in danger of passing him. For this trait we have nicknamed him 'Victor' after the giraffe that collapsed at Marwell Zoo, near Southampton, and couldn't get up.

Chapter 4

'It's good being underdogs'

Wednesday 13 May

The county circuit is not meant to be a culinary tour of Britain, but the restaurant in Cardiff tonight was a huge open-plan fish place called 'Le Monde' with all the various creatures exhibited (dead) in a large glass-covered display – a bit like an upmarket Billingsgate. The sea bass baked in about a hundredweight of salt was superb.

Sitting in a large armchair at the head of the table laden with food, Wayne Larkins, with his moustache and longish curly hair, looked exactly like a medieval king. So from now on we are calling him Henry.

Thursday 14 May – Glamorgan v. Durham
Championship match, first day, at Cardiff

Sophia Gardens has always had the unenviable reputation of providing the lowest bouncing pitch on the county circuit – it's no wonder that their last real pace-bowler, Greg Thomas, left for bouncier pastures. This wicket looked a disgrace. Tufty grass in places, bare in others, no real substance. I doubt if it will last two days, never mind four.

Seventeen-year-old Paul Henderson is making his Durham debut. He is a solidly-built lad from the Middlesbrough area, a bit stroppy, but very talented – already has a hat-trick to his name on the Zimbabwe trip and can bat too. He knew the day before that he was playing, which is more than can be said for my Middlesex debut. The first day was washed out, we declared on the second afternoon, and I was just looking out for the umpires as all good twelfth men should when Mike Brearley said, 'Hey, what d'you think you're doing standing around? You're playing.'

Today's debutant was soon required to perform. Glamorgan had progressed comfortably to 90–2, with Maynard looking dangerous. But with customary beginner's luck, Henderson had Hugh Morris caught at cover, slashing, Viv Richards lazily top-edging a long-hop, and Maynard chasing a wide one. Glamorgan declined ineptly to 224 all out, in the face of our persistent, if hardly terrifying bowling. Graveney bowled only two overs, observing from mid-off most of the time. He was required to pursue one ball to a very long boundary. The batsmen, aware of the identity of the loping fielder, tried to run 5, at which Botham shouted from slip. 'Kick it over, Victor, for God's sake.'

Later Larkins chanced his way to 49 not out, interspersing fine shots with swishes at thin air. I don't think this pitch will suit him.

Friday 15 May – Glamorgan v. Durham
Second day

Just after lunch Larkins was out for a scintillating 143 – which just goes to show what a good judge I am! I must say he has the most laid-back approach of anyone I know, even Botham. He arrived this morning at ten past ten, carrying only his essential equipment – a bottle of shampoo and 20 Benson & Hedges. He did deign to do the warm-ups but then sat in a cloud of nicotine until eleven o'clock after which he pummelled the bowling to all parts. Neville Cardus's description in *Autobiography* of Frank Woolley could also apply to Larkins: 'He is always about to lose his wicket; his runs are thin-spun. An innings by him is almost too insubstantial for this world.'

Dean Jones, itching for the big punch like a middle-weight boxer, restrained himself well to make 94 on the far from perfect wicket. Then Parker, the stabilising influence in a flamboyant batting order, made another chanceless century. He is playing better than he has for some time and is worth two men in the field. I hope it continues, for there isn't a nicer, more enthusiastic man in the game.

Glamorgan took the second new ball, and suddenly we looked vulnerable. I had my doubts that Botham, coming in at 317–4, would make many. So did Viv Richards who greeted his friend's arrival with 'OK, boys, we're down to de tail now'. The thing is, his technique is so good. He rode the swing and lift beautifully, and belted anything loose. You could see the bowlers growing more apprehensive every passing minute. 'What were you trying to do?' I asked, after he was out for a swift 40. 'To get as many as quickly as possible without having to run,' he guffawed. Oh, to have the ability.

Spent most of a hot, sunny day relaxing in a pair of shorts by the sightscreen. Had an interesting discussion with Mark Frost, the Glamorgan 13th man. 'I just can't get it right at the moment,' he said. 'I run up with a new ball and I can't swing it away. And I keep overpitching. What am I doing wrong?' Far be it for me, as a beggarman's Brian Statham, to try and advise first-class bowlers, but this is a common problem which I too have experienced. In fact, bearing in mind the complexity of a bowling action, I am frequently amazed that the ball lands on the cut strip as often as it does. But it boils down to run-up and timing. The shorter the delivery stride, the more the bowler's front leg braces at the point of release. This gives a more upright position of the wrist and a better follow-through. The back foot take-off is all-important. Leaning back even a minuscule amount on delivery leads to a loss of momentum and usually of control.

On the other hand, maybe he isn't polishing the ball vigorously enough, although with this current crop of balls you couldn't get up a good shine even with Cherry Blossom and a chamois leather.

Saturday 16 May – Glamorgan v. Durham
Third day

Our first Championship victory, so a red-letter day. Basically, we won because they didn't make enough on the first day, and we made too many on the second. Bowling them out again, though, would have been much harder if we hadn't got six of them with the new ball. Four went to Simon Brown who has improved one hundred per cent with every game and is now a hostile performer. Two of them were caught in the slips by Botham. But how understated scorecards can be. They were both stunning catches taken by a man wearing skiing glasses and standing far too close with his hands on his knees. If he hadn't caught the second, the ball would have rearranged his nose.

It took the best part of fifty overs to flush out the last four batsmen. The job was all the harder because the pitch had deadened, it was hot, and Henderson was already confined to the pavilion with sore shins.

'They don't make 'em 'ard like they used to, 'appen.'

Celebrations postponed as it's Sunday tomorrow and we've earned a day off. Everyone is anxious to get home and clock up a few bonus points with the missus.

SCORES: Glamorgan 224 (Maynard 88) and 193 (Cottey 112*, Brown 5/66); Durham 521 for 9 declared (Larkins 143, Parker 124, Croft 5/105). Durham won by an innings and 104 runs.

The Four-day Debate

On Tuesday English cricket's own Politbureau, the TCCB, decided to approve the recommendations made by Mike Murray's working party on the layout of the English season. This means that, from next year, we are to have a Championship programme of seventeen four-day matches each, a Sunday league of 50 overs per side with a midday start, and a termination of the zonal section of the Benson & Hedges Cup.

Most players prefer the four-day game because there will be

fewer contrived finishes and the better team will win more often. The downside is that, as far as the public is concerned, a game of county cricket that could last for 2,592 balls and still be a draw is about as inspiring as watching paint dry. Team members not actively involved in the play sometimes feel this, too. There may be more carefully compiled innings in the first-class game next year, but more yawning mid-offs as well.

Mind you, discuss the four-day approach to batting with some of the more flamboyant exponents and they'll say it's business as usual. 'I don't care if it's one-day or five-day, the first five overs or the last five, if I see a bad ball I'll go out and whack it,' says Wayne Larkins. The problem is that four-day wickets are even blander than the three-day variety, as groundsmen, terrified of surface deterioration, water and roll their strips to death. But I don't subscribe to the uncovered wicket argument. Balls popping off a length on a sticky dog do nothing to improve a batsman's confidence and only flatter ordinary bowlers. No other country plays first-class cricket on uncovered pitches and you can't expect trained professional athletes to risk life and limb in unsatisfactory conditions. Surely in this technical age, if you have sophisticated machinery to make play possible after a downpour, you should use it, for the benefit of everyone.

The powerful lobby favouring 50-over matches on Sunday is somewhat disturbing. This cannot be a panacea for dwindling 40-over game attendances. People have far too much on their Sunday plates to consider scrambling off to cricket at midday. There is going to be trouble about this before the month is out, with players threatening action and captains petitioning each other. Predictably, sponsorship may decide the issue. BSkyB are rumoured to be reluctant to cover the League unless it conforms more to the World Cup rules with coloured clothing and longer matches. No TV, no sponsorship, which would mean in the long run some players losing their jobs as counties economised. So the complaints will probably be revoked, continuing the trend towards professional sport being tailored to the demands of the electronic eye rather than the naked one.

I have often aired the idea of a 25-over Sunday League. It is a form of cricket played all over England on weekday evenings that is great fun and not too tiring. Most Sunday League innings only break out of a trot after 20 overs anyway. Such matches could begin at 3.30 pm, allowing ample time for the roast to digest and be over by 'Songs of Praise'. It would fit neatly into a TV slot too, and might woo back the people whose Sunday afternoon entertainment consists of a trip to a DIY store or another encounter with GameBoy.

Monday 18 May

We are third in the County Championship with more bowling points than batting. I hope the cynics who have referred to us as 'joke bowlers' have noticed that.

Friday 22 May

Heatwave in London, so I travelled up by train to Durham in a pair of Australian beach shorts. Arrived to find mist and a temperature around 8°C. Felt silly walking about the town with everyone else in overcoats.

Saturday 23 May – Durham v. Northamptonshire
Championship match, first day, at Stockton

Anyone would think we were in Iceland rather than England. A real pea-souper enveloped the entire north-east region, which only made the job of finding Stockton CC for the first time even harder. It was chilly as well which meant that hot water bottles filled from the canteen tap and personal primus stoves were de rigueur for spectators. What our loyal supporters suffer to see a bit of ancient sport!

The sea-fret (or was it acid rain from the nearby chemical works?) wafted in at midday and wouldn't budge. Which meant that the ball got wet and severely hampered our bowling. Ian Botham pointed this out to the umpires every ten minutes but they didn't seem interested.

Umpires have a hard, unrewarding job. On their feet six-and-a-half hours a day, required to find their own B&Bs, never mind adjudicating tricky decisions with no help from the batsmen. Judging fair conditions for play is about as easy as a tight run-out, and someone always moans, whether it's a batsman who can't see, a bowler who can't stand up, or a spectator bored with staring at a pitch covered by tarpaulins.

Northants made 340–6 in a mist that hampered us far more than them, but the game seemed incidental to the racing from Redcar as far as Lamb and Botham were concerned. Jokes and tips were exchanged almost every over.

At the Mayor's reception in the evening, I found out a bit about Stockton. It has the widest (and most nondescript) High Street in Britain, and a haphazard-looking shopping centre appropriately called The Shambles. It used to be a fisherman's town until the sea receded; now it seems to be populated by groups of chunky girls wearing short skirts and too much rouge.

24 May – Durham v. Northamptonshire
Sunday League match at Stockton

Classic example of non-familiarity with your own home wicket. Shaved to the bone, it seamed, stopped and snaked, and four of us dragged balls into our stumps. This was a shame since the Teesiders had turned out in their multitudes with their pet Rottweilers and German Shepherds – maybe the burglar alarm phenomenon hasn't reached here yet. Still, the next three home Sunday matches are sell-outs.

No chance of defending a total of 124, but we were still able to have a laugh. Botham showed off his new England floppy hat to Geoff Cook who has a particularly conservative attitude to headgear. 'What d'you think, Tosh?' he said, looking like Freddie Parrot-Face. 'You're a bloody pillock,' said Cook, and walked out.

Monday, 25 May, was not a day I shall remember with much relish. It began with Fothergill dropping a straightforward chance, and the Northants seventh-wicket pair, Ripley and Curran, then extending their partnership to 180, much of it off my bowling. So – perfectly respectable figures of 1–39 declined to 2–93. Simon Brown finished with five wickets again. It doesn't make me feel envious, just a bit baffled and more disappointed than ever that I am 5ft 10in., not 6ft 4in.

Mind you, that's nothing compared to Curtly Ambrose's 6ft 7in. He touched the roof of the showers tonight with a bent arm, while I, stretching to tiptoe, was still six inches short. I asked him if he had any advice on how to grow taller. 'Give eet a few years,' he said, smirking.

I think I would be smiling too if I was capable of getting the ball to lift nose high from a good length. That was the one he reserved for me, first ball, thank you very much. I suppose I should be thankful that my nostrils are not now spread across my face, but somehow being on a king-pair is worse.

Northants hustled us out 13 short of the follow-on and look a formidable side. Lots of batting, and plenty of bowling variety, the pick of whom is the left-arm quickie, Paul Taylor, formerly with Derbyshire. There is something about left-arm-over bowlers that English batsmen seem to find tricky. Presumably it is the different angle, or the fact that sometimes the sight-screens do not roll far enough across to accommodate them. Curtly comes over the top of them, of course, which is probably why Phil Bainbridge has a nasty bruise under his left arm-pit. He has been out of first-class cricket for a year and it showed a bit, particularly against the bouncer. He did make a valiant 92 not out, however.

Glorious weather on the Tuesday, but not such a glorious prospect of us having to bat all day. We managed it for all but nine overs, thanks to a technically brilliant century from Jones. I batted with him for two hours, putting on 87 for the ninth

wicket, and found it a fascinating experience. His foot movements are so quick, his hands so fast, enabling him to play back
to balls which I would be lunging at. His judgement of line –
particularly balls from Ambrose he left alone – was impeccable.

Two other things were noticeable. One was his constant
encouragement as I defended staunchly. The other was the
cacophony of shouts and claps from the multiplying slip cor-
don. The longer I survived, the more feverish it became. You
get used to it, in fact, learn to shut it out. It helped that the
crowd gradually got behind us, even applauding me for one
over when I played and missed at five out of six.

While Jones was facing, Lamb pushed men deep to give him
the single (hoping to have a crack at me), then brought them in
for the last two balls of the over to try to keep him up that end.
Instead of looking for a single, Jones counter-attacked, helping
to extend our narrow lead and adding to their frustration.
Offering the senior batsman a single early in the over never
seems to work – bowlers tend to go through the motions with
the first four balls, then accidentally concede a run somewhere
unlikely off the fifth or sixth ball, leaving the tailender usually
with only one to survive. A pointless exercise.

Lamb gazed from slip through his kaleidoscopic sunglasses
with less than total interest, I thought. I don't get the impression that many of his players would sacrifice themselves for
him, which perhaps explains why they don't win more often.

He did, however, manage to drag himself away from
monitoring his bets at various race meetings to win this one. If
there is one man who knows how to score 90 off nine overs, it's
Allan Lamb. After I had been hit for 25 off two overs, I
considered running him out at the bowler's end as he backed up
too far, but thought better of it, not wanting to cause a rumpus.
He is a brilliant player, and has taught Alan Fordham a thing
or two about improvisation.

Eventually Rob Bailey had to hit one run off the last ball and
I could hear the Durham spectators all muttering, 'Miss it,
miss it,' with screwed-up faces and clenched fists. But it wasn't
to be.

Felt later as if I had rather shot myself in the foot. If I hadn't

[63]

batted for so long, then we wouldn't have needed to field again, and I wouldn't have conceded 38 off three overs. That's life, I suppose.

> SCORES: Northants 420 for 9 dec. (Ripley 104, Curran 82, Lamb 58, Brown 5 for 124) and 95 for 2; Durham 258 (Bainbridge 92*) and 253 (Jones 157). Northants won by 8 wickets.

Wednesday 27 May – Hampshire v. Middlesex
Benson & Hedges Quarter-final

Plying my alternative trade as BBC TV summariser at Southampton today. I realise now that the reason why I wore a chestpad and arm-guard against Ambrose yesterday was so that I was fit for this opportunity. Strange priorities?

I should have been distressed to see my old Middlesex colleagues go down without so much as a whimper, but I wasn't. Perhaps they were over-confident, they certainly got out in some horrendous ways. Of the bowlers, only Angus Fraser seemed to be really trying, and he is still short of match fitness after a twelve-month hip problem which has had about five different diagnoses. Sadly, I don't think he will ever be quite the same again.

Great fun working with the real pros, Tony Lewis and Richie Benaud. It's been my life's ambition to commentate with these two and they are both absolutely superb, as is the director who is burbling in your ear all the time, but can still respond to your words of wisdom, changing shots and angles at the touch of a button.

Apparently it costs about £25,000 to cover a county one-day match. That's seven hours of very cheap TV.

Thursday 28 May

Reading the paper, I discover there are 36,800 electric pylons traversing the British countryside. I don't know why I'm

1. Durham's first first-class match, a 'friendly' against Oxford University, 14 April 1992. Graveney (*left*) and Lovell toss for innings.

2. (*Below*) Team photocall before Durham's first Sunday League match v. Lancashire: (*left to right*), Bainbridge, Parker, Graveney, Botham, Larkins, Jones, McEwan, Hutton, Berry, Brown (S), Briers, Blenkiron.

3, 4. Non-paying spectators outside the Durham University Racecourse ground during the Lancashire Sunday League match, 19 April. (*Below*) In the dressing-room afterwards satisfaction after a nailbiting finish.

5, 6. Different ways of loosening up: (*above*) Larkins and Botham get in some alternative putting practice at the St Lawrence ground in Canterbury; (*below*) team callisthenics.

7, 8. Durham's first
championship win, against
Glamorgan at Cardiff,
Botham toasts it; Larkins
takes it lying down.
(*Below*) The problem
of being Ian Botham.
Whenever he leaves the
pavilion he is besieged
by fans and admirers.

9, 10. (*Above*) John Wood's first delivery in first-class cricket, Tony Middleton caught behind at Southampton. The sun-shaded Jones and Botham appeal, Umpire Constant adjudicates. (Wood finished with 5/68.) (*Below*) Simon Hughes bowling, also against Hampshire. He usually kept the runs down but captured fewer wickets than he hoped.

11, 12, 13. (*Above, left*) Larkins, the dashing and aggressive opening bat. (*Above, right*) John Glendenen hitting confidently to leg. (*Below*) A satisfied group of the directors of Durham Cricket Club.

14, 15, 16. (*Above*) David Graveney, a popular captain, was unlucky with injuries. Here he is hit on the helmet during an eighth-wicket stand of 63 against Hampshire. (*Below*) No shortage of work for the physiotherapist, although Sheila Job had occasional difficulties in penetrating male sanctums. (*Left*) she treats Darren Blenkiron; (*right*) she ministers painfully to Dean Jones.

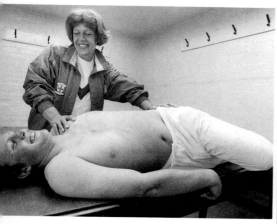

17, 18. 'Dean Jones has boundless energy, infectious enthusiasm, and the quickest turn for two in the business.' Two moments from the dramatic match against Sussex at Horsham.

fascinated by that, but I am. Actually, I have always found them rather frightening.

Friday 29 May – Hampshire v. Durham
Championship match, first day, at Southampton

Cloudburst and torrential rain on the way from London. Basingstoke flooded, but Southampton OK. The rest of the team had done the 350-mile trip from Durham by coach. It took seven hours mainly because the driver had evidently been trained on a milkfloat. Ian Botham is sponsored by Newcastle Breweries so he had no trouble organising twenty crates of Newcastle Brown. They ran out of Sauvignon Blanc at Doncaster, though, and had to stop for more. No wonder one reporter has described us as 'the happiest band of travellers you could wish to meet'.

Prompt start on relaid strip a short hit from the hospitality boxes, so the ball could have come back from the boundary covered in chicken leg and squashed strawberry, especially while we were batting. Larkins, Parker and Botham took full advantage of loose bowling, particularly by Kevin Shine, who had lured thirteen Lancashire batsmen to their doom in the last match with a run-up of 45 yards.

Usual mid-innings collapse staved off by Graveney and myself – we have a £10 bet on which of us will score more runs this season. I'm odds-on to win, because he is always contracting some ailment or other and dropping himself down the order. Helped in this game by the absence of Malcolm Marshall with a back strain. He's not as fast as he was in the mid-1980s, but he has straightened his run-up and seems to have even better control as a result. And that, with a weird grip that has two fingers either side of the seam and the thumb tucked into the palm. I've tried it, but all I can bowl is slow beamers.

[65]

Saturday 30 May – Hampshire v. Durham
Second day

Slightly groggy from dinner out with Botham, Graveney and
Nicholas, the Hampshire skipper, but suddenly looked up at
the scoreboard and realised I had 30. No-one noticed, they
were too busy laughing at me playing and missing and at
Graveney being hit on the head by Cardigan Connor. Unique
name that – Cardigan Connor – sounds like the new range in
M&S autumn wear.

Durham then let loose another newcomer, John Wood, on
Hampshire. His first ball was fast and short and gloved Tony
Middleton, the country's leading run-scorer; his sixth bounced
off the ridge and had Gower, slashing, caught at slip. 0–2.
Robin Smith then bumped a sharp catch to short leg (27–3)
and retired to the nets. Sprinkled in among the half-volleys
were some really good balls, and the sixteen-stone Wood, the
first twenty-year-old fast bowler I've ever seen with a hairy
back, finished with 5–68. A dream start. Hampshire, meanwhile, top of the table before this game, conceded a lead of 94,
which was doubled by the close. Yet again, we have sneaked up
on an unsuspecting team just when their guard is lowered. It's
good being underdogs.

31 May – Hampshire v. Durham
Sunday League match, at Southampton

There has been quite a rumpus regarding some comments
made about Gower by Graham Gooch in his autobiography.
It's the tabloids at it again, lumping distant sentences together
to make a sensational story. But Gooch does seem to have overstepped the mark, and I guess Gower may sue.

It doesn't seem to have affected his batting, though. He
stroked it around today as if in a dream, seeing Hampshire to
150–1 with the pugnacious Smith. After that, they contrived to
try and lose the game, and it was only Raj Maru with 8 off the
last two balls who saved them from ignominy. The presence of
Botham put 2,000 extra on the gate, and they saved their

biggest cheer for his comic attempt to catch a swirling skier which finished with a full-length dive still a yard from the ball. The thud as he hit the ground registered 6.5 on the Richter scale!

It was a perfect day's cricket for the local punters. The top stars all made runs, there was a nerve-jangling finish, and Hampshire won. Afterwards they mobbed Smith as he climbed into his sponsored car with the personalised number plate J11DGE (the nearest he could get to the nickname derived from his bouffant hair). Gower is not so lucky – he is obliged to drive his own private car, one of only a hundred special XJI2s built to commemorate something or other. But then he is a bit of a collector's item himself.

Monday 1 June – Hampshire v. Durham
Third day

'Flaming June,' they say, but it was teeming rather than flaming. By eleven o'clock the outfield was a lake, so we were denied the chance of trouncing the current champions. Botham was ecstatic. 'It's two days late, but it's finally here,' he exclaimed, peering out into the gloom. 'Now how about a few bottles of Burgundy for the coach-trip back?' I took the train – a safer route. (The guard used a word new to me during the journey – 'Will the passengers make sure they have all their belongings when they *detrain*,' he announced.)

Tuesday/Wednesday 2/3 June – Durham v. Somerset
Championship match, first two days, at Darlington

This is the first year Somerset haven't had a world-class batsman to kick off their innings and it's quite a relief. Obviously Jimmy Cook had sensational success, but he was preceded by Martin Crowe, Steve Waugh, Viv Richards and Sunil Gavaskar. Now it is apparently their young bowlers who represent their strength. I watched them warming up, trying to assess their actions. You know you are getting past it when you don't recognise half the opposition!

[67]

They are an impressive bunch: André van Troust, the Flying Dutchman, only eighteen but 6ft 7in. and lightning quick; Richard Snell, the South African paceman with the mop of scraggy hair; and Andy Caddick, the spitting image of Richard Hadlee even down to the sweat-bands, and a potential Test bowler with height, pace and direction – all at once. Perhaps their most exciting player is Mark Lathwell. Born in Bucks, but raised on the creamy wickets of North Devon, he is that rare phenomenon, a back-foot player with nice touch and very fast hands. He has already taken blistering fifties off good attacks.

Had some difficulty gauging the Darlington strip – it looked like a furrowed vegetable-patch, but turned out relatively benign. Somerset were 150–1 by mid-afternoon but this Durham team's sneaky mentality worked again. Suddenly we had bowled them out for 270, and that without the hypnotic traps of Ian Botham (away on Test duty).

Chris Scott, the former Notts wicketkeeper, has made it back into the team for the last two games, and is slowly coming out of a dark shell. He actually uttered a couple of words on Tuesday, complimenting Phil Bainbridge on a good delivery. Wicket-keepers are a very important source of motivation for a team – but Scott seems to go about his work in a state of silent apprehension. You feel like saying to him, 'Don't worry, Scotty, it will never happen'. He will have to sort it out, because otherwise it will be a waste of a silky set of gloved hands and impish batting.

I have never had a clue about 'keeping but observed that, when he takes deliveries down the leg-side standing up, he watches the ball from the off-side of the batsman. 'Knotty told me that,' Scott explained, 'to leave my movement as late as possible.' But, like umpires, 'keepers rarely get the opportunity to practise new techniques. Their day consists of fielding the wayward throws during pre-match warm-ups, then the real thing.

Elsewhere, Phil Edmonds made an unexpected comeback for Middlesex at Trent Bridge. Phil Tufnell has had an appendix operation, and Edmonds was suddenly re-registered to fill the breach. He always aspired to the luxuries enjoyed by Imran

Khan – captaining his country, a house in Chelsea, good looks and a part-time contract. He has finally achieved the last anyway. Although his bowling skill was untarnished in spite of five years spent monopolising an office telephone (he took 4–48) it may be some while before he is able to summon up the energy to play again. A combination of 28 overs and pain-killers for a familiar old back injury left him weak at the knees, and he could barely make it on to the field when Notts followed-on. Later, he had to be helped out of the bath and into his suit and tie.

What makes Edmonds almost unique is that few men would have had the confidence to return after such an absence, let alone the ability. But then he was never short of self-belief, usually declaring, as everyone took the field, 'Oh, well, I suppose I'm going to bowl immaculately again'. After strug-gling down the Trent Bridge steps and into his E-registration Rolls, which required about a nine-point turn to get out of the tiny car park, he was asked how he would manage 40 overs the next day. 'You don't think it will take me that long, surely?' he replied.

For the team's sake I hope he was given a single room. He used to be a very disruptive room-mate, leaving the TV on until the National Anthem at 12.50 am, and priming the radio for the 6 am news and 'Farming Today'.

Thursday 4 June – Durham v. Somerset
Third day

After two relatively balmy days, a cold snap returned, but no rain. Every other game in the country is off, including the first day of the Edgbaston Test, and even a 2nd XI match just down the road. Our second team has been doing extremely well, scoring quick runs and humbling opponents on a variety of grounds from Sunderland to Philadelphia. I should imagine it's pie and mushy peas for lunch at some of those places.

Darlington is one of Durham's pleasanter venues. The pavil-ion has a large upstairs terrace with sunshades where this morning we ate a breakfast of bacon and tomato muffins. I remember sitting up there once during a pre-season 'warm-up' match for Middlesex against Durham. It was the year Jeff Thomson was the Middlesex overseas pro. 'Jeez,' he said, shrouded in sweaters, 'it's not as cold as this in my fridge back in Brisbane.'

The Feetham's ground also boasts the largest sightscreen in England – the back of Darlington FC's grandstand painted white – and the lowest bouncing wicket (apart from Tring). This presumably explained Somerset's unadventurous tactics in the morning. They even patted back the leg-spin of debutant Mark Briers given its first outing. You would have thought that, with an attack of quick, bouncy bowlers, they would have fancied setting us a target, but Chris Tavaré dragged an attempted cut limply into his stumps and the innings plodded on. Essex apparently always put on short, stumpy people to bowl at Tavaré because he has a tendency to inside-edge low, skiddy balls directed wide of the wicket.

Suddenly, and inexplicably, with 38 overs left and a lead of 212, Tavaré declared. Whether, with his team second in the Championshp, he felt he had to make some token effort, or whether he was taking account of the fact that we had only ten men (John Glendenen was laid up after contracting some kind of blood infection which at one point made him look as if he were about to explode), the ploy failed. Jones demanded to open, and he and Larkins were soon racing along at 7 runs an over. They were a substantial danger to each other: the Australian running his partner ragged, while Larkins unleashed skimming lofted drives which nearly decapitated Jones.

Larkins is such an uncomplicated batsman. He wields a very heavy Stuart Surridge (one of the rare players to use the bats he is supplied with rather than a preferred make disguised by sponsor's stickers), and plays old-fashioned shots – dumping opening bowlers back over their heads, or flicking them to square-leg with a short punch of the arms and lovely timing. It's a real plus playing with, rather than against, him. His secret, he says, is being 'a natural batsman, not over-coached'.

With about 40 runs needed, Jones skied a catch to third-man, but Richard Snell dropped it. Mrs Jones, watching from the pavilion, jumped up and cheered excitedly. The local vicar was sitting beside her and when she had calmed down, he said, 'I was praying, too, but I did it quietly'.

Perhaps the two most satisfying things about this our first *home* Championship win, were that it was achieved without Botham, and in the presence of a number of Durham's directors. So a case of Moët & Chandon soon materialised, organised by the county club president, Ian Caller. He's a marvellous man. Despite considerable wealth achieved through the success of the Callers-Pegasus travel group, he is never reluctant to get his hands dirty, humping advertising hoardings, and helping to erect marquees. On this occasion he trailed right across the field brandishing a glass of champagne for Durham's bravest supporter, Malcolm Rooney, a promising young cricketer who was seriously injured on the road. He can now take one step every ten seconds only with the aid of his father and a Zimmer frame. Yet he still struggles to every home game.

SCORES: Somerset 270 (Hayhurst 76, Lathwell 53) and 192 for 6 dec. (Lathwell 50); Durham 250 (Scott 57) and 213 for 2 (Larkins 92, Jones 78). Durham won by 8 wickets.

Chapter 5

Last-over equations, and a visit to Dublin

Friday, Saturday, Sunday 5/6/7 June – Derbyshire v. Durham Championship match at Chesterfield

The lovely Queen's Park in Chesterfield seems to have attracted the summer's first monsoon. At one stage the ground looked more suitable for boating than batting. By Sunday, with more coconut matting in evidence than you usually find at a fairground, we managed to slither our way through a Sunday League game.

No wonder the Derbyshire wicketkeeper, Karl Krikken, looks as if he's trudging through mud if they always play in conditions like this. I must say, he looks to me the best stumper around at the moment. Despite a strange technique which involves incessant fidgeting, and a goalkeeper's stance standing back rather than the usual crouch, he takes brilliant diving catches with both hands, and makes it all look ridiculously easy. True, with an attack featuring Devon Malcolm and Ian Bishop he is rarely required to stand nearer than about twenty-five yards from the bat, but if he played for a more fashionable county . . .

Nothing could look more unfashionable than Kim Barnett's stance, shuffling across from a guard at least a foot outside leg-stump, but it does give bowlers problems trying to lock their radar on him. It's a bit like shooting at those moving plastic ducks you get in arcades.

For some odd reason we seemed lacking in desire in this match, and lost by a distance. Their match-winner was Peter Bowler, a man who opens the batting, and bowls both right- and left-arm spin, and can keep wicket, too. Almost a team in one. As he came off with 75 not out, the announcer with the sibilant s's said over the tannoy, 'Well played, Peter,' just like his captain might have done. (The Derby players once persuaded that same announcer to read out the following message: 'Will Sydney Spencer of Sissinghurst please sidle over to the sponsors' seats to see Cecil Spicer.')

Monday 8 June – Derbyshire v. Durham

If two whole days of a Championship match are lost, the conditions of play allow a one-innings match for 12 points. Despite the light-meters indicating that it was almost pitch-black outside, the Durham openers were obliged to face the two swarthiest bowlers in county cricket – Malcolm and Bishop. But some collusion, and an extraordinary innings by Paul Parker, who currently seems to be more on edge every day, resulted in Derbyshire being set a target of 250.

The wicket, not as quick as in its heyday (the old grounds-man fell out of a tree and had to retire), is still bouncy and we had a chance. Not when the heavens opened, though, half an hour later, so we took an early drive to Harrogate. As we left, Queen's Park looked like a paddy field. I doubt if they will play there for a month.

Met Sussex's David Smith in an Indian restaurant in Harrogate at about 11.30 pm. They are our opponents in the Tilcon Trophy tomorrow. I have bet him £20 that he won't be able to lay a bat on my first ball, and I've guaranteed it won't be a no-ball or a wide. I have something up my sleeve.

Tuesday 9 June – Sussex v. Durham
Tilcon Trophy match, at Harrogate

Smith took guard at 11 am and I marked out my run, mean-while slipping the new ball into my pocket. I then ran up and let go another one which had been sliced in two by a machine. One half finished up at long-leg, the other rolled to a stop in the slips. The umpire called 'Dead ball'. Smith, to his credit, laughed, then produced a cheque book from his hip-pocket and began to write one out. He also cheerfully gave up his wicket to Graveney after a breezy 28.

That's when the relaxed nature of the game ended. I always thought the Tilcon Trophy was festival cricket which was competitive but enjoyable, emphasised on this occasion by the disappearance from the field of Parker and Jones at one stage to help a waitress carrying a heavy crate. Not too conspicuously in front of an ample crowd, we 'allowed' Sussex back from 57 for 5, and eventually required 215. They then took the whole thing extremely seriously, Franklyn Stephenson finishing the match with a nasty bouncer at Graveney in half-light. 'You played that pretty hard,' I said afterwards to the Sussex wicketkeeper, Peter Moores. 'We're skint, we had to,' he replied.

The match revealed deficiencies in our side when we chase runs. The middle order tends to collapse whenever the pressure is really on, inexperience is exposed. We need a good hitter – a DeFreitas – to come in at no. 8.

From a selfish point of view, I didn't mind our getting knocked out as I have to get to Canterbury to commentate on tomorrow's Benson & Hedges semi-final, and would have then had to slog all the way back from there for Thursday's Tilcon decider. Still, it was nice to have the opportunity to play in a (for me) new tournament, and in a spa town like Harrogate, still redolent of its affluent Victorian past.

Wednesday, 10 June – Kent v. Surrey
Benson & Hedges Semi-final, at Canterbury

Back to the commentary box. I still have a soft spot for Kent and hoped they would put on a good show against Middlesex's old rivals. There is always said to be animosity between the two sides on opposite sides of the Thames but I've never noticed it. It may have been something to do with the rather complaining lbw appeals of Arnold and Jackman.

Canterbury is just about the best spot in the country to watch a big one-day match. Cars park all round the banks and their occupants unfold picnic tables, barbecues, the works. It's a bit like a summer version of Twickenham's west car park, only you can see the game as well. Many had queued from 6 am to get a good spot. They were rewarded with a nail-biting home victory, and the satisfying fact that the BBC generator went on the blink, so those who plumped for the armchair angle missed some of the action.

Commentating on TV is quite a complex process. You have to keep one eye on the game and another on two monitors to see what they are showing, as well as listening through an ear-piece for action-replay instructions from the director, and checking that the other commentator isn't about to raise his microphone to say something. Once you get the hang of it, it's rather like driving a car.

Of which I am having to do very little at the moment, thank heaven. Instead I have already clocked up 5,225 train miles this summer, costing in all £625 (most of which I won't get back). In the old days everyone used to travel by rail. Harry Dickenson, one of the first players for Glamorgan once it had achieved first-class status, remembers their finishing at Hull at 5 pm and catching a train for London which arrived just in time for a late Movietone showing. Then they caught the milk train from Paddington to Swansea, which got them there for breakfast after stopping at every station on the way. They had hardly slept because of the din of milk-churns being constantly unloaded.

Friday 12 June

At least their journeys weren't disrupted by the IRA. When I got on a tube train for King's Cross from Ealing at 7 pm it took an hour to reach Knightsbridge because of a bomb scare at Piccadilly. Which meant I had to get the 10 pm train to Durham, arriving at 1.30 in the morning. Not ideal preparation for facing the best side in the country (Essex) at Hartlepool today. I was a touch apprehensive about it, but discovered that Cook and Graveney had decided to play an extra spinner and I would be rested. 'But there's a Second XI Bain Clarkson Trophy game at Bishop Auckland today, and I wondered if you wouldn't mind helping us out, we're one short,' the Director added. I didn't mind at all, as it happened, but was disappointed not to be playing at what looked a very civilised, intimate little ground.

While I was away checking the form of the 2nd XI – which wasn't at all good on this occasion – the plan back-fired. Simon Brown limped off with recurring back trouble, and John Wood contracted shin soreness. Botham was already nursing a groin strain. So Bainbridge and Graveney did the bulk of the bowling on a sporty pitch, and Essex made 360.

Meanwhile news had leaked out that Botham had been awarded the OBE in the Birthday Honours list, and by tea the place was swarming with photographers and pressmen all trying to get their twopennorth. But the information was embargoed till midnight, forbidding interviews, so Mike Gear kindly sent Botham a police escort as the players came off the field. 'Blimey, I was a bit worried,' he said afterwards. 'I thought they were coming to arrest me.'

Saturday 13 June – Durham v. Essex
Second day, at Hartlepool

Coming over the hill to Hartlepool from the A19 offers a view that perhaps best sums up the north-east. Rolling fields and small cottages give way to denser terraces further down. Vast chemical works dominate the coastline, belching smoke in angular plumes. On the horizon, tankers wait their turn to come inshore. The scene is like an up-to-date version of the Industrial Revolution, as chimneys, vents and pipes spew forth their effluent. With such a hinterland, the sea at Seaton Carew doesn't look particularly inviting but the beach was packed. In 1926 Hartlepool was depicted as the health resort of the north-east on posters of the period, though the monkey that was hanged by locals during the Napoleonic Wars because they thought it was a Frenchman, probably wouldn't have agreed.

The town, once the domain of millionaires, has a tired sort of appearance, but the Park Drive ground, set amongst sprawling detached houses in Ward Jackson Park, has a leafy ambience. And, such is the public interest in our venture, it has a struggle fitting everyone in. Temporary stands overhang adjacent back gardens, makeshift one-way systems disorientate local traffic, and membership of Durham CCC, at 6,464, is officially closed.

Stood on a TV gantry for a while watching another debutant, Stewart Hutton, battle it out against Neil Foster who seems to have lost a bit of pace. Hutton, predictably nicknamed Lenny, is a left-hander with a penchant for hitting boundaries. He acquitted himself well and continued the trend of gradually easing younger players into the side. He has displaced John Glendenen whose defensive technique has been shown to be a bit suspect.

Having decided that Foster had got slower, I watched as he suddenly produced a wicked delivery that thundered into Dean Jones's 'box'. Jones was doubled up in agony for some time, and eventually had to retire hurt. On inspection in the dressing-room, it emerged that his essentials had turned black.

Despite these mishaps, we hauled ourselves up to 300 for 7 and declared, Phil Bainbridge playing a cultured innings of off-drives and cuts, while towards the end Botham twice launched Childs into the road. But Gooch, Stephenson and Prichard put the pitch and debilitated bowling into perspective by plundering 245 in the final session. While Prichard swept, Gooch hit the bowling anywhere he wanted, treating Berry and Graveney with the kind of disrespect he reserves for spinners, even one as good as John Emburey. Having lofted and chipped them everywhere, he then dabs boundaries through the vacant slip area. It is mickey-taking of the highest order. I was obliged to field as twelfth man (some rest!) and, as it was bright, decided to try a pair of those new-fangled sunglasses which Botham wears. Verdict – excellent, and a good disguise if I dropped a catch.

Five hours later I was sitting up a large lime tree sharing a Wolf Blass (£150 a bottle) with Derek Pringle. A secret party had been arranged by Kathy Botham to celebrate Ian's OBE and we had raided his wine cellar. The Bothams have the sort of house you might expect. Large, old, and next to a pub. It has sprawling grounds, mature trees, a lake stocked with trout, and stables. How had he found it? I wondered. 'Well, I was sitting on the loo reading *Country Life* one day and I saw it pictured. I rang the agent immediately, saw the place and put in an offer that day.' Inside, it is cosily furnished. A shrunken grandfather clock stands on the landing, a grand piano in need of a tuning dominates the formal dining-room.

At first Botham looked slightly put out by the surprise. Whatever he is doing, he likes to be in control. He took out his initial irritation on Jones, saying, 'This house has a 350-year history, y'know, a lot more than your entire country'. Various other luminaries showed up, notably Brian Close as dogmatic as ever. He plays golf both right- and left-handed and at one stage could sustain a handicap of two with either.

At about 4 am in the bar of a nearby pub I reminded Graham Gooch, who had also been sampling the wine, that in a few hours' time he would be facing my bowling from the pavilion end. He shook his head and wobbled off to bed. Another adversary crippled by Botham's midnight trap.

Sunday 14 June – Durham v. Essex
Sunday League match, at Hartlepool

There is something about playing a one-day match with a hangover that focuses the mind admirably. Basically you know that if you fail to perform you will deserve a rocket. Clearly I emerged from the evening's ordeal better than Gooch because he missed my third ball and was adjudged lbw for 0. Essex are unbeaten in the Sunday League, but after 15 overs they were 53–3, most of the runs and one of the wickets coming from the gangling medium pace of Gary Wigham, making his first appearance. But Essex bat a long way down and managed 220. I had a £10 bet with Pringle that he wouldn't hit me for a boundary, but lost miserably.

In reply Dean Jones made a brilliant 100 – only 26 in boundaries which illustrates his skill at finding gaps and picking up ones and twos – but we lost too many wickets at the other end. The most crucial was Botham who was opening, cut off in his prime by a breakback from John Stephenson. The dismissal betrayed Botham's irritating side; he complained that he had been distracted by a man flashing a mirror behind the bowler's arm. He was so churlish about it that an official was dispatched to flush out the culprit. In vain, of course: this is County Durham, not Delhi.

Monday 15 June – Durham v. Essex
Third day

By now the excellent pitch was behaving a touch unreliably, but luck went against us. Jones was not permitted to bat until five wickets down because of his absence from the field on Saturday (a fatuous rule, surely, when a player has a genuine injury sustained during the match), and then Mark Ilott struck a cruel blow, breaking Phil Bainbridge's arm just below the elbow with a ball that took off from a ridge. The impact made a sound like hammer on wood and we knew it was bad. He still managed to clip the next ball to the boundary before retiring hurt. Two hours later he returned from Casualty, his arm in plaster, just as his wife arrived on the ground. He is a key man in our team, chipping in with runs and wickets, never complaining, always cheerful. He will be much missed for the next six weeks.

Our other invalids struggled out to bat, but did not detain Essex long. John Wood had his shins heavily strapped with sticky tape which looked more painful than the actual injury. 'Go away and get fit,' he was told afterwards. 'And that doesn't mean eating scones laden with jam and cream,' added Botham, eating a scone laden with jam and cream. Fitness is the one aspect of cricket that you can control, and Wood needs to put in a lot of work if he wants to progress. He has the talent, but has he the desire?

Ian Botham, OBE – an Admiration

After six weeks spent constantly within twenty yards of Ian Botham, it is safe to say that he is larger than life. Arriving in his black Mercedes at 9.55 am, brandishing a copy of *The Independent* ('we get it delivered at home'), he has a bath or a massage to loosen up a back that has broken down twice and been rebuilt. Then he dials some crony on his mobile phone. 'Oi Jez, I've got a bit of info on a filly in the 3.30 at Redcar. D'you think I should put some on?' He takes an interest in anything that involves an element of risk.

'He's fat, he's round, he hits them out the ground,' a contingent of spectators chants at Gateshead after a massive six. Botham is a vast man with a deep growly voice. The excess accumulated from years of socialising spreads out evenly round his ample frame. He grins boyishly while excusing himself from practice because of a throat infection. The bowlers are glad. At least they won't have to trudge half a mile to fetch their ball back.

He may turn up only a few minutes before the start but he still addresses the initial stages of a match with great enthusiasm. Despite his breadth of achievement, deep down he still covets the applause, the compliments – from colleagues and opponents as well as spectators. His anxiety shows as he puffs on a cigarette. He bats more circumspectly than he used to, knowing that to get out is a brutal sentence. Once back in the pavilion he is a prisoner there, unable to venture out because he will be immediately harassed as a starstruck public quizzes and stares. Instead he snoozes, shuffles papers, thinks up silly nicknames – he should try finding one for himself – 'Mr Creosote' wouldn't be bad (after the huge 'Monty Python' character with a mammoth appetite).

Cricket has given him fame and fortune, money is no object nowadays. Recently he bought a £50,000 timeshare in angling rights on the River Tay. With paparazzi hounding him everywhere during a two-month ban in 1986 for admitting smoking cannabis, fishing was his last great retreat. He bought a rambling house in Alderney for that purpose, and to be near his dying friend John Arlott. 'He's taught me everything I know about the quality of life,' Botham said once. Presumably that was a veiled reference to fine wines which he drinks now in preference to beer.

He has been selected in the England one-day team for this summer, though you hear some people claim that he is still living off his 1981 heroics. But while he has not made a Test century for four years, and tends to lure batsmen to their doom with an ordinary delivery, he is still an awesome opponent. His skill is in his eyes, which remain razor sharp and sanction reflexes of astonishing speed, and in his hulking shoulders ever able to propel awkward bouncers to the unsuspecting or launch the bat in that distinctive wide arc. He is like the ageing cat that can still pounce and grab the errant mouse.

Frustratingly he does make excuses if things go awry. He may blame uneven footholds after a long-hop has been thumped to the boundary, or the distractions of a spectator when he is unexpectedly dismissed. But that trait is common amongst superstars and part of the remarkable self-belief which makes them great – they are never in the wrong.

Some days his enthusiasm wanes, and he is only interested in putting money on horses. There are any number of willing friends who will give him tips, act on his instructions and collect his winnings. He is the pied-piper of English sport.

But you have to like him. For his humour, his generosity, and above all his loyalty. Whether he's playing cricket for England, or a golf match for Darlington, he spurs on his team-mates to pull their weight, to win. 'Anyone I see not trying will feel the force of my boot up their backside,' he will say. Despite little preparation, his extraordinary cricketing skill lives on, and is being translated into golf too which he now plays off seven. 'It's funny, I never have a net, but I'm always on the driving range,' he says as he arrives at the course with two sets of clubs.

His winter schedule is heavy: the 22-day walk for leukemia research across the south coast of England, another series of 'A Question of Sport', a pantomime somewhere, and an extensive speaking tour with Viv Richards called 'The King and I' going as far afield as Australia. He is inundated with letters, requests for what has become the world's most unreadable autograph, and invitations. Yet does he have any real friends, I wonder? His wife, definitely. But it is so hard for anyone else really to relate to him. He has such a powerful aura that sweeps past, leaving everything else in its wake. Pressmen who privately ridicule him daren't do so in print. Rightly so too. They are wary of writs arriving on their desk and mindful also, perhaps, of a remark of Dr Johnson: 'A fly, Sir, may sting a stately horse, and make him wince; but one is but an insect, and the other is a horse still'.

Tuesday 16 June

Doing my washing, I discovered I have only three cricket socks left, and one pair of flannels. I don't know where they all go. Someone somewhere must have a whole truckful of used gear!

Thursday 18 June

A day at the Lord's Test, something worth keeping my MCC membership on for. The pavilion may be stuffy but it does serve delicious carvery sandwiches and you always run into someone you know. The City must have closed down for the day, to judge by the number of pin-striped skivers around. I also spied John Paul Getty, Mick Jagger, Michael Parkinson, and, of course, the inevitable John Major. Spent most of the day in the Upper Mound Stand from where it looked as if you could play

Waqar Younis with a stick of rhubarb. It was only when I inspected the television highlights later that I could see he was undoing England with his vicious brand of inswinging yorkers. This delivery has coined a new phrase – 'Getting Waqared' – which is either painful or terminal or, in Ian Botham's case, on the fourth day, both.

Friday/Saturday 19, 20 June – Sussex v. Durham
Championship match, first two days, at Horsham

One of the odd things about this season is that we have got to this stage and still haven't played on a Test ground. Having said that, some of the best wickets are on the out grounds. Uxbridge, Cheltenham, for instance, and this one. When I say 'best', by the way, that doesn't mean a belter, a shirt-front, but one that gives everybody a chance. Batsmen have it all their own way: one bouncer per over, heavier bats, flatter wickets, light meters, ample protection. What developments are there to a bowler's advantage? And if this sounds like a whinge, get hold of a 1950s *Wisden* and see how many batsmen averaged over 50 then. Not many.

A 'good' pitch
What makes a good cricket pitch? The answer is: it depends. On the type of match, the ability of the players, the state of the soil, the time of year. The groundsman's first objective is to find a balance between a surface which causes danger to batsmen and an unresponsive one that is a complete disincentive to bowlers.

The spectator's ideal is somewhat different. There is a public outcry after a spate of pitches giving assistance to the seamer, but no-one complains (except the bowlers themselves) when ball is paying total homage to bat. Bill O'Reilly, the great Australian leg-spinner, sums it up one way, saying, 'Batsmen are the pampered darlings of the committees, while the bowlers are classified as necessary appurtenances of the game best designated as "cricket's labourers".'

[84]

The pitch at Horsham is white and, with a parched outfield as well, fielding sunglasses are de rigueur. Apparently shielding your eyes from the sun will be one of the health fads of the 1990s. So should be protecting your body from Franklyn Stephenson's bouncers! His action is definitely the hardest to pick up in the country. It's his height, flailing arms, and changes of pace. Although his quick one is awkward, it's his slower ball you really lose. It looks destined to hit you on the head, and you stand transfixed like a rabbit in headlights until it dips, missing the off-stump by a whisker. Even Wayne Larkins rates him a tricky proposition.

It was a red-letter day for Paul Parker, returning 'home', if you like. He used to live in a house backing on to the ground, and he made several centuries for Sussex here. His departure at the end of last season could have been due to his losing the county captaincy as well as philosophical differences with Norman Gifford, the coach. What these were is hard to fathom but Parker is at his best launching an offensive, Gifford is naturally more cautious.

The former Sussex captain, John Barclay, whom everyone affectionately knows as 'Trout', put it into perspective. 'I've never seen Paul so relaxed,' he said. 'He's obviously having a great time with such a variety of characters. Playing positively he's an awfully good batsman, isn't he?'

Oh yes, what happened in the match? Well, Parker took four fours off an over from Stephenson who bowled a liberal sprinkling of bouncers at everyone. (Each ball of one over he bowled at me hit my bat or my body before I'd moved.) Having invested in a substantial new pair of boots, John Wood retaliated, taking the first three Sussex wickets, all caught on the boundary by Steve McEwan – one cutting, two hooking. As he took a single David Smith ran into Wood accidentally-on-purpose, knocking him out of stride. In the next over from Wood, Smith couldn't avoid a bouncer and took it painfully on the shoulder, though he didn't flinch. Our rookie paceman is progressing rapidly.

20 June – Sussex v. Durham
Sunday League match at Horsham

What with the Biggin Hill airshow, and the London–Brighton bike ride, I suppose I should have expected some trouble on the M25, but not an hour at a standstill. At least it gave me the chance to listen to descriptions of the Pakistanis winkling out England in the gripping Lord's Test. Managed to get to the ground by 1 pm, for which I would have been reprimanded at Middlesex. David Graveney is more lenient.

Don't know how anyone can argue against a 40-over Sunday League after this match. It swung one way and then the other, produced 545 runs and brilliant fielding, all under a hot sun. It seems extraordinary that 479 swishes at a piece of moving leather during the day can leave the match hanging in the balance until the last ball, but it seems to happen quite regularly. Even more often, I seem to be bowling the last over. The equation this time was 12 runs to win, two wickets left. Facing was the Sussex all-rounder John North, who had just completed a whirlwind half-century off 21 balls. He had even been hitting yorkers for four.

So where does one bowl? I tried to find the block-hole first ball, but he countered that by advancing down the wicket and lacing the extra-cover boundary. Eight runs needed off 5 balls. Obviously the yorker ploy wasn't going to work, so next ball I attempted a bouncer, a risk with nobody behind the wicket on the leg-side. Fortunately, he had decided to charge me again and could only jab a top edge to the 'keeper. This brought the last pair together who scrambled 3 singles, leaving them to make 6 off the last ball. Crucially the no. 11 was facing and he had obviously lost the thread: instead of unleashing a huge swipe, he glided the ball delicately down to third-man and we were home by 5 runs.

Such a finish saps all your energy and concentration, but I must confess I do enjoy them – for one simple reason. Whoever wins, the twenty-two players have done their job and provided a breathtaking climax. We are, after all, entertainers first and foremost. True, it took a long time for the nightmare of losing

[86]

the 1989 NatWest final off my last over to fade, but I still felt that the entire crowd would have gone home sated. That's the bottom line.

Hardly feel today's modest achievement merits a magnificent hotel bedroom complete with four-poster, and separate sitting-room, but that's what I've ended up with. Makes a nice change from sterile cramped cubicles and a concave mattress.

Monday 22 June – Sussex v. Durham
Third day

If ever there was a 'déjà vu' in cricket, this was it. Set 340 to win, Sussex required 270 at tea, from 40 overs. Precisely what they needed at the same juncture yesterday. The only difference was that this time, if necessary, we could put every fielder on the boundary (rather than only five on Sunday), and we could bowl wide of the stumps and get away with it.

It didn't help us much. Sussex players, reared on beautiful batting wickets, love pursuing big targets. They bat a long way down and hit plenty of sixes, no-one more than Martin Speight, who conspired to sweep everything the spinners bowled at him and a couple of my faster deliveries as well. Wish he'd stick to painting landscapes rather than larruping bowlers.

Such is the precise charge of these run-chases that yet again it was down to the wire. 12 runs off six deliveries. Only this time we couldn't win unless I got a hat-trick or something.

As I turned for the first ball of the over I caught sight of a T-shirted Botham on his third jug of Pimm's giving me the thumbs-up through the pavilion window. I then ran in, stopped in mid-delivery and half-heartedly ran-out Franklyn Stephenson as he backed up too far. It was only a joke, but it made a point of sorts. Umpire David Shepherd drew a red-card from his pocket and pretended to send me off, which caused general amusement. It riled Stephenson, though, and he somehow managed to flick my second delivery just over square leg for six, and my last through mid-wicket's outstretched hands for the winning two runs. Oh well, three days' cricket and no positive result does seem a bit of a waste of time, I suppose, but, although we lost, we've gone up the table through bonus points. We're seventh.

These last two days have certainly stretched our younger contingent. Stewart Hutton has been severely tested by the short ball, and survived, just, though he got a nasty one in the gonads. He hasn't had much protection from umpires who are having difficulty distinguishing a short ball from an intended bouncer, particularly when the batsman ducks. The leg-spin of Mark Briers has had a couple of airings, and he notched a crisp maiden fifty as well as fielding agilely under pressure. And John Wood has been taught a salutary lesson in bowling at the death. It doesn't matter how fast or tall you are, if you don't cramp the batsman for room you'll be caned. But they have all come through relatively unscathed which bodes well for when we old lags bow out.

Protect yourself!

'Struck amidships', 'hit in the nether regions', 'a blow to the abdomen', 'a fate worse than death'. All these phrases are commonly used to describe a batsman's most painful experience – receiving a ball in the testicles, if you see what I mean. And whereas most cricket equipment is constantly improved – lighter pads with Velcro straps, gloves with extra padding and built-in sweat bands – the design of the abdominal protector, or 'box', has remained more or less unchanged for a century.

Yet players unlucky enough to receive a bouncy nip-backer still suffer considerably. Leicestershire's Tim Boon spent two days off the field after such a misfortune last week, Stewart Hutton vomited violently after being led off, and Dean Jones's experience brought tears to his eyes. It is on occasions like this that the employment of a female physio is counter-productive. Sheila Job, running to the aid of a convulsed Jones at Hartlepool, commented, 'I knew what the problem was and that there was nothing I could do'. Which reminds me of the

[88]

player who, in a similar condition, said to the approaching lady, 'Get rid of the pain, but keep the swelling'.

In the 1930s, the box – a dome-shaped codpiece – was made of tin. 'They used to knock the dents out if they'd been hit there,' the umpire David Shepherd remembers. Plastic replaced metal in the 1950s and some came with their own waist straps. Today's model has padding round the rim and slips into the pouch in jock-strap or briefs. But it has a habit of moving sideways if struck, with the awful consequences. Yet no-one has thought up an effective alternative, although Allan Border and Sussex's David Smith swear by a longer, sleeker version used in baseball which, if cracked, can be repaired with Superglue.

Mind you, it's the extreme ends of the body that need protecting when you play the Pakistanis. Wasim Akram threatens your head or the base of the stumps, while his partner Waqar Younis spears them in at your toes – Ian Botham is only the latest casualty of the most devastating yorker in the game. Discussions continue about the extravagant swing purveyed by these bowlers. The umpires have examined the ball constantly but have found no sign of tampering. Sri Lankan-born Gehan Mendis, of Lancashire, who has played with both Wasim and Imran, has an amusing theory: 'The reason that the Pakistanis get the ball to swing so much more than anyone else, may in the end boil down to the racial characteristic,' Mendis says. 'Perhaps their sweat has different properties to other people's, that makes it ideal for shining the ball!'

Mike Gatting always achieves an exceptionally good polish on the ball. He certainly has no distant Pakistani relatives, but he does eat a lot of curry.

Wednesday–Friday, 24–26 June – Ireland v. Durham
NatWest Bank Trophy, first round, at Dublin

There is a general feeling that all major counties should play their first-round NatWest ties away. Certainly, if the destination is Dublin, they should. Even the slightest whiff of a celebration and Dubliners are out till all hours – no-one seems to have any conception of time in the bars and clubs dotted about Lisson Street. For a region of widespread unemployment, the people seem amazingly content, too. They take immense pride in their city and countryside, I suppose. The corpulent barman of the gleaming Mount Juliet Golf Club was still feverishly pulling pints at 2.30 am. The establishment was heaving. 'When does this bar close?' I enquired. 'OCTOBER!' he roared. It summed the place up.

We took thirteen players, one scorer, one female physio, and Tommy the Tourist, alias I. T. Botham. Still inconvenienced by his damaged big toe, he arrived in shorts and T-shirt armed with golf clubs and extra drinking capacity. Oh, and his wife, who was heading for the stores. 'If my husband's going golfing for three days, I'm off to spend his money,' she said saucily.

Golf is, of course, meant to do injured big toes some good. Tuesday's round at the Royal Dublin Club didn't. Asked by his opponent, Dean Jones, to putt out an 18-incher, Botham missed, and hit his foot with the club in annoyance. Unfortunately, it located the same spot that the Waqar Younis missile had three days earlier. What he yelled echoed round the entire harbour, but I wouldn't know how to spell it.

Having played in Ireland twice before, I know their tactics. They always organise a pre-match dinner and attempt to get the opposition plastered. Last year, against Middlesex, the plan failed, largely because the hosts allowed themselves to get drawn into the festivities as well. This time it was even less successful as our two chief guzzlers retired to bed at 7 pm after an extensive afternoon session, and the third, Botham, wasn't playing.

He was in fine arguing form at the table, however. Sitting opposite Trevor Bailey, the Man of the Match adjudicator (which always seems just an excuse for wheeling out the old 'uns for a mid-week outing and is regarded with little interest by the players), the two soon became embroiled in an argument over (1) the wearing of helmets, and (2) injuries to young bowlers. The debate progressed precisely nowhere, neither of them listening to, nor appreciative of, the other's opinion. It was a bit like two bull-elephants meeting head on. I moved away and talked to Tom Moffat.

One of the founder-directors of the new county and formerly treasurer of Durham, Tom is a genial, diligent man, passionate about his birthplace. He tours the county, giving heartfelt speeches on the continuing need for progress. You could say that he is the voice of the members. So unassuming that he is occasionally taken for granted by the other club officials, he was perhaps the most influential of all in getting the wheels in motion back in 1989.

The match was of little consequence – well, you don't come to Ireland to worry about the cricket. There was some consternation among officials at the pleasant Clontarf ground that, last year, I had denigrated their wicket by describing it in *The Independent* as 'like playing on Weetabix'. It was a bit insensitive perhaps. This time the wicket was greener – more like dried seaweed. 'It needs some time under a seven-ton roller,' I said, when pressed afterwards by the groundsman who was not sober. 'The heaviest we've got is a two-tonner,' he slurred. A problem.

The Man of the Match award went to Steve McEwan for a quickfire 34 and 4 wickets although he also delivered 11 wides. Wayne Larkins' 113 had been the most decisive contribution, but he was ignored. 'Trevor Bailey's always had a thing against me,' he said, which makes me think even less of Man of the Match awards.

It has often been suggested that the adjudicator spends most of the day sozzled in a sponsor's tent, then takes a quick look at the scorecard before selecting the batsman with the highest score. Statistics tend to bear this out. There have been 949 Gold Awards since the Benson & Hedges Cup began in 1972. Graham Gooch heads the list with twenty, followed by Barry Wood and Mike Gatting (eleven each), Kim Barnett, Chris Balderstone, Ian Botham (ten each), Boycott, Greenidge, Edrich, Stovold, Tavaré, Lamb, and Rice (nine each). Malcolm Marshall has won only one, Curtly Ambrose and Courtney Walsh, none at all. Wicketkeepers, of course, need not apply.

[91]

Chapter 6

'Dean Jones got us out of jail'

Back to the real world and the terraced house in Durham I've recently moved into. The news on the home front is that our Second XI have lost in two days to Somerset, but still stay top of the table, a great effort. The spindly paceman, André van Troost, exploited a ridge on the Eppleby wicket, and Durham succumbed. Our young lanky medium-pacer, Gary Wigham, commented, 'Why can't I bowl as quick as him, I run in just as fast?'

Saturday 27 June – Durham v. Kent
Championship match, first day, at Gateshead Fell

Extract from the memoirs of a seasoned seamer, aged 32½.

9 am. Miss lift from Paul Parker, so take taxi from Durham to Gateshead. 'It's bloody greet this Durham thing,' says the driver. 'Never thought you'd do so well.' Costs me £10, partly offset because I donate match-tickets to driver.

10 am. Mad fielding games with Dean Jones, criss-crossing each other, balls flying everywhere, a poor-man's version of those army acrobatic teams at the Festival of Remembrance.

10.30 am. Win toss. David Graveney asks Kent to bat to slight surprise of Kent captain who would have chosen to bat anyway. Daunting prospect of fielding till 7 pm, as we are playing a truncated third day to allow Kent to get off early for the long drive to Maidstone.

11.30 am. Fortunately, we take two early wickets. On the other hand, I am asked to bowl at Carl Hooper who has just taken guard. Bowlers always prefer their first couple of overs at a lesser batsman, to get their rhythm and confidence. As it happens, he is dropped at mid-on off my second ball, then launches a couple of decent deliveries over cover. He is an astute man, Hooper, with gunslinger eyes under a white sun-hat.

12.00 Mark Benson stops me in mid-run because someone is moving behind sightscreen. As I run in again, the same thing happens but Benson ignores it and edges to the 'keeper. He walks off looking daggers at the miscreant, but shouldn't he have been watching the ball, not the background?

After taking a good catch, nervy wicketkeeper, Chris Scott, shouts, 'Come on, Yozzer' – the first time he has spoken on the field since early June.

12.45 pm. Hooper gradually assumes control, lacing the boundary with drives and cuts. Dean Jones jabbers from second slip, cajoling the bowlers, suggesting the odd short delivery. Graveney claps heartily, and looks rather red in the face. Either he's embarrassed or had too much sun.

1.15 pm. Lunch. Lamb curry and rice, and gallons of orange squash. Outside the dressing-room an errant cigarette butt sets Neil Taylor's thigh pad on fire.

1.45 pm. Botham arrives for treatment, his bandaged big toe protruding through a pair of flip-flops. He is interviewed by an eleven-year-old for a children's magazine.

2.30–3.50 pm. I bowl lengthy, probing spell for no reward, moving the ball away from the right-handers but never getting a touch. Edges and sliced drives fly to the boundary. Usually I can keep tally of how many runs I've gone for, but now I've lost count.

4.10 pm. Retire to long-on and manage to watch final set of Bates v. Champion singles match at Wimbledon through pavilion window between balls. At tea Kent are 230–4.

[93]

4.40 pm. Begin two-and-a-half hour last session. I am bowling again and immediately beat Matthew Fleming three times outside off stump. Fleming apologises for not getting an edge, then tonks two fours over mid-off. Eventually trap him at deep cover, but not before I've got my ton from 30 overs.

5.45 pm. Mid-session tea-break while umpire Meyer pops off to relieve himself. Caterers have gone home so 12th man has to raid sponsor's tent for tea-bags.

6.15 pm. Supporter asks me why Kent players are all so broad in the beam. I am nonplussed. Perhaps they all grew up with pictures of Colin Cowdrey in their bedrooms.

6.40 pm. We winkle out Kent for 392. We have 12 overs' batting in which time Wayne Larkins will probably score 40, while Stewart Hutton nudges 2 with his Harrow-size bat.

7.20 pm. Hutton 16 not out, Larkins 4. What a good judge I am! Looking forward to mulling over play with the opposition but they leave for their hotel immediately afterwards. I assume this is the influence of their Australian coach, Daryl Foster. Or perhaps they don't want to listen to my whingeing.

Sunday 28 June – Durham v. Kent
Second day

Very good opening partnership developed between Larkins and Hutton, although the latter was nearly felled again. Dean Jones not required until 2.30 by which time the portly quickie Martin McCague, from Western Australia via Northern Ireland, had embarked on a fiery spell. A snorter, third ball, smacked his compatriot on the cheekbone. Jones, who doesn't wear a visor, collapsed, kicked his feet, then got up unaided and marched off, blood seeping from below his left eye. Nearly another injury as he angrily flung his bat across balcony. No major damage revealed, but interesting that none of the Kent players enquired after his well-being at tea. It didn't really surprise me. While he has been of immeasurable value to us, his confident demeanour at the wicket probably drives opponents wild. And he did admit to having made McCague look a bit of a fool in a recent Sheffield Shield encounter.

For all the acclaim from commentators for the one bouncer per over per batsman rule, it hasn't prevented a gentleman like McCague from propelling three or four short ones an over, and getting away with it. The intimidation law was quite satisfactory, but the umpires always seemed reluctant to enforce it. My vote (and that of Derek Pringle, Imran Khan and many other players I've talked to) is a return to that law. Anyway, if anyone claims they can accurately judge whether a 90mph ball was over shoulder height as the batsman ducked, then my aunt's the Queen of Spain. How else, I wonder, can the authorities handicap the fast bowler? Restrict them to only one inswinging yorker per over, I suppose, in the light of Waqar Younis' recent successes.

Monday 29 June – Durham v. Kent
Third day

Game petered out into a draw, Kent setting us too many in the time. This often happens in three-day cricket; not many county captains seem to realise that you have to be prepared to lose to have a chance of winning. During Kent's final onslaught, I bowled a yard down the leg-side to Fleming who countered by taking guard on the return crease. It's at times like this that you wonder what is the point of having the wickets there at all.

Thursday 2 July

The left hand is in vogue at the moment. John McEnroe has won through to the Wimbledon semi-finals; also Goran Ivanisevic – the first Croatian ever to do so – with his 140mph serve. And David Gower is back in the England squad for the first time since his well-chronicled flight over an Australian ground in a Tiger Moth. Martin Johnson put it beautifully in *The Independent*: 'The return of Wing Commander Gower is even more apposite now that England's batsmen are beginning to associate the sound of the pavilion bell with an air-raid siren'. He needs thirty-four runs to become England's leading Test-match run-maker and thus displace 'Sir' Geoffrey. I hope Gower does it. Quite apart from his entertainment value, he is a very genuine, self-effacing chap who becomes embarrassed at all the cooing of the crowd when he plays a regulation off-drive.

Friday/Saturday 3/4 July – Durham v. Gloucestershire
Championship match, first two days, at Stockton

Rain for 48 hours, which makes any ground look depressing but Stockton unusually so. 'At least it'll make the sightscreens grow,' the groundsman suggested, alluding to my previous comment on TV that they were rather short. You can't get away with anything these days!

Took the opportunity of a bad forecast to try out the night spots of Darlington with the local lothario, Andy Fothergill, as my guide. It proves to be a remarkably lively place with everyone under the age of forty getting togged up to cruise round garish bars full of loud music and gyrating waitresses. Thought I'd better do my bit and chat someone up, so in Buzz's bar I sidled up to two girls having an animated conversation. 'You seem to have plenty to say to each other,' I yelled above the din. 'Yes, we have, thanks,' they both answered, and turned their backs.

Sunday 5 July – Durham v. Gloucestershire
Sunday League match at Stockton

Just as well Geoff Cook forced us to turn up for a net on Thursday because we haven't done anything for nearly a week. In Botham's case it's more like three.

Exciting match, well attended again. They can't sell many tickets to the local population because the County members keep applying for their entitlement. 'Sometimes we even have to turn members away,' Tom Moffat said. 'It's a bit embarrassing.'

I'm being entrusted with opening the bowling in these games, which takes the pressure off some of the younger guys. At first I was a bit nervous about it, but I don't mind now. A lacklustre display in the field materialised though, which particularly annoyed Graveney, watching from the pavilion as his old county feasted on a juicy diet of ill-directed bowling. (He had begun the match, but then, trying to stop a drive, he fell like a lopped tree and twisted his knee. So we have changed his nickname to Human Chernobyl – walking disaster!)

Fortunately, the batsmen did their job this time. There's something quite reassuring about sending in Larkins and Botham to chase a big score. They bring out the best (or worst) in each other. 'He always bowls in my slot,' Botham said to Larkins, having taken 12 off Babbington's first over. 'Now it's your turn.' Whereupon Larkins smote his second ball over the sightscreen. 'Ooo, I like the look of that one, Neddy,' Botham cheered, as the ball soared upwards. Then Dean Jones took over, and with his familiar mixture of nurdles and clips and frenetic running, progressed to 50 almost without noticing. He is not what you would call a pretty player – all bustle and confidence with fast hands and quick feet – and he works hard for his runs. He scored only four boundaries in 92, and two of those were inside edges past the 'keeper.

As Graveney pointed out afterwards, Jones got us out of jail, helped by the hapless Gloucester bowlers and the imperturbable Ian Smith who seems for ever destined to come in with 25 runs needed off three overs. 'Our out-cricket was crap today,' Graveney said, in a post-mortem conducted amidst the entangled contents of thirteen cricket cases in a room the size of a prison cell. 'And if we're like that on Thursday against Middlesex, they'll annihilate us.'

Drove home in my sponsored Astra diesel which I lent to Mark Briers in April when it had done 343 miles. The clock now reads 6,785.

Happily Gower achieved his goal at Old Trafford, passing Boycott's aggregate in a blaze of shots. They were interviewed together on the balcony afterwards. 'Yes,' said Boycs, 'cricket has always needed flair players like myself and committed professionals like David.' In truth, the way Gower wafts his bat outside off stump is a reminder that, in this game, genius and folly are rarely far apart. He does not walk out to bat having signed a commercial undertaking with the spectators, but plays spontaneously as the mood takes him.

Gower's triumphant match was soured by the outrageous behaviour of some of the Pakistanis. First, Aqib Javed was warned by umpire Roy Palmer (standing in his first Test) for intimidating Devon Malcolm. He responded by running through the crease and bowling yet another bouncer, and finally, having been handed his sweater, threw it back childishly. All this provoked an ugly scene involving Miandad, the other umpire, and a threatening Pakistan supporter.

The Test Match events overshadowed a dreary attempt at a one-innings match at Stockton. Gloucester batted on too long, and bowled and fielded too defensively to engineer a result. Spent part of the afternoon talking to two dishevelled supporters. One, known as Jesus for his shaggy hair and long wispy beard, is particularly put out by nearby Redcar Cricket Club having banned him because his dog supposedly soiled their square. He will only be allowed back in if he brings a poopa scoopa. 'One of those isn't big enough to clear all the crap out of that club,' he said belligerently. Anyway from listening to them I've learnt some more phrases from the new Geordie Bible of Cricket:

'Canny Knacker' – good ball;
'slog oot, sorn' – get on with it, mate;
'hossin' down' – very heavy rain;
'wad yer or wadn't yer' – eligible girl in grandstand.

Thursday 9 July – Middlesex v. Durham
NatWest Bank Trophy, second round, at Uxbridge

Apart from our opening match, the biggest game of the season so far. Middlesex have been in fantastic form, winning every Sunday match and half their Championship ones. Their batting is looking awesome – Gatting is currently averaging 125 – so we will do well to limit them to 270. Particularly with Bainbridge still injured, and Graveney due for the surgeon's knife on Monday.

Crucially it was damp and quite un-Uxbridgelike (it's usually a batsman's paradise), and we won the toss. Botham for once led the pre-match psych-up.

'They're over-confident at the moment, and vulnerable,' he said. 'We can beat them, but everyone's got to believe it. We must all identify a member of the opposition and try 100% to outplay him. And if I see anyone not giving everything, you know what'll happen.'

It was well spoken, and motivated John Wood to such an extent that he tore in for the first ball with special vigour. Unfortunately, the groundstaff had mistakenly left the crease areas uncut and, as Wood took off, his foot slipped and all sixteen stone of him went crashing to the ground. He moaned in agony. Oddly, instead of bringing on a stretcher, a lawnmower arrived, and the creases were given a short back and sides as Wood hobbled off with a twisted knee.

Steve McEwan stepped into the breach. A nervy character we thought early season, who ran in faster than he bowled, he has now harnessed control to outswing, and he kept the pugnacious Haynes and Roseberry in check. So, too, did Brown, though his early season venom seems to have gone.

After twelve overs, three things had emerged: (1) Roseberry was back in the pavilion; (2) Parker, as captain, was calming down after initially impersonating Corporal Jones of *Dad's Army* ('Don't panic, DON'T PANIC'); and (3) I was due for a bowl. At this point the Middlesex batsmen noticed a distracting flag fluttering over the sightscreen. Umpire Dickie Bird was at great pains to get it taken down which took several minutes.

When I said, 'Hey, Dickie, we need all the help we can get, y'know,' he shouted, deadpan, 'PUT THE FLAG BACK OOP AGAIN.'

I had been mulling over the game for a week, and subconsciously I was fired up. After taking an over to settle, I bowled brisk and straight ('You seem to have put on a yard of pace,' Fothergill exclaimed.) I didn't manage to get Gatting, but I visualised he might run himself out at some stage, and said so. He rarely makes big runs in big games.

Sure enough, he chanced a quick single on 57, off the last ball of the over, and Larkins hit the stumps from short-extra. Brown and Carr added a thrust, but it was left to Emburey to try to boost the score. 'Please let me survive Botham's over so I can heave you just once over extra-cover,' he said to me. The result – a thin edge to the 'keeper, first ball, and I finished with 4–41, my best Durham figures. 'Oh, Simon, why did you leave Middlesex?' a kindly woman supporter asked. 'We rather liked you.' 'Because I was asked to,' I replied, matter-of-factly. They say absence makes the heart grow fonder, but it has to be said, it only took a couple of misfields for the shouts of 'Eeyore!' to return.

I suppose playing against your old county does tend to lift your game as you strive to remind them of what they are missing. I thought I perceived a certain reluctance of some of the Middlesex committee to speak to me afterwards, although I did try to catch their eye!

After an early success, Middlesex conspired to lose the game with a succession of wides and no-balls totalling 27 in all. Their bowling really isn't the strength it was – Fraser and Williams only at medium pace, Chas Taylor too wayward, and Tufnell inexplicably left on the bench. What also didn't help was Gatting's strange decision to field on the boundary most of the time, instead of being in the circle, urging on his team.

A composed century partnership between Botham and Parker won us the match. Neither took any risks, until Botham attempted a mortar attack on the sponsors' tent late on, and both proved that once partnerships are established in one-day cricket, anything is possible. As is now customary, Ian Smith popped up in the last overs to provide the final impetus. Paul Parker, quite rightly, won 'man-of-the-match' for his innings and three fine catches; I didn't even get a mention. What was I saying about bowlers never getting any recognition?

It was a tremendous victory, against all the odds. What gave me particular satisfaction wasn't that we had beaten my old colleagues, but that we had played so well as a team to do so. Most of the Middlesex side were too dejected, or annoyed, to socialise, and our team was disappearing off in various directions (four to stay at my house), so the celebrations petered out.

Friday 10 July

The good news is that we have drawn Leicester in the quarter-final; the bad news is, it's away. So, not only are the Durham supporters deprived of a home tie, but we have to eat again in the dining-room where, if the roast beef's that tough, you can always use it as boot insoles.

Saturday 11 July – Kent v. Hampshire
Benson & Hedges Cup Final, Lord's

Easily the highlight of my journalistic career so far – commentating for BBC TV on the Benson & Hedges final. Went to examine pitch with Ray Illingworth – to do the 'key test' – and was immediately told off by officious MCC representative. 'The BBC knows nothing about your presence here,' he said, 'and the Colonel is doing his nut. Please leave at once.' A shame, because I was having an interesting conversation with Mick Hunt, the MCC head groundsman, about scuff marks on the square made by over-enthusiastic Middlesex fielders. 'Thank God you lot beat them in the NatWest the other day,' he said. 'It gives us all a day off.' Groundsmen the world over are so protective about their wickets and hate them being overused.

[101]

Despite dark skies and an even darker forecast, the match started on time. After my first stint at the microphone I was just enjoying a glass of Lançon to celebrate the B&H's twenty-first year when in walked the BBC Director of Sport, Jonathan Martin. Felt a bit of an ass drinking on the job, but he didn't seem to notice. 'How are you enjoying it?' he asked. 'Great,' I replied, 'I think I'm learning.' 'Just imagine you're talking to three or four friends in a room,' he advised, 'and if you haven't got anything interesting to say, don't say anything.'

Made one or two faux pas during the day, especially when I described Malcolm Marshall's hand as 'slightly darker than those belonging to the Kent attack'. 'D'you want to take the phone call from Bernie Grant or shall I?' said Richie Benaud off-mike, with a sly grin. Generally, though, I felt I handled things OK, particularly when I suddenly had to discuss the issue of neutral umpires to camera, sandwiched between Tony Lewis and Sunil Gavaskar!

Rain ruined the match with only one innings completed, so it will continue tomorrow.

Sunday 12 July – Somerset v. Durham
Sunday League match, at Taunton

Arrived by train at 11.40 and hailed taxi for lift to ground. 'Arrr, Oi'd be rippen you arf,' said the driver, and pointed to the ground barely 400 yards away. When I got there, ample, ruddy-looking families with rosy cheeks were already filing in with their picnics.

Team talk at 1.50 pm. Paul Parker: 'Right, lads, important game this one. Five hours' concentration and we could be up among the moneyplaces. They've had a nightmare recently, Somerset. They've got Caddick [the Hadlee lookalike], Mallender, Lefebvre (he skids a bit). And MacLeay – bowls very, very slow outswing. Hit him back where he comes from.'

'What, Perth?' said Jones. 'That's a bloody big hit.'

'Anyway, lads,' continued Parker, 'we'll enjoy the evening a lot if we win.'

[102]

'Well, I'm going to get pissed anyway,' said Botham, and guffawed.

Fortunately, things went to plan. After a brisk start, Parker clubbed 70 and Jones made a crisp 80. 'That's your fifth consecutive Sunday 50,' I said, as the Australian passed, sweating profusely.

'Sixth,' he corrected.

Victory was never in doubt, except while Tavaré was breaking out of his weekday shell as he often does on Sunday. Stonewall Jackson one day, Slogger Smith the next. Botham bowled aggressively and seemed anxious to show his old county supporters a thing or two. This included an astonishing catch off his own bowling. As the ball disappeared into orbit he yelled 'BEEFY'S!' and the fielders scattered. He eventually took it horizontally about a yard from the wicketkeeper.

Monday 13 July

Travelled back to Durham on the 11 am flight from Taunton in Botham's Mercedes. On the way he opened a new office complex in Cheltenham, pocketing a fat cheque for the trouble. For most of the rest of the journey, he gave instructions on various business matters on his portable telephone, or discussed racing tips.

When we had reached Wetherby, he said with a degree of concern, 'What are you doing tonight, Pluto?' I replied that I had planned nothing in particular. 'Come and stay with us, if you like,' he went on. 'Better than going on to an empty house.' It was too good an offer to refuse, so I spent the evening round the table devouring two huge roast chickens with the family, Liam, Sarah (13) and Beccy (9), and Kath. We emptied three bottles of New Zealand Sauvignon Blanc to accompany the meal, then watched *Tough Guys*, a comedy with Burt Lancaster. During News at Ten I went for a row on their private lake. Further afield they have a racehorse, a goose and two goslings, and any number of rabbits and hares which Liam tries to shoot.

[103]

On the rare occasions they are all together, they seem a very happy, contented family.

Tuesday–Thursday, 14–16 July – Durham v. Pakistan
Three-day match, at Chester-le-Street

The Pakistanis have to be the noisiest touring team ever encountered. The din of ball on helmet or stumps being shattered is exceeded only by the constant jabber from the fielders. Shouts of 'Bowling Wicky, Shabash!' rent the air one end, while at the other Wasim Akram queried the adjudication of no-balls and bouncers.

Fortunately they batted for most of the first day, on a lovely even-paced wicket. The extravagant opener, Aamir Sohail, chipped balls into gaps and rode his luck to record a rapid 50. No-one else was very impressive and we held them to 300–7 declared. They obviously weren't aware of our ability to lull teams into lethargy. This left eleven overs of potentially torrid batting, but it turned out to be the fielders who were more in danger as Larkins and Glendenen thrashed 64. Larkins has always said he likes these short aggressive sessions because he can take advantage of the close-set fields to knock up a quick 40.

Botham arrived on the second day complaining of a chipped thumb (the result of a caught-and-bowled attempt), and took no further part in the match. He wasn't even at the ground for most of it. With a sniff of a spot for the Fourth Test, he probably wants to avoid possible jarring. He is said to have lost a stone in weight although, typically, his diet is tailored not to interfere with his lifestyle – it consists of fish and champagne.

Nevertheless, at lunch we were 215–1. Larkins, having played the most marvellous array of shots on that lovely wicket, walked straight over to his girlfriend, while Jones marched off nursing a bashed finger. With two weeks of his stay left, his wife decided to head back to Australia early – she was fed up with being in Durham on her own. The repercussions were evident as Jones took the field in a pair of woefully crumpled whites.

Both batsmen notched their hundreds as I was collecting my soiled whites from the launderette. It was rewarding stuff for the spectators who had come in droves; in fact, tickets were in such short supply the players donated a dozen complimentaries to a queue of Geordies outside.

As we continued to lash the Pakistani bowling – including Wasim Akram ambling in off six paces (they play their strongest XI in every County match, mindful of the £50,000 bonus if they win eight games) – I inspected the site of the new ground, just a good three-iron away. Giant earth-movers rumbled around the flat churned-up plain on the banks of the river, beneath Lumley Castle. Workers wielded pickaxes laying the service road, and I could just make out the shape of the square (marked by pegs in the soil) and outfield. Judging by the drawings it will be an impressive sight, with all sorts of sporting facilities. At the moment it looks like a collection of fallow allotments.

Bowled tight spell after tea and was unlucky not to take a wicket, particularly when Aamir Sohail top-edged two bouncers (in consecutive overs). We had the following altercation:

Me: You jammy sod!

Umpire: That's your one for the over.

Sohail, provocatively: Let him bowl another one then.

Me: I don't break the rules.

Sohail: What rules?

Chester-le-Street produced more glorious weather and keen crowds for the third day. It is a charming ground, very lush, and overlooked by temporary stands while the austere castle, now a hotel, looms in the background. On the commercial side the club has done brilliantly, selling four hundred covers a day in the hospitality tents pitched on a nearby school play area. With a profit of £15 on each one, some healthy revenue is coming in from these home games.

And some runs, too. Before the match I asked Dean Jones how many he needed for his 1,000. '220 or so,' he reckoned, which would take him several innings. In the event, he got them in two, with successive hundreds against Akram and Co. This was an outstanding performance, particularly in the light of the phenomenal pace generated by Waqar Younis. I doubt if the people of Chester-le-Street will ever again see bowling of this ferocity, countered with such skill and panache. Glendenen fought bravely at the other end for 36 and will have grown enormously in stature after this harrowing experience. But once we lost a couple of wickets, we were never going to make 300 without Botham batting, and the innings quickly subsided as the Pakistanis sensed another notch in their quest for eight wins and a cash windfall.

It was left to Brown and myself to fend off the last ten overs, hemmed in by those umbrella fields last seen when Lillee and Thomson were in tandem. Some people might imagine that the experience of facing Akram bowling round the wicket, running up behind the umpire before popping out in the last three strides to let you have it, while Waqar sought the vicious yorker the other end, was exhilarating. It's not the word I would use.

The saddest aspect of this defeat was that we had really played the superior cricket until tea on the last day. If it had been a football match we would have led 3–1 until suddenly conceding three goals in the last ten minutes. Worse still, Miandad put up the shutters when we bowled accurately in the morning and wouldn't budge until we offered up some friendly spin with inviting fields. He even jokingly offered me £100 to give up my wicket at the end. 'Why should I?' I said, laughing. 'You wouldn't give me yours!'

You can only admire their team's skill, though. Even their reserve quick bowler, Ata-ur-Rehman, looks impressive, despite running in like a headless chicken. No-one is sure how old he is. Apparently he played in an Under-18 tournament recently, claiming he was born in 1974, but when an official allegedly visited his mother's gravestone, he noticed that she died in 1969!

Over the three days they were reasonably well-behaved and I had a good chat with some of their reserves, who all made it on to the field at some stage. It's well-known that the Pakistan cricket team has more subs than the American Navy. Whether this is due to laziness or the anxieties of their physio – a

Pakistani called Eric Johnson – no-one is sure, but I find it hard to believe that Ramiz Raja has an upset stomach every time they are in the field.

Friday/Saturday 17/18 July – Nottinghamshire v. Durham Championship match, first two days, at Trent Bridge

Life at Trent Bridge has always been a combination of enterprise and stagnation. Ever since William Clarke, the Kerry Packer of the mid-nineteenth century, first established cricket there in 1840, the ground has been characterised by mostly progressive and sometimes mystifying behaviour. Clarke didn't pay the players so they earned money through side bets. Many of them were small-time crooks. When Clarke left Nottingham to create his touring England XI the ground was less in demand and all manner of other activities were staged. These included football, archery, and even an annual cricket match between one-legged and one-armed XIs.

The inventiveness continues today. On Saturday there was a display of medieval fighting, the combatants dressed up as local heroes, Robin Hood and Little John; a demonstration of elementary mountaineering on a climbing wall; news items printed on the scorecards; and Bruce French proposing an abseil down a nearby tower-block. But a certain resistance to change is still evident. The sightscreens at the pavilion end are inadequate, and when a request was made to move spectators sitting above the bowler's arm at the Radcliffe Road end (from where many a top batsman has failed to sight Franklyn Stephenson's slower ball) there was a committee meeting to discuss it. The request was refused.

The players' dining-room is dual purpose. On match days you can enjoy a choice of sausage and onions, leek pie, or quiche Lorraine. Outside the hours of play it doubles as a museum, packed with memorabilia from Nottinghamshire's chequered past: Jessop's bat, Larwood's cap, Hadlee's sunhat, a kangaroo foot presented by an Australian touring team, and Arthur Shrewsbury's 1887 Testimonial certificate on receipt of a purse of seventy-two sovereigns. Shrewsbury eventually shot himself during a match in 1903. The game was abandoned as a mark of respect.

For such a talented team as the present one, the disappointing performances in the early part of this season are a bit of a mystery. Mike Hendrick took over coaching duties in June and for him life has been transformed. Two months ago he spoke dolefully of his inactivity apart from the odd stint on Test Match Special. Now he has his hands well and truly full. A country man reared on the green pastures of the Midlands, he disputes the assumption that seam bowlers deliver deliberate leg-cutters, arguing that he could land the ball on the seam six times out of six, but had no idea which way it would go. Hendrick was an upright cricketer who has brought his sense of discipline to bear on the Notts players, even down to fining them if they arrive unshaven or bring copies of *Mayfair* into the dressing-room. Results, other than on Sundays, have improved significantly.

Which is about time, considering the abundant talent at Trent Bridge. On Friday it was very much on show. Tim Robinson compiled a typically sedate hundred, Derek Randall (the only forty-one-year-old trying to talk himself *into* a Sunday League side) played a brief cameo combining exquisite drives with airy wafts for which he constantly admonished himself, and Chris Lewis injected impetus with an afternoon century. One six off Mark Briers landed just below the pavilion roof – a massive carry. I fear for the future of spinners if bats can deposit the ball this far. Our lack of bowling firepower was exposed here. Simon Brown has no zip at present, and Botham, McEwan and I are failing to paper over the cracks.

In contrast, Chris Cairns blew away our top order with pace and aggression, and broke Jones' finger – next to the one smashed by Waqar Younis yesterday. Already three down, we needed a circumspect innings from Botham but he missed with a huge drive and was bowled. There was a depressed silence when he walked into the dressing-room, eventually broken by 'Cor, how was I expected to play that, it came back miles!' 'How would you know, your head was in the clouds,' someone mumbled under their breath. We couldn't recover, and followed-on.

Jones, making light of his injury, thumped length balls back over the bowler's head, and rapidly reached three figures, with Larkins a mere spectator at the other end.

We went for an Indian meal at midnight in a buzzing Nottingham (there is supposed to be a ratio of three women to one man here, which perhaps explains why it's where Boots the Chemist was born), but were soon nearly thrown out when one of our number declared the establishment null and void for having a West Indian head waiter.

Sunday 19 July – Nottinghamshire v. Durham
Sunday League match, at Trent Bridge

Usually on Sunday mornings you can lie in and enjoy a peaceful read of the papers. It's not quite so relaxing when the windows of your hotel room are sealed and you're next door to Ian Botham in good burping form. At least the hotel is large and central and most of us have singles, which makes a change from the ordeal of a room-mate's snoring or early wake-up calls (the captain and the senior pro never have to share). But they will insist on cramming the room with every type of free sachet, from hair gel to boot polish. No doubt it's just an excuse to put up the price.

Good solid League win against inexperienced Notts side languishing at the foot of the table and missing six regulars. Tim Robinson threatened, but was brilliantly taken in the deep by Glendenen, at last erasing the memory of those early season blunders.

Monday 20 July – Nottinghamshire v. Durham
Championship match, third day, at Trent Bridge

Showers never long or heavy enough to be terminal made us hang around for most of the day, but not even a greased wicket could dislodge the determined Jones and, when play was abandoned at 4.15, he was 157 not out. What a triumphant finish to his abbreviated season. The middle finger of his right hand is broken, and to play again before he goes to Sri Lanka with the Aussies would be putting his entire career at risk. But he's staying with the lads till next week to lend moral support.

Took the short hop to Leicester through the country down the A46. Stopped off at Ansells' pub in the village of Thrussington on the way. Anything to delay actually arriving in Leicester!

Dean Jones – One-day legend

1) Dean, if you hadn't chosen your current career, what would you have done? *Become a prison detective for correctional services.*
2) Who were your biggest influences/heroes? *Keith Stackpole, Bob Simpson, Allan Border, and my father, Brian.*
3) Biggest regret? *Missing Ashes tour of 1985.*
4) What would you like to be doing in five years' time? *Playing for Australia.*
5) Favourite place? *Home (nineteenth-century farmhouse, north of Melbourne).*
6) What was your worst job? *Taking out the rubbish (at home) – I class that a job.*
7) What do you like about the north-east? *The people, the countryside, and my team-mates.*
   Dislike? *The A1, noisy ground announcers, regulated taps on showers.*
8) What would you most like to change about yourself? *My golf handicap from 12 to scratch.*
9) What makes you angry? *Roadworks, people not coughing up, three-putting.*
10) Players admired? *Allan Border, Viv Richards, Malcolm Marshall.*
11) Suggested changes to improve the appeal of county cricket? *Coloured clothing for Sunday League; four-day cricket will improve play but may not improve attendances.*

12) Special hobbies? *Golf; walking my two Rottweilers, Jess and Stanley.*
13) Pet hates? *Queueing; batsmen having to ask spectators to sit down or be moved.*
14) How in your wildest dreams would you like to spend a day/night? *To play and win a final at Lord's, then celebrate with players and friends all night long. I love winning!*

Dean Jones arrived in Durham with a big reputation and left with a vast one. Almost singlehandedly he has set the place alight and provided a superb role model for all and sundry to emulate. Few could doubt his status as the best one-day batsman in the world – seven consecutive fifties on Sundays is testament to that – no-one could dispute his commitment. Always first in the nets, constantly assessing his technique, batting is his obsession. Fielding too. We lost count of the number of new catching games he introduced, making practice fun as well as instructive.

I was amazed how dedicated he was. Bowlers' weaknesses and strengths are jotted down meticulously in the kind of little black book that would in the old days have been associated with activities that had nothing to do with cricket. 'Just a few tips for the other Aussies when we tour here next year,' he said once when I peered over his shoulder. He also records his own scores and modes of dismissal each day, and number of deliveries faced. He ought probably to make a note also of how many ones and twos he's run – it would be a useful indication of how tired he should be feeling at the end of the day.

He's essentially a workmanlike batsman with no real frills, yet he's exciting because a typical innings involves a flurry of activity. A crisp on-drive will be followed by loud yells of 'Yes . . . Hustle!' and as often as not, a scampered two. What he lacks in pure speed he makes up for with a swift turn, despite a left knee completely rebuilt five years ago after a collision. For this reason he can only push off with his right leg and uses his hand on the ground, sprinter style, for extra leverage. This explains why he wore out eighteen pairs of batting gloves during his short stay.

[111]

No-one could have relished more becoming the first batsman ever to score 1,000 first-class runs for Durham, yet no-one worked harder on behalf of whoever was batting up the other end. His encouragement to youngsters or tailenders significantly raised their expectations, and was a source of inspiration to older ones. Watching him and Parker chasing madly up and down the wicket like two March hares made fielding sides wilt appreciably. His esteem as an aggressive boundary fielder put hesitation in the minds of opposition batsmen as another flat throw came winging in from deep square.

At first he found it hard adjusting to the plasticine wickets and quiet pubs of the north-east, preferring bouncy hard surfaces to bat on and a place with more action after hours. But he soon acclimatised, revealing an almost childlike enthusiasm – a willingness to take guard with that rigid, slightly closed stance, in any conditions at any time. He rarely even asked for a night watchman, and several times insisted on continuing in the middle in spite of obvious injury. He would be the first to admit that his own game benefited as a result. 'Mind you,' he said, 'it's actually cost me money coming over. I would have grossed twice as much appearing at clubs and functions back home. But it's been worth every cent.'

In common with most Australians northern sarcasm passes him by, and his drinking capacity is limited – he slipped off to bed if there was a dangerous session developing. But he kept us entertained with lurid tales of his exploits with Big Merv Hughes and early encounters with Rod Marsh. He was universally liked and made a huge impact on Durham's people and players. His absence will leave a yawning chasm in the batting we can't hope to fill.

Chapter 7

Digging deep

Tuesday/Wednesday 21/22 July – Leicestershire v. Durham
Championship match, first two days, at Grace Road

Stayed in a bizarre hotel, next to the racecourse, called Leicester Squash. This was not an allusion to the size of the rooms (minute), but that you ate breakfast hemmed in on all sides by people thrashing rubber balls about in those claustrophobic square chambers. It was a friendly club, with a good snooker room, but somehow the smell of stale sweat doesn't really go with scrambled eggs.

Twiddled thumbs, played snooker, looked glumly at Grace Road lunch of stewed giblets, while rain lashed an already moist square. The NatWest pitch for next week was under water, but there was obviously no prospect of moving it as they were erecting the TV commentary box directly in line.

Eventually play started at 4.30 pm. Very damp conditions under a hot sun – you could almost feel the moisture being drawn upwards. Graveney lost an important toss, and in came David Millns tearing down the hill. The Leicester paceman already has 53 wickets to his name this season, and in six overs he made it 57, as the ball flew through chest high off a green ridge. The West Indian Winston Benjamin was a positive relief the other end. Larkins gloved a brute of a ball that almost cut him in two, Hutton edged to the 'keeper, Briers and Glendenen were beaten for pace. Botham was away in London collecting his O.B.E. We finished the day at 100 odd for 8, and it was quite a relief to escape to the Royal Leicester golf course for 9 holes with the umpires, Meyer and Balderstone.

Driving to the ground on the second day past rows of drab council housing evoked a depressing going-to-the-office-on-a-Wednesday feeling. It doesn't help that the street leading to the players' entrance deserves to be renamed DisGrace Road. It is choked with vans and lorries all servicing a collection of decrepit-looking factories manufacturing knickers and socks. The mood is slightly alleviated by a marvellous tuck-shop selling delicious filled cobs, which at least take the edge off the terrible lunches.

It was soon our turn to try to exploit the seaming conditions. The ball made a sort of splat as it pitched, emphasising the dampness under the surface. It helps the seam to grip, makes green streaks on the pitch and exaggerates the bounce. All countered with aplomb by the crooked bat but boundless patience of the Leicester captain, Nigel Briers (93). It was a turgid innings but it was invaluable for his team. During one over, I beat him several times outside off stump, before delivering a half-volley last ball which he swatted for four. As the ball returned from the boundary I took an angry kick at it, accidentally volleying it head height to third-man. I apologised, but Briers said, 'I like to see a bit of emotion, shows you're competing hard', which was decent of him.

The form of Paul Henderson continues to baffle. Having taken crucial wickets on Sunday at Trent Bridge and scored 30 under trying conditions yesterday, he bowled like a drain today despite strangling two wickets late in the innings. Marking out his run-up for a second spell, he was asked by the umpire what he would be bowling (over or round the wicket). 'Right arm shit,' he said, and delivered a leg-stump full toss. It's wrong to get too impatient with him, though. He is only seventeen. At that age I didn't even have a proper run-up.

Rotating the bowlers, we winkled Leicester out for a lead of 110; Graveney helped, tricking three batsmen into the assumption that the wicket was turning. I donned the pads and survived a dozen balls as night watchman, in partnership with Larkins who somehow avoided getting a touch to six ferocious deliveries from Millns. 'Piece of piss,' he said, walking up the wicket at the end of the over.

Thursday, 23 July – Leicestershire v. Durham
Third day

The tiny Grace Road dressing-room – a sea of coffins and bats – has a mid-season reek about it, as if it needs fumigating. All the more reason, you would have thought, to spend some time in the middle, but soon five batsmen were back in the hutch. Including myself, lbw ducking what I thought was a bouncer but which rapped me on the knee, and Larkins, acrobatically taken by a pirouetting second slip. The Leicester players are on a tenner a catch – almost as much as their daily meal allowance – giving rise to the new local motto, 'Cling for your supper'.

Millns finished with ten wickets in the match, damaged several more fingers (including that of Graveney who is doubt-ful for the next game), and looks a good bet for the Fifth Test if he stays fit – a big if. He attributes his improvement to long sessions spent with Ken Higgs, bowling at one stump. Young players need this level of scrutiny, not some cursory glance between fielding practice and the arrival of the morning tea trolley. Conversely, it was the umpire, Allan Jones, who had the most profound influence, pointing out that his angled run was ungainly and pointless. Now the only thing that curves is his late away-swinger.

During a rain stoppage, I picked an alternative England XI with Millns' opening partner, Winston Benjamin. It was: Gooch, Bowler (Derbys.), Stewart, Speak (Lancs), Ramprakash, Smith, Krikken (Derbys.), DeFreitas, Millns, Taylor (Northants), Tufnell.

Friday, 24 July – Middlesex v. Durham
Championship match, first day, at Lord's

So, the mass Durham exodus to the headquarters of cricket, marking, for many supporters, the county's real stamp of approval. For me, of course, it was strange going back as a visitor to the place that was my home for twelve years. The visitors' dressing-room wasn't so alien, though – twice in NatWest finals Middlesex lost the toss for choice of dressing-room and had to move. It's not just a matter of popping next door, incidentally, but entails lugging kit about half a mile to the other end of the pavilion.

I always pride myself on being completely unable to predict or read a Lord's pitch, and today was no exception. 'What can we expect the strip to be like?' Graveney asked, as we walked out to the middle. 'Oh,' I said, 'there's been a lot of rain and Middlesex never get what they want. It'll be damp as hell.' Wrong again. It couldn't have been more of a desert if it had been pitched in Abu Dhabi. Clearly it would turn from ball one, so Graveney took a gamble and, with only one able leg and the fingers of his bowling hand strapped together, declared himself fit, hoping to win the toss, bat first, and be OK to bowl tomorrow.

Trouble is, he lost it. You could tell that as soon as Mike Gatting uttered an ugly chuckle, looking down at the Queen's head glinting up at him from the 10p piece. Friends they may be, but there are few gratuities in county cricket, and Gatting was intent on quashing any flickering romance associated with Durham's first appearance at Lord's.

At 220–1 by mid-afternoon, you could say he had achieved that fairly efficiently. There was no absolute domination, however, mainly because Phil Berry turned in a long and restrictive spell from the off-spinner's favourite pavilion end. No-one took excessive liberties, though Mike Roseberry – Durham born and bred, of course, and in a rich vein of runs – tried hard, unveiling a newly-learned reverse sweep which drives spinners to distraction.

Once Gatting was out at 239, a succession of Middlesex

[116]

batsmen came and went, uncertain as to whether the captain wanted to press for a very large total, or ensure 300 by a hundred overs, thus securing maximum batting points. (Ideally he would have liked both.) But where was Gatting? No-one knows.

Suffice it to say, they lost five wickets trying for the 300 and failed by 2 runs, largely because I located the block-hole with some frequency. The day ended with Middlesex 340–8 (Roseberry 169 not out, Phil Berry 6/71), and a rumpus between Gatting and Roseberry about the squandering of a good position, which nearly came to blows. When all's said and done, the Middlesex captain should have been in the dressing-room directing his charges. Something far more calamitous happened to me. My treasured Reebok bowling boots finally gave up. Two spikes sheared off in my fifteenth over, and they are beyond repair. So ends their two-year career of more than 1,000 overs, umpteen nets and about fifty rounds of golf.

Saturday 25 July – Middlesex v. Durham
Second day, at Lord's

Took Durham players for a tour of the ground – Fothergill had never been to Lord's before. It is much maligned because of its formality, its indifferent public facilities, its quaint rules. If you're a man, though, it has a certain irresistibility. Having played there for over a decade, it's easy to become blasé about the austere elegance of the Long Room, the palatial nature of the refurbished dressing-rooms with their brass fittings and plush seating, or the enquiring stare of the members as you walk out to bat. (Certainly the Middlesex members seemed more pleased to see me this year – with the opposition – than they did last!)

My favourite place at Lord's is not Nancy's dining-room nor the Bollinger Bar, but the Print Room, hidden away under the Grandstand. Vince Miller may not be a household name, but he is Lord's longest serving employee, first handling the letter-

[117]

presses in the days of Compton and Edrich. Last year, the room that reeks of ink and machine-oil produced 170,000 scorecards, each one meticulously hand-set by the assistants, Chas and Dave. The cards are updated three times a day, a process which has continued probably since the days of John Lillywhite and his portable printing tent in the 1840s. On non-match days, the presses churn out tickets, passes, circulars, menus, and pro-grammes by the thousand, as the commercial arm of the MCC grows longer.

Watched a few overs from the top of the new Mound Stand – the breeze billowing the canopy roof. It is a spectacular view from here, deserted as usual during a county match. Then we climbed up to the scorers' nest at the top of the Grandstand, and watched Brian Hunt and Harry Sharp dotting and cross-ing while Pam operated the electronic scoreboard via a compu-ter. Harry is a marvellous stalwart of Middlesex whom he joined after the war as a stolid opening batsman. The story goes that a spectator once approached him practising his whelk-like defence in the nets before a match. 'Are you playing today, Harry?' the man enquired. 'Oh yes,' came the dignified reply. 'Well I'm off home then,' the spectator declared.

Now Harry's views are much sought after by the Middlesex players when he returns to the dressing-room for his Scotch at the end of play. 'Not a bad day,' is the perpetual summit of his compliments, mumbled as he puffs on a relit cigarette. He always reserved his greatest praise for a rapid Gatting century. 'Brutal, bloody brutal,' he would say, wincing in sympathy with the unfortunate bowlers.

Lord's is moving ahead slowly. There are more eating points, better loos, and organised tours of the pavilion and other quaint exhibits, including some of the spectators. There is even talk of staging a baseball match here in a year's time, which will advance the number of sports played at Lord's to nine; the others, apart from the obvious, being lacrosse, hockey, tennis, boxing, soccer, real tennis, and squash.

Old habits die hard, though, and women are still not allowed in the pavilion during a match. Which caused a problem when Durham arrived with Sheila, our female physio. A series of

phone calls were necessary for her to gain admittance, and once she reached the relative sanctuary of the dressing-room it was hard for her to leave. She was told she wouldn't be allowed on to the field at any time, but was soon summoned to treat Botham's damaged finger. 'Hey, women can't go on there,' a flustered steward shouted as she hurried down the pavilion steps, while startled members sat agog and grumbled, 'Whatever happened to the British Empire?' A few years ago, a young eccentric MCC member turned up in the pavilion wearing long hair and a pink suit, and was not admitted for looking too effeminate.

In keeping with the friendly welcome accorded me by all the stewards and other employees, the crowd and the Middlesex players gave me a lengthy ovation when I walked out to bat. It made the hairs on the back of my neck (there aren't many on my head) stand on end. But, having survived Phil Tufnell's wiles for half an hour, I was confronted with the pacemen. 'Come on, Chas, stick it up his nose,' the left-arm spinner urged. The warmth, then the chill, of an English summer's day.

Hemmed in by four close fielders and the expertise of Emburey, we had subsided to 102–7, although, ironically, Tufnell had taken most of the wickets. With a mixture of force and fortitude Berry and I put on 89, and we eventually not only achieved two batting points but saved the follow-on. The Yorkshireman finished 75 not out, a career best, to add to his seven wickets – doubling his career wickets total in the process. Seeing him bat in pre-season nets I assumed he was the resident no. 11, but he is actually a solid competent player. A direct contrast to his physical constitution which is decidedly fragile. He visits the physio as often as Graveney with anything from a 'bad knee' to a 'bruised shoulder'. He has that slightly puppyish physique that looks as if it likes being mothered.

Dinner tonight in our honour at the Swiss Cottage Holiday Inn, but also to raise money for the Middlesex County Cricket Club Benefit. Hey, something fishy here. What are 250 Geordies doing lining the pockets of a profit-making southern business?

Sunday 26 July – Middlesex v. Durham
Sunday League match, at Lord's

An education received today in how to pursue a total. It wouldn't have mattered what we had scored, Middlesex would have passed it. Geoff Cook made his first appearance as preparation for possibly playing in next Wednesday's quarter-final, and contributed a pleasant 49. But a total of 198 was never going to be enough. Haynes and Roseberry milked the bowling, never taking undue risks. They are a hard pair to bowl at – the West Indian gliding a length ball on the off stump through cover, his partner punching an identical delivery past mid-wicket. Gatting came in to add impetus, giving the off-spinner a bit of a pasting as is his wont, until I satisfyingly got him two short of 50. I think I have illustrated during the course of the last month that Middlesex didn't really get the best out of me in recent years, perhaps because subconsciously I didn't have the greatest respect for Gatting as a captain, although I did as a batsman, of course. You have to make players feel wanted and important in a team, not just a last resort.

Barbecue at my parents' home for both teams afterwards, during which we dressed up John Glendenen as a long-lost childhood sweetheart of a blindfolded Dean Jones. He carried it off rather well in blonde wig and fishnets until the calls to 'stick your tongue in, Glendo,' broke out!

Monday 27 July – Middlesex v. Durham
Third day

While Graveney lay next to the juice machine, wired up to an electronic gadget which appeared to be feeding him orange intravenously (it was actually treating his finger), we considered our position. Middlesex were 140 ahead, all second innings wickets standing, on a deteriorating wicket. We had one fit spinner with six first-class matches under his belt, they had Emburey and Tufnell with seventy Tests under theirs.

The anticipated capitulation began at 2.12 pm when Botham rushed up the pitch to Tufnell, and was stumped by a mile. By 4.15 it was all over as our brittle batting submitted meekly to the leg trap. At least I had the satisfaction of getting the ball as far as deep square-leg.

Oh well, we still have a run in the NatWest to look forward to.

Wednesday 29 July – Leicestershire v. Durham
NatWest Bank Trophy Quarter-final, at Grace Road

Or did have. But the chance went begging. Never, surely, will Durham have a better opportunity of a semi-final spot. Was 250 in sixty overs too many to chase? Not if you liken it to the third day of a championship match on a flat pitch, when you know that the opposition's best bowlers are restricted to twelve overs each. For five of our team – Glendenen, Fothergill, Smith, Berry and Brown – this was the biggest match of their careers and to be let down by some of the senior players was a calamity. At 100–1 Larkins casually lobbed to long-off, Cook over-balanced and was stumped, Bainbridge played a loose shot, and Parker ran out Botham. Then, when we still had a sniff of a chance – though by this stage it was only ten parts per million – I ran out Parker. It was a game we lost from the jaws of victory, and everyone knew it. Cook summed up the mood afterwards. 'I am utterly downcast,' he said.

It's a mistake to get too romantic about cricket. Yes, it would be lovely to score 100 on your debut, or make a final in your first first-class season, but these things rarely happen. Grace Road, Leicester, on a Wednesday in late July, is not a dream; it is stark, naked reality, from the precipitous steps back to the pavilion to the warm bottled beer and gnarled spectators.

The build-up to such matches is never entirely what you expect. Having taken our minds off cricket with a round of golf the night before (Cook and Hughes lost to Parker and Botham whose finesse round the greens was surprising), we arrived in good time at 9 am, only to find our route to the players' car park

[122]

blocked, and then the gates to the nets padlocked. Well, you don't want a net at this stage in the season anyway. The pre-match discussion didn't materialise either. We had so many players that half of us had to change on the balcony in full earshot of the opposition. When all the injuries had been taken into account, the team was: Larkins, Glendenen, Cook, Parker (capt.), Botham, Bainbridge, Smith, Berry, Fothergill, Hughes and Brown – seven genuine batsmen and six bowlers. Just before we took the field, Peter Willey, doing a stint on the BBC commentary team, popped his head in the dressing-room. 'And I don't want you bowling from this end, Prof'. (He thinks I'm intelligent.) 'The glint off your head will blind me.'

Although the pitch was sporty, six batsmen were run out in the match. Two in the Leicester innings were pure farce. Parker threw to the 'keeper's end as Parsons came back for two, but Fothergill conned him, pretending the ball was elsewhere, the batsman eased off and was a yard out. The next delivery rapped into the no. 11, Mullally, prompting a loud lbw appeal. The ball, meanwhile, trickled back down the wicket and into the stumps as the batsmen attempted a leg-bye. Bainbridge yelled gleefully as the bails came off with Benjamin out of his ground, but no-one had touched the ball. Parker, ever alert, seized it and threw down the striker's stumps with Mullally stranded.

As the match was covered on BBC TV, this incident is guaranteed to reappear on *A Question of Sport* in the 'What Happened Next?' category. It was a hysterical end to the Leicester innings; but they had the last laugh.

SCORES: Leicestershire 249 (Whitaker 63, Hughes 3 for 34); Durham 204 (Parker 54, Wells 3 for 38). Leicestershire won by 45 runs.

31 July–6 August. A week in Durham

August is for arguments. It's the time when players' limbs are weary; they lurch in pairs from one cramped hotel bedroom to another, waking up in the morning unsure of the day or the way to breakfast. There are injuries, long days in the field, and the cordial early season atmosphere, when players applauded every delivery, has degenerated into silence and bickering. Hanging on to your marbles is imperative, especially if you lose the toss.

The flick of a coin is the age-old method of deciding who goes where at the beginning of a match, and it is hard to convince the team that, even though you've lost eight in a row, mathematically there is still a 50-50 chance of losing the ninth. The moment of the toss is a focal point of any cricket match. Beforehand, there is any amount of pushing and prodding at the pitch, car-keys pressed into the surface, balls surreptitiously bounced on it, trying to ascertain how this strip of turf will behave. The groundsman is sought for his opinion, the weather forecast checked. Committees of players stand about discussing the various permutations.

Half an hour before the game the captains exchange teams. Chris Cowdrey often relates the time he stood in mid-pitch at Headingley, proudly wearing his England blazer, as Viv Richards, in lycra shorts and baseball cap, ran through his team. 'Now let me see,' the West Indies' captain mused, 'there's Greenidge, Haynes, Richard-son, Richards, Logie, Dooojon, Marshall . . . Man, you can play who you like.'

The other participants have long since retired to the pavilion for tea and bourbons, but as the coin goes up you can be sure that most will be watching anxiously from the window for a signal. Irrespective of the conditions, bowlers want their team to bat first, batsmen want to field, thereby delaying the moment of personal performance for a while. Colin Cowdrey had a simple philosophy about winning the toss: 90% of the time you batted first, the other 10% you contemplated fielding, but batted anyway.

'Durham are second from bottom in the Championship, but have the chance to pull themselves up with home matches against fellow strugglers Surrey and Yorkshire this week,' *The* (Newcastle) *Journal* reported. Graveney announced a team meeting. 'Oh God,' Chris Scott said, 'I'm terrified of meetings in August.' (It is usually at this time that the contracts for next season are announced.) But with injuries to Parker and Wood, and Jones now departed, the captain was only clarifying the need to dig deep into our reserves of physical and mental energy, otherwise we will gather pace down the slippery slope. He's good at putting such things in a nutshell.

At lunch after 32 overs the Durham score was 160–6, which suggested that Graveney's words had not been heeded. It was certainly entertaining, but depressing too, especially when Surrey's Alistair Brown emerged at 5.10 pm to clobber a century before the close and put his side firmly in the driving-seat.

From Caterham School, Brown is flaying county attacks with a combination of brazen stroke-play and urban bravado. There is a confident self-belief about big-city boys that our meeker people like Scott and Brown just don't have. During his breathtaking assault, he swatted a high bouncer from Ian Botham to the boundary. 'That was a bloody slog,' the bowler grumbled. 'I'm only copying the way my idol plays,' Brown replied, with a mixture of cheek and respect. As he launched one ball in the direction of Durham prison, I noticed scaffolding above the jail. 'What's that?' I asked a local. 'They're erecting a platform for the prisoners to watch Durham. It's their punishment,' came the reply.

His team already out of the match, a beleaguered Graveney returned to the pavilion at the end of the first day, his head bowed under the pressure of poor performances and cynicism from press and supporters. 'The honeymoon period is over,' he said sadly.

Things are not all dark and dismal, however. As Geoff Cook says, we are building for a future. People should not expect instant results, and good things are emerging all the time. Mark Briers looks a class act with the bat, but he is constantly lumbered with taking guard at 20–2; Stewart Hutton's taciturn nature is loosening and he could become a fine player; John Glendenen is allying technique to indisputable power. To be fair to the majority of members, they do acknowledge all this – sympathising with unlucky dismissals and revelling in the general situation. Some have become regulars at certain parts of the boundary (it always seems to be where I'm fielding), and are teaching me various Geordie pronunciations.

Surrey arrived with a squad of fifteen and the familiar figure of Graham Clinton, glinting bonce and all, as coach. I bet he still breaks fingers just taking fielding practice. They are without Keith Medlycott whose bowling skill, by all accounts, has deserted him. This seems constantly to afflict left-arm spinners; one year they are close to England selection and the next can only propel a long-hop or a full toss. When this malaise befell Phil Edmonds, he couldn't remember with which foot to start his run-up, never mind what to do with the ball. Derbyshire's Fred Swarbrook was in an even worse state. When asked by a sports psychologist why he persistently bowled head-high full tosses, he said, 'I envisage a wall somewhere down the wicket that I have to lob the ball over'.

Alistair Brown's bat looked a bit like a wall all weekend in Durham. He fired off a volley of shots on Sunday, rubbing our noses in the dirt to the tune of 330 – the highest total I've ever experienced in a 40-over match. (During our fielding the combined ages of the men in the circle – Cook, Graveney, Larkins and Botham – was 153 years, surely some sort of record?) Just to underline Brown's domination, he then ran round the boundary, picked up and threw in one movement, hitting the stumps direct as Botham came back for two.

Tuesday 4 August – Durham v. Yorkshire
Championship match, three days, at the Racecourse

The Surrey match, then, was a watershed. The one against Yorkshire was a different matter entirely. It coincided with another 'first' for me. Having relinquished my sponsored car to team members living further out, I walked to the ground from my Durham cottage. It was a far more pleasant route, much of it beside the river, than that which the Bedser twins would have taken when they allegedly travelled on foot to The Oval. They must have been good walkers living, as they did, in Woking!

Matches against Yorkshire are always to be savoured. The side is full of characters and they're always humorous, even in adversity. They have some funny nicknames, including 'Daisy' for Peter Hartley. 'Some days-ee does it, some days-ee doesn't,' is the explanation. You fancy beating them, too. An added incentive this time was the presentation of a trophy donated by the Durham Light Infantry – the Lahore Cup, reputedly the largest cup in the world.

While Larkins was rediscovering lost form on a brisk wicket, I examined Botham's mail. He gets about fifteen letters a day from all sorts of loonies. One from Cochin, India, read: 'Dear Mr Botham, We very much enjoyed the way you danced after taking a wicket in the World Cup '92. This letter is to ask if you would be interested in importing cashew nuts from factories here in Kerala . . . you might be able to set up a shop.'

But a peaceful afternoon watching our chaps cream it about was ruined by the clatter of wickets which continued unabated for two days. Ten of these (in two innings) went to Mark Robinson, an honest into-the-wind toiler, who left Northants two years ago mainly because Allan Lamb habitually ignored him. Then five went to me as Yorkshire capitulated from 82–1 to 108 all out. The collapse was so sudden that Robinson, the last man, had to be retrieved from a shop, and came bolting down the hill in a tracksuit as no.10 was making his way to the wicket. Mind you, as Robinson's career batting average is a little over 2, we would have been prepared to wait for him to get ready.

Chris Scott and Graveney rescued our second innings from a calamitous 68–8. By comparison with his early season reticence, Scotty is positively extrovert now, patting bowlers on the back, cajoling fielders and even offering Botham a few words of encouragement in a tremulous voice. He is still living in the sparse conditions of the flat on the Great Lumley housing estate, where the TV and the bed satisfy his every need. He is also an expert washer-upper which is just as well as all the other birds have flown the nest. Bainbridge has been back in Bristol until this week, Wood in Wakefield, and I've taken my Coronation Street house near Durham station. I saw three kids playing with a bat and tennis ball in an alley today, perhaps the embryo of a cricket boom in the north-east.

Barely out of short trousers himself, Sachin Tendulkar piloted Yorkshire to a five-wicket win with an immaculate century – his first in the county championship. The loss of the Lahore Cup was greeted with some dismay by the Durham faithful, but they were philosophical. 'Ay, he's a little master, Tendulkar, canny lad. There's always next year.' And they trooped off to watch the White Water Rafting finals of the Barcelona Olympics, or maybe drown their sorrows.

Scores: Durham 214 (Larkins 67, Robinson 6 for 57) and 155 (Scott 54); Yorkshire 108 (Hughes 5 for 25) and 263 for 5 (Tendulkar 100). Yorkshire won by 5 wickets.

Sachin Tendulkar – Child prodigy

Most nineteen-year-old youths are preoccupied with girls, clothes and resenting their parents. India's batting prodigy eats, sleeps, and talks cricket in a relentless quest for perfection. Tendulkar's meteoric rise confirms him as a rare player. A century on his first-class debut followed by his first Test at the age of 16 years, 205 days. In that match Tendulkar was struck in the face by a ball from Waqar Younis. Battered but unbowed, he hit the next two deliveries to the boundary, but was out soon afterwards for 15. Only a year later he made a composed Test century at Old Trafford.

The key to Tendulkar's extraordinary achievements is his sporting maturity. Lack of experience is irrelevant. He seems to know instinctively what to do. 'He has a remarkably old head on young shoulders,' Allan Border said. Tendulkar seeks advice from India's greatest batsman ('Mr Gavaskar', he reverentially calls him) and helps himself by being extremely self-critical. He noticed how fielders like Dean Jones were respected for their speed to the ball and quick release, so he concentrated hard on that area of the game. 'Now batsmen think twice before taking two to me on the boundary,' he said.

19, 20. Paul Parker, (*above*), one of the country's finest fieldsmen, takes a high catch Australian-style in the Benson & Hedges match against Middlesex at Uxbridge. (*Below*) A splendidly athletic attempt by Botham to run out Emburey.

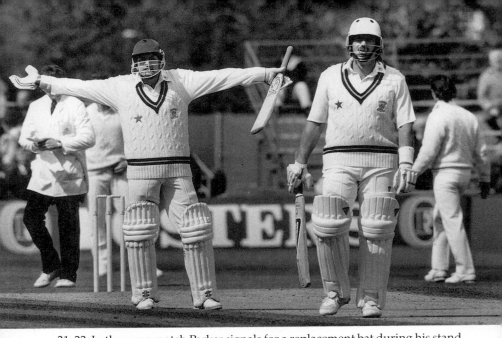

21, 22. In the same match Parker signals for a replacement bat during his stand of 123 with Botham. His 69 won the Man of the Match award, but it was Botham (*below*) who hit the winning single.

23, 24, 25. The Durham batting depended heavily on three players: (*top, left*) Dean Jones was the first Durham player to reach 1,000 runs; (*top, right*) Larkins, cutting savagely square; (*below*) Parker finding a gap on the leg side.

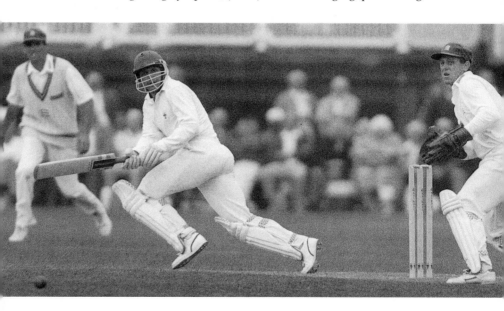

26. Durham players: (a) Geoff Cook, Director of Cricket; (b) Wayne Larkins; (c) John Glendenen; (d) Phil Bainbridge; (e) Chris Scott, wicketkeeper; (f) Brian Hunt, with his scorer's paraphenalia in the Stockton crow's nest.

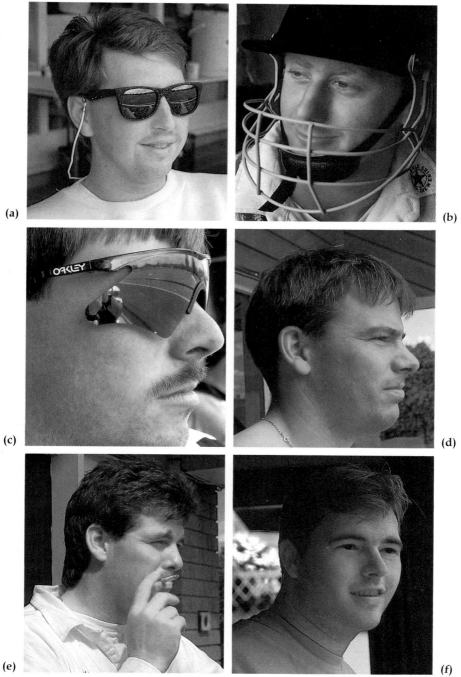

27. More Durham Players: (a) Phil Berry; (b) Mark Briers; (c) Simon Brown; (d) Steve McEwan; (e) Ian Smith; (f) John Wood.

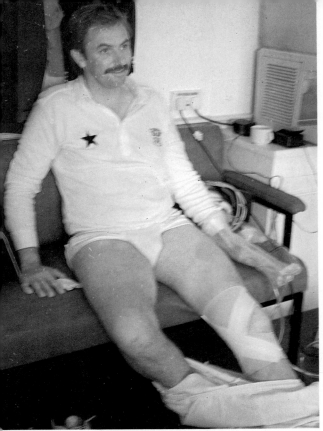

28, 29. Graveney,
desperate to make
himself fit to play against
Middlesex at Lord's,
receives finger treatment
from a 'juice machine'.
(*Below*) Chris Scott about
to stump Desmond
Haynes during Phil
Berry's marathon
bowling spell of 7/113.
He took 10 for 191 in the
match and also made 76
and 14 not out.

30, 31. (*Above*) Durham's one-day wicketkeeper/batsman, Andy Fothergill, applying insect repellant to Larkins' face. (*Below*) The Feethams ground at Darlington, one of six on which Durham regularly played. Bainbridge taking strike.

32. Player of the future: Jimmy Daley. His first two Championship matches brought him scores of 88 and 80 not out. (*Sunderland Echo*)

33. Ground of the future: Chester-le-Street. The area is being levelled to provide an international standard cricket ground and leisure and conference centre. When it is finished, in 1995, it will be England's first modern Test arena.

His meticulousness extends beyond his play to his smart turn-out, even to the way he packs his kit, but it was not always so. The fourth child of a Marathi language poet, Tendulkar was an unruly seven-year-old with a huge mop of curly hair, who regularly broke windows hitting balls around the apartment compound. About the time Ian Botham was mauling the Aussies at Headingley in 1981, Tendulkar's hero was John McEnroe. His studious father had no interest in cricket (he has only seen him play once), but his brother, Ajit, ten years older, noticed a special talent. Ajit sacrificed his job and got Sachin installed at a school where the celebrated coach, Ramakant Achrekar, taught.

By fourteen Tendulkar was a phenomenon. He made consecutive unbeaten triple centuries in the Bombay inter-schools trophy, sharing a partnership of 664 with Vinod Kambli – now also in the Indian team – the highest stand in cricket history. Soon afterwards he made a century on his debut in each of the first-class competitions and finished the season as Bombay's leading scorer. Initially his Test batting was indiscreet. 'He was a flashy player,' Azharuddin recalls, 'who attacked without much purpose. Now he's the pillar of our innings. In three years he could be captain.'

At first glance Tendulkar is an unlikely-looking god. The bandy legs, the stout physique, the quiet, thin voice, and the meek grin do not quite fit the bill. The bat, at over 3 lb the heaviest in the team, looks too large as his bottom hand grasps it round the splice. But that chunk of wood is Tendulkar's mouthpiece and he has become alarmingly articulate with it. His trademarks – a scything cut and a controlled punch through wide mid-on – carry the stamp of Viv Richards. So does the exaggerated block to the immaculate delivery. He can throw powerfully with either arm and bowl leg-spin or off-breaks as well as tantalising little seamers.

But it is his astuteness that astounds team-mates more than anything. Tendulkar sets precise fields for his bowling (similar in style to Barry Wood) and admonishes anyone who strays fractionally. He makes strategic comments to his captain constantly. 'His perception is amazing,' Ravi Shastri said. 'We are learning from him rather than the other way round.' He has had no trouble fitting into the Yorkshire side or understanding their earthy humour, and has been weaned off Lucozade and on to a curious mixture of Bailey's Irish Cream topped up with Tia Maria.

The trappings of success are rolling in – a handsome salary from a marketing conglomerate, plus advertising contracts – but the price of being a leading cricketer in India can be high. 'One spectator had so much money on our match against Australia in the World Cup, he hanged himself when we lost by one run,' Shastri said, 'and my Bombay home was stoned by a mob who blamed me for slow scoring. At the moment Sachin is exempt from that sort of treatment because of his age, but it won't take long.'

Most of the time it is hard to believe how young Tendulkar really is but occasionally there is a reminder. During a domestic flight in India the players were offered refreshments. While others chose tea or coffee Tendulkar was handed a bottle of warm milk and a dummy. 'But I don't drink this,' he said blankly, failing to see the joke. Which only goes to show that gullibility is a better guide to age than sporting prowess.

Friday–Monday 7–10 August – Warwickshire v. Durham Championship and Sunday League matches, at Edgbaston

An appointment with the world's fastest bowler is not what you want as the culmination of twenty-six days' cricket in the last twenty-eight. Usually on arrival at Edgbaston, batsmen look round anxiously for some sign of Allan Donald at pre-match warm-ups, hoping he is confined to the physio's table; then, when they realise he isn't, they practise jerky head movements. After twenty minutes ensuring every vulnerable part of their body is well padded, they nervously take guard, flick tentatively at a wide loosener and are trudging disconsolately back to the pavilion.

To say that this befell us on Friday would be grossly unfair to our batsmen. They were undone by blistering pace, searing bounce and prodigious swing as Donald exploited moist conditions with 7–37, his best-ever figures in England. He seemed to be bowling faster than ever, and with far better control. A genial man without the ball, he attributes his progress to an improved run-up which is more steady and less like a bull at a gate. Much of the credit for this and other Warwickshire successes must go to Bob Woolmer who, having inherited the job of coach from a series of old pros, has initiated much closer scrutiny of technique and abolished the old 'bloodhound' mentality. There were times during the mid-1980s when the Warwickshire players were doing so many long-distance runs, they appeared too exhausted to play cricket.

The Edgbaston ground can't quite seem to make up its mind whether to retain its rather worn 1960s' image or move into the modern era. It doesn't have much atmosphere, though the facilities are marvellous and they have George, the best dressing-room attendant in the business who will attend your every whim including washing the dirty whites – vital during a lengthy sequence of away games. A decent crowd rarely turns up here to watch Warwickshire, but there's a reason for this. A good hit beyond the Eric Hollies stand and over the River Rea takes the ball into Worcestershire, and half of Birmingham is in Staffordshire. A Brummie XI, on the other hand, would get excellent support.

John Glendenen had the dubious pleasure of being restored as opener for this match, having made a hundred in the second team, but it's a bit like going from the seal pool to the lions' den. Stewart Hutton has failed to negotiate the new ball recently and is starting to despair. It's not surprising, considering he made a record 1,500 runs in League cricket last year and was persuaded to sacrifice a steady job with ICI to join Durham. He even took a drop in salary – a serious matter for a Yorkshireman. 'But I would always have regretted it if I had turned down the chance to find out whether I could make it at this level,' he said.

Mark Briers came in at 0–2 and made a courageous 15 against some ferocious stuff. Dismissed by an unplayable delivery, he mooched back to the pavilion, head bowed, embarrassed by another failure. He has to be consciously reminded that his technique is excellent, and as long as he hangs on to his marbles, the runs will gradually come. Unfortunately he is being cruelly exposed by hungry bowlers preying on our brittle middle order deprived crucially of Jones and the still-injured Parker. There is talk of Martin Crowe or Richie Richardson being the overseas target for next season, and they would certainly fill the breach. Other prominent county players have been mentioned as possible recruits, although some of them are just temporarily disgruntled and will be reluctant to move when pursued. They might even look for an overseas bowler – especially after the lack of response I got from a pitch on which we had just been rounded up for 136!

But, as Geoff Cook says, it is a building process, and we still have a few supports to lay. The trouble is, Glamorgan have beaten Notts and we are now propping up the Championship table.

The survivors – Fothergill and Glendenen

On the other hand, we are progressing in the Sunday League. We trounced Warwickshire this weekend and the two longest-serving Durham players played a significant role. Andy Fothergill took four catches and an excellent stumping, and John Glendenen contributed a strong-arm 78 despite ducking every time he received a short ball, which was often. It seems that at last these two are turning the corner on the field which is heart-warming for they have been the life-blood of team morale these last three months.

Both natural satirists, they have borne disappointment with great strength of character and been able to laugh off a mistake. At the beginning of the season Fothers had no idea where to stand to Botham's bowling and dropped a crucial snick in a Benson & Hedges game. 'The trouble was,' he said then, 'no-one said "hard luck" or "well tried!" at the time. The silence was deafening.' Now he is a vigorous, competent performer in one-day games (he and Chris Scott job-share – the latter playing most of the three-dayers), motivating everyone when the spirit begins to sag. A live-wire in the dressing-room and on various social excursions, the County experience has brought both intrigue and fatigue into Fothergill's life. 'God, I'm so tired I could sleep on a clothes line – with a knot for a pillow,' he said, after the tense NatWest encounter with Middlesex.

Originally from Newcastle where his father was a welder and 'probably a good scrapper', he learned his cricket at Darlington CC and played for Durham as far back as 1982, combining that with all manner of labouring jobs. He played in Neil Riddell's victorious team that beat Derby in 1984, and also in a FA Cup tie for Bishop Auckland during which, he sadly recalls, he gave away a penalty shortly before the end with his side 1–0 up.

Inevitably he's found the demands of concentration in first-class cricket wearing, but he continues to practise with a vigour that is infectious. What he hasn't come to terms with is the infrequency of getting to the wicket. At one stage he hadn't played a serious innings for three weeks and yet was required to pop up and squirt a quick 25 at the end of a Sunday League innings. His batting is typical of a thirty-year-old who's been brought up on low, sluggish club pitches. He tends to plunge his front foot down the wicket as the bowler releases, favouring a solid plonk over mid-wicket given the chance. Unfortunately in first-class cricket you don't get many balls to deposit in that direction and as soon as a fast bowler sees someone intent on lunging forward they are likely to be fending it off their nose for a while. Fothergill has the aptitude to improve, however, and I dare say he'll finish with a very healthy Sunday average.

At twenty-six John Glendenen has time on his side and was first selected for Durham in 1988 after good club performances for Ormsby. A snappy dresser, he turned up for the first match in a suit only to discover the rest of the team in T-shirt and jeans. 'I felt a bit of a fool,' he recalls. He is still the team scapegoat when things go wrong, mainly because he seems the sort of laid-back personality that a ticking-off wouldn't affect. It was this apparently casual attitude that dissuaded Yorkshire from signing him after a lengthy trial in 1989.

He does seem a relatively slow learner – he still stands too fine at third-man for a medium-pacer, or too far away to save two for a spinner – and he tells funny stories in an unbelievably long-winded way. But he has undoubted talent, is very fast over the ground with a sharp, straight throw, and a hilarious mimic. The occupants of a pub were in stitches the other day when he did his impression of the giants writhing on the floor during *It's a Knockout*.

The two of them are a great double-act, constantly picking up the irony of other people's remarks or chiming in with lyrical references. But whereas Fothergill has a good cricket brain and reads situations, Glendenen seems less focused. He was better at remembering the name of the first girl he ever kissed than those of the Australian bowlers whom he plundered while making an unbeaten 200 for Durham last year. The pressure of opening the batting during the week, then coming in lower down on a Sunday run-chase, is percolating through, and he hasn't yet realised that, when you do come across a weak attack on a flat wicket, you've got to cash in. The daily concentration levels required are sapping his energy and last week he declared he needed some time off. 'How could I get injured for about a year?' he asked. Life on the county treadmill gets like that.

Chapter 8

Life in the old ball yet

Tuesday 11 August – Yorkshire v. Durham
Flamingo Land Trophy match, Day/Night, at Sheffield

The Don Valley Stadium, on the outskirts of Sheffield, was originally built for the World Student Games in 1990. It looks as if it has never been used since. The changing-rooms are pristine, the varnish on the public seating is unstained, and the running track hardly has a spike mark. An artificial green wicket was laid on a sand base in the centre, with a close-cropped outfield, the boundaries of which were indicated by motorway style bollards. Australian-type floodlights towered over the arena like giant spatulas.

The players gorged themselves on supplies of pork pies and quiche before taking the field at 7 pm, Durham in a rather deeper shade of blue than their pastel-clad opponents. A scattered crowd, many of them Asians, had assembled. As with the World Cup, two white balls (one at either end) were used, which the Durham players had difficulty negotiating. Not because they couldn't pick up the flight – the lighting and black sightscreens were adequate – but because the wicket was unpredictable, and Paul Jarvis seemed intent on whacking the ball in halfway down. This was a little ungentlemanly, but Yorkshire don't win much these days, and a competition between only four teams does perhaps give them a better chance. The trophy was named, I was told, after a nearby wildlife park in need of some publicity.

We had been soundly beaten by pub-closing time – the latest I have ever been still involved in a cricket match, and Graveney was seeing red – or should I say white? The ball had certainly kept whistling back past him wherever he bowled it. Yorkshire TV had attempted to wire him up to the commentary box for live on-field analysis at various points, but during his spell all they probably got were expletives.

For all but the beleaguered spinners the general day/night concept had been a success, but it also illustrated the problems of floodlit cricket in England. There is no point in playing these matches in mid-summer because daylight lasts until about nine o'clock; if you play them later in the season, however, it gets too chilly for most people to sit about for long periods.

The TCCB has announced that coloured clothing and white balls will be used in the 50-over Sunday League next year. The drawback here is that matches will be played in broad daylight, and most seats and fences at county grounds are white. And I can't quite imagine what it will be like trying to catch a skier with a background of fluffy cumulus cloud. On the other hand, sales of the coloured shirts worn by the teams in the World Cup are nudging up towards 100,000 in England, so clearly the idea has captured the public's imagination. I would advocate football-type numbers on players' backs, anyway, to make identification easier.

Wednesday 12 August – Warwickshire v. Northamptonshire
NatWest Bank Trophy, semi-final, at Edgbaston

Returned to the commentary box today during a cloudburst, to find Edgbaston two-thirds drowned. Three hours later play had begun. This was due entirely to the extraordinary 'Brumbella' – the huge roll-on cover that once squashed the groundsman's cat as it unwound. As the rain ceased, and six men held up the edge of the 150-yard tarpaulin to prevent leakage, the engines creaked into action and the cover was rolled off, creating a veritable tidal-wave that surged towards a huge drain. No water escaped and play started at 1.30 pm. At Lord's it would have been off for the day.

Richie Benaud, Jack Bannister and Paul Downton were the other commentators. Benaud is a genius, managing to do about three things at the same time and yet still produce a concise assessment of each incident. In a sense this makes him tricky to work alongside; he describes everything so completely there is almost nothing left to add. He researches every player thoroughly and, despite having no real contact with them, always seems extremely well-informed. Beneath that angled smile and those famous exclamations ('I'll get it!' when the ball disappears into the grandstand) he is a serious man, dressed neatly in a cream suit, watching intently, frequently consulting the scorer, or tapping furiously on his micro-computer in the back of the box. I was amazed to find that he talks in real life with that same sideways glance, raised eyebrows and lilting voice. 'I remember you once saying that captaincy was 90% luck and 10% talent,' I said to him on air, when Allan Lamb had won the toss on a damp wicket. 'Yes, that's quite right,' he replied. 'You need the luck as captain, but don't try it without that 10%!'

Despite the combination of Allan Donald's furious pace and the loopiest slower ball in the world, purveyed by Dermot Reeve, Northants are in the final to play Leicester, for whom the BBC cricket correspondent, Jon Agnew, made an unexpected return.

Thursday 13 August

Some early autumn nip in the air reminded me that the new football season is only two days away. There are to be no back passes to the goalkeeper which seems to have caused a bit of a stir. Most of the players appear to be in favour, not so many of the managers.

Friday, Saturday 14, 15 August – Durham v. Glamorgan
Championship match, three days, at Hartlepool

A fine blustery morning, team selection delayed until extent of
people's injuries known. Parker not confident of hamstring,
Wood apparently lacking durability, Bainbridge still can't
bowl though he has toiled manfully and his throwing arm is
gradually coming back. So Glendenen gets another chance,
Hutton is omitted. Briers, despite looking increasingly like a
case for the Samaritans, included for his versatility, McEwan
ignored because he hasn't taken wickets. The stoical Gary
Brown is twelfth man. The nice thing about that job in this side
is that you're not made to run about like an eighteenth-century
chambermaid. Our scorer, Brian Hunt (or 'Wottack' as we
know him), puts complimentaries on the gate, Steve, the
dressing-room attendant, pours drinks and fetches lunches,
and senior players like Botham and Larkins are undemanding.
Larkins never complains about anything – injury, batting in
half-light or on dodgy wickets. The spirit within the team is still
predominantly excellent.

By the end of the first day of this bottom-of-the-table clash, it
wasn't quite as good. Glamorgan had made a healthy 390–6,
and we had already lost Glendenen for 0. Our bowling just isn't
penetrative enough, and for some reason, Ian Smith, a happy-
go-lucky sort of chap who plays cavalier innings and stands
jovially at slip, doesn't get a bowl despite an ability to swing the
ball more than anyone. Sometimes captains have fixed ideas
about players which they find hard to relinquish.

This is not true of Glamorgan, however, who appear to have
rather changed their tune about Viv Richards. Their players
now suspect he is not interested, tends to contract injury easily,
and has lost his trademark flip through mid-wicket. I guess you
can sympathise – after what he has achieved you can hardly
expect him to put his heart and soul into a five-hour fielding
session at Ebbw Vale with his side meandering along at the foot
of the table.

Sure enough, Richards made a sketchy 30, two vast straight
drives off Graveney a salutory reminder of his capabilities,

before playing loosely at a weary-looking Simon Brown and departing lbw. He loped off lazily, almost like a cat that is barely awake. Somewhere, somehow, he will catch someone unawares, you bet.

Sunday 16 August Hartlepool

Easily the most unpleasant day of my cricket career. An article has appeared in the Hartlepool *Mail* quoting me at length about alleged divisions in the Durham camp and lack of enthusiasm from certain senior players. The piece is entitled 'The Outsider' in large thick capitals and depicts me as a mediator between the old lags and the young bucks. I am even supposed to have said, 'Wayne (Grandad) Larkins doesn't give a stuff when he's out . . . ' What I actually said, and I can remember it clearly, was – 'Wayne Larkins might sometimes look as if he doesn't give a stuff when he's out, but he does really, he's devoted to the team's cause.'

Needless to say, Graveney, Larkins and Botham (all referred to in the story) are very put out, and relations are extremely tense. Obviously I am bearing the brunt of it despite my remarks to the particular journalist (who until last year was confined to writing the 'Uncle Charlie' column on the kids' page) having been grossly misrepresented. My tone during our conversation two weeks ago had been 99% complimentary and constructive, my attitude in this rag comes over as 99% cynical and destructive. It is a sad day when journalists on local papers resort to the tabloid mentality, but as we languish at the bottom of the table, without a win in the Championship since early June, reporters' knives are sharpening.

The episode is particularly upsetting as it jeopardises my long-standing friendship with Graveney, and ruins a six-year sequence of writing a column for *The Independent* with only one isolated complaint from another player. I'm not sure how I can regain the team's trust except by putting everything into my performance. After a lengthy discussion of the issue, the club has disciplined me for talking about team members publicly without prior consent. The punishment is fairly lenient, I'm glad to say.

It all overshadowed a disappointing 16-run loss in the Sunday League in which Ian Smith took great satisfaction from dismissing three of his former colleagues, including Richards for a duck, at a personal cost of 32.

Monday 17 August – Durham v. Glamorgan
Championship match, third day

Summoned to Botham's 'office' (the changing-room) at 10.15am – a terrifying proposition. The real tabloids have been on the phone pursuing rumours that he is a disruptive influence. Assured him that I had been thoroughly misquoted and would be giving the said reporter a piece of my mind; he couldn't have been nicer. But then this issue is piffle compared to what he has been through in the past.

Good rearguard action on the field, match saved – crucial as otherwise Glamorgan could have widened gap between them and us. Fifty to Mark Briers at last after suffering a poor run. At least now he looks happier to be alive.

The groundsman's craft

Must mention good old Tom Flintoff at this point. The former Hampshire groundsman, he has moved lock, stock and barrel to the north-east and has supervised the creation of ideal three-day pitches from turf more acclimatised to league scraps on Saturday afternoons. They have all offered some incentive for the bowler while still promising lots of runs. This is partly due to the proliferation of postage-stamp outfields. He must ensure that the new ground at Chester-le-Street has ample boundaries, otherwise I fear for the state of spinners' necks as they follow the path of yet another massive blow. At least the arena will be flat. They are levelling off the surface with the aid of lasers.

What will the wicket be like, I wonder? There is a very fine balance required to achieve an ideal surface – something on which quality players can flourish. Cracked, patchy or damp wickets behave unpredictably, placing uncertainty in the batsman's mind. If the ball lands on a crack, for instance, the rebound will be less than if it hits the firmer patches in between. This unevenness is exacerbated as cracks widen during the match. The action of the ball pitching gradually wears down the top surface of pitches devoid of grass, damp ones 'hold' the ball, and a pock-marked appearance results. These wickets are the batsmen's bêtes noires where they flounder in the lap of the moderate medium-pacer.

Glass would probably be the perfect surface for batsmen, but for a proper contest bowlers have to be encouraged, so grass is more appropriate. An even covering will hold a pitch together, thick green on a hard wicket will make the ball fly through and probably deviate. The right moisture content is crucial; too dry and the top layer will disintegrate, too wet and the match may be decided in a few hours. Most importantly, bowlers want reward for effort. Deliveries dug in firmly should bounce up; if spin is imparted the ball should react accordingly. No paceman really wants an attempted bouncer to shoot along the ground. Once Joel Garner, bowling for Somerset on an overused pitch, remarked – 'Man, she gone to sleep'.

So how does the groundsman reconcile all these aspects? In park cricket the pitch might consist of flattened grass interspersed with bare patches, perhaps the odd clover, but be quite adequate for a club fourth XI. At the other end of the scale first-class pitches need to be nurtured like vines. Special rye grass is sown in heavy Surrey loam. Usually the strips are watered and compacted up until a week before use, then carefully tended with brush, mower and heavy roller. Each groundsman has his own formula, like butchers making sausages.

Now, after thirty-one days' cricket in thirty-six, we have a three-day respite. Just to illustrate the diversity of characters in this team and the complexity of getting them all to one place, here is a run-down of each one's destination:

Larkins – resting in Sedgefield
Glendenen – 2nd XI match, Sunderland
Bainbridge – three days in Bristol
Briers – home: Middlesbrough
Botham – one-day international, Trent Bridge
Smith – home: Blaydon
Scott – resting in Nottingham
Graveney – home to Bristol
Hughes – Darlington, then train to London
Berry – Redcar, then Sunderland
Brown – wiring up converted warehouse, Newcastle.

Thursday 20 August

England achieve world record 363–6 in one-day International
v. Pakistan. Hick scores astonishing 63 in 42 balls. If only he
had the confidence to play like this in Test matches. Wasim
Akram has had a brilliant summer – 82 wickets, over and round
the wicket, inswingers and outswingers, but he'd be better off
spending his spare time working on his run-up than sueing
English newspapers for accusing him and co. of doctoring the
ball. Today he reached a century of no-balls in international
matches this summer. It's a statistic that may baffle the
dogmatists who claim that a fast bowler should 'just move his
mark back a bit'. This doesn't necessarily work. For a start,
Wasim doesn't seem to have a proper mark – he starts running
from wherever he feels like. Also, he looks at the crease as he is
running, which means that his stride pattern automatically
adjusts so he finishes in the same place regardless of where he
starts.

This is a problem afflicting other good bowlers – Derek
Pringle and Phil Newport among them – not easily solved. The
key is to mark out a run-up carefully (I use the heel-toe method
for accuracy, as plain walking steps can vary too much), then
train yourself to fix your eyes on the batsman's off stump rather
than the bowler's no-ball line. It requires discipline and practice, but it works. I used to have no-ball trouble. In around 700

overs this year, I've overstepped about five times. Ted Dexter identified this cure to my problem in 1982, but it's taken me about a decade to work it out.

Friday – Monday, 21–24 August, Worcester v. Durham
Championship match, and Sunday League match, at Worcester

Didn't appear on field for entire four days. Rested for the Championship match, Sunday League rained off. What cricket I did see was pretty anaemic, unbecoming of Worcester's magnificent setting. You can't quite see the River Severn from the ground, but it has a major influence on the cricket. Even in August the outfield is green and lush, cut in concentric circles by the meticulous ground staff. In winter it is a haven for water-sports. Masochistic wind-surfers and swimmers have braved the floods on New Year's Day, and a previous groundsman once rowed across the square and caught a 45 lb salmon. Occasionally the fire brigade has to be drafted in to pump out the umpires' room. Not surprisingly, the wicket always has that mottled appearance that batsmen tend to mistrust.

Plenty of rain around, so the conversation centred on people's winter plans. With the recession biting harder in Australia and New Zealand, winter coaching jobs are harder to come by, and it may be time the Cricketers' Association hired someone full-time to find its members off-season jobs. It doesn't much matter what these are. In the past they have included performing the hindquarters of a horse in pantomime, chasing free-range chickens with a large net, and examining sugar-beet crop for moisture content, which is what Chris Scott will be doing in October. Several others face the weekly trek to the dole office. There are still leading players in their early twenties who earn less than £8000 a year. Calculated on an hourly basis that is less than the average wage of an office cleaner.

Sheila Job can go back to her Newcastle health clinic with a rich catalogue of experiences. It hasn't been at all easy for her surviving in the male-orientated world of county cricket. At some venues she has had nowhere to change into her tracksuit

[143]

and has encountered occasional hostility from the 'home' physio. Then she habitually has to wait outside for what probably seems an eternity until the team have washed and changed. It was quite odd initially having a woman around all the time, and players curbed their language and lewd stories. Everyone has relaxed now and she has been completely accepted. It's vital to have a travelling physio. There is so much misunderstanding about injury and at least she provides continuity of diagnosis and treatment. But it must seem an awfully long day for a non-cricket fan.

Highlight of the match was John Wood's innings of 28 in which, during one scamper for two, he shoulder-charged the bowler, Neal Radford, who was foolishly blocking his path. This earned him the Champagne Moment award from Bollinger, the sponsors for the day. Unrelieved mizzle and bad light relegated the game to a dull draw on the third day, although Parker contributed a frenetic 94 between the showers.

As a change from selecting Ugly or Bald XIs during the frequent stoppages, we voted for cricket's version of the Grammy awards. Here are the results:

Best forward defensive: T. J. Boon (Leics)
Hardest hitter: A. Fordham (Northants)
Best reverse-sweeper: M. A. Roseberry (Middx)
Best expectorator: I. T. Botham
Most fidgety cricketer: D. A. Reeve (Warks)
Most histrionic bowler: N. A. Radford (Worcs)
Most exaggerated follow-through: T. A. Munton (Warks)
Quietest wicketkeeper: C. W. Scott
Noisiest wicketkeeper: K. J. Piper (Warks) – shouts 'Come on, let's bubble' before every ball.

Tuesday 25 August – Durham v. Pakistan
Floodlit match, at Gateshead International Stadium

The Pakistanis' demeanour was exemplary despite a damning article by Allan Lamb in the *Daily Mirror* alleging they had been doctoring the ball throughout the summer. Waqar Younis joined in the Kwik-cricket with schoolboys before the match, and later took 5–13 without ever remotely threatening life or limb. From high up in the stand the white ball is far more visible than the red one, of most benefit to the spectators who can follow the game without assumptions or consultations with sharper-eyed neighbours. In fact there weren't all that many, partly because of the chilly evening, but probably more to do with the prohibitive admission price of £12.

Our dressing-room conversation revolved around the ball row, particularly as the ICC announced that a ball had been replaced during the second one-day international. They refused to say why. Meanwhile, any county cricketer under the age of about ninety is being canvassed for his opinion. David Lloyd said, 'It's a hoot. People have been picking the seam for years. I used to do it myself', which perhaps puts the issue in perspective.

Ball doctoring – an ancient art widely mastered

'Any member of the fielding side may polish the ball provided that such polishing wastes no time and that no artificial substance is used. No-one shall rub the ball on the ground or use any artificial substance or take any other action to alter the condition of the ball.' From *The Laws of Cricket*, Law 42, Paragraph 5.

The great ball debate rages on. Do they or don't they? Of one thing there is no doubt; Waqar Younis and Wasim Akram swing the older ball prodigiously and at great pace. This fact is not new. They devastated a New Zealand side that visited Pakistan in 1989 with the same combination of lifters and dipping toe-crushers. There were rumours then that they scuffed the ball using the top of a Coke bottle. The trick, it was said, was to keep it in the hip pocket, corrugated side outwards, then rub the ball over the area as if polishing it. The result would be a scuffed ball and, often, ripped trousers.

Old bowlers and other sages remain bewildered at the logic

[145]

of roughing up one side of the ball when for years they have been teaching their protégés to keep a new 'cherry', in mint condition as long as possible. Polishing one side and leaving the other dull was supposed to encourage movement through the air. The new formula for swing has reversed all the theories. By concentrating on exaggerating the difference between one side and the other, the ball swings even more. Assisting the natural deterioration of the rough side – manicuring the worn areas – and saturating the polished side with sweat makes the ball extremely unbalanced. The heaviness of the soggy side contrasts with the lightness of the scuffed side and drags the ball in the direction it is positioned. So for an inswinger the ball is projected with saturated (polished) side facing mid-wicket, the opposite of traditional techniques. Vice versa for the outswinger, of course.

The current crop of Pakistanis are not the first to discover the 'reverse swing' phenomenon. Imran Khan made a ragged old ball bend alarmingly in the Lord's nets one day in the early 1980s. He used various fingertip skills some of which he demonstrated. One of these was to manoeuvre the quarter-seam so that it acted like a rudder, pulling the ball in the direction it was intended to go.

A few years later I was bowling in a benefit match in tandem with Angus Fraser. From his cricketing travels, Angus had got wise to the scuffing system, and we experimented with it. The ball started to swing around and one edge was fielded by the Pakistani-turned-Lancastrian, Mudassar Nazar. He examined the scratched ball and then exclaimed, 'Hey, who told you about this?'

From the authorities' point of view, ball tampering is very difficult to detect. The abrasion of a dry wicket soon removes parts of the leather coating, and the Pakistanis accentuate this process by bowling a spinner (Mushtaq) early in the innings. Bare areas appear on the ball which could then be enlarged by subtle attention from fingernails. It is quite easy to do this gently while walking back to your mark, under the guise of polishing the ball. This way it would be almost impossible for the umpire to determine that anything improper had occurred.

[146]

The secret to this whole matter is to avoid discovery. At all levels of English cricket, slip or gully fielders have lifted the seam, so much so that, at times, you might cut your fingers on it. There are several first-class players who have transferred oily substances from their clothes on to the ball, and one team used non-scented talcum powder in their pockets.

Why fiddle with the ball at all? Simple. As bats get bigger and better, and protective equipment lighter and more effective, the bowlers have to strike back. The bouncer has been rationed, seam-size reduced, the reverse-sweep officially sanctioned. Understandably, the propellers of the red missile are seeking ways to combat the batsman's advance. Regardless how you interpret their methods, you have to admire the skill of Waqar and Wasim. It's all very well to be in possession of a lopsided ball, but the regularity with which they can make a delivery which spends two-thirds of its life heading towards the slips, suddenly home in on the base of leg-stump, is quite astonishing. There is no noticeable change of action, and hawk-eyed batsmen can't even spot how the shiny side is positioned in mid-run as both bowlers cleverly conceal the ball in both hands on their approach.

The Pakistani bowlers have two other advantages. First, I mentioned earlier Gehan Mendis' theory that their sweat may have certain properties that help to get up a good polish, useful in the lush, moist conditions prevalent in English domestic cricket. Other players of Asian descent are the best shiners in various county teams – Asif Din at Warwickshire, Damien D'Oliveira at Worcester, for example. Second, they are brilliant exponents of the swing art, partly, perhaps, because they have a more round-arm action than their English counterparts, who are high, 'over-the-top' seam bowlers. With Championship pitches becoming consistently slower, more home-grown bowlers are experimenting with swing. But there is no-one with the skill and speed of Wasim and Waqar and they deserve their admission to cricket's Hall of Fame.

Wednesday 26 August – Durham v. Hampshire
Championship match, four days, at Darlington

Four-day cricket is back, three-day cricket is gone for ever – well, at least until 1996. It doesn't seem to make any difference to Essex who are heading towards their sixth Championship title in twelve years. Hampshire have slipped quietly away, partly, perhaps, because Malcolm Marshall has lost a bit of potency. There was no sign of him at all at Feethams, and nasty rumours that he was on his way up the A1 were dispelled when it was revealed he had a bad ankle. Remarkably he has missed only nine Hampshire games through injury in thirteen years.

Reduced Hampshire to 71–4, but they then recovered to 250–4 before rain set in. This gave our three diligent administration girls, Nicola, Louise and Sarah, ample time to prepare us a vast spaghetti Bolognaise in a nearby flat they have borrowed for the week. Apart from their culinary expertise, these females have contributed a vast amount to what is, of course, essentially a male-run organisation. While Sarah and Louise have used their PR skills to woo sponsors into entertaining their guests at matches – four hundred are expected to the Yorkshire match on Sunday which means erecting a separate marquee in the football ground car-park – Nicola has been doing sterling work selling merchandise to spectators. The turn-over of caps, ties, sweaters, tracksuits and T-shirts has surpassed all expectations.

Thursday/Friday, 27/28 August – Durham v. Hampshire
Second and third days

Because of bad weather, two more days in the field as Hampshire prolonged their innings. Some members of the opposition who were already out didn't even show up, and one story has it that Gower went out for lunch with Botham, who has a sore shoulder. Players of this stature deserve to be let off the leash from time to time. Their past successes have earned it, and by being lenient with them, they probably respect you more. Sometimes the exceptional flair in their performances is born out of being a shade non-conformist.

Saturday 29 August – Durham v. Hampshire
Fourth day

Talking of which, throughout my career, there is nobody I have bowled to so consistently badly as Gower. But then he makes ordinary balls into rank ones with eyes that are reputed to be able to read the manufacturer's serial number at the bottom of an eye-test card from a distance of three feet. The delight is in the ease with which he coaxes the ball to the boundary, and I must confess I like experiencing him make runs as long as it doesn't go on for too long. I complimented him on one flick over square-leg and asked how he would describe the shot. 'I suppose you'd call it an underhand pull,' he said, slightly embarrassed. Two overs later I got him out playing exactly the same shot. After lunch, I chided him – 'I guess that has to go down in the book as caught pulling surreptitiously?' I suggested, and he laughed. Robin Smith was also out playing loosely, though you could understand why. He has had particularly trying physical (and verbal) confrontations with the Pakistanis, and has played some quite breathtaking innings. What he needs now, more than anything else, is a bit of time off.

A combination of timely showers and Phil Bainbridge conspired to save the match, when at one stage a Durham defeat was looming. Bainbridge made two silky fifties in the game and never looked like getting out until Shine found a bit of extra lift. It was a shame, as it diddled him out of a maiden Durham century.

Phil Bainbridge – a man for all seasons

'Wo kick a bo agin a wo an 'edit til it bosses?'
  'You what, Bains?'
  'Cos kick a bo agin a wo an'et it til it bosses!!'

'Eh?'

'It's Potteries lingo. It means, 'let's go and kick a ball against a wall and head it till it bursts.'

Phil Bainbridge was born in Stoke-on-Trent and is proud of it. He retains his rather nasal Midland accent and was at great pains to point out that his favourite breakfast consists of Staffordshire oatcakes. In some ways too he has rejected his background. He owns horses and a mobile phone and dresses affluently in pastel trousers and bright shirts. This together with his styled grey hair and love of socialising has earned him the nickname 'Osty', standing for 'Oldest Swinger in Town'.

He's not old really, only thirty-four, but has had a lengthy career starting with Gloucestershire in 1977 where he had a benefit twelve years later. But disillusionment with the Bristol set-up persuaded him to join Durham minor county in 1991, knowing that within a year he'd be back in the first-class game again. At first, this year, his season away from the higher echelons showed, and there were signs of vulnerability to quicker bowling. He even admitted it. A bruising battle with Curtly Ambrose at Stockton soon sharpened his reflexes and, but for an unlucky injury at Hartlepool, he might well have finished up the county's leading run-scorer.

In retrospect, that match against Essex was probably Durham's watershed. Three players hobbled off injured – Bainbridge, Wood and Brown – and though we won subsequent games, the drain on resources was severe, and when in late July we needed to 'dig deep', as Graveney put it, there was nothing left. What was missing as much as anything was Bainbridge's effervescent spirit. Once Jones had gone too there was no-one to gee up sagging fielders or fiddle a few wickets when the main seamers were tired. There was no-one to inspire a bit of hilarity into dejected troops.

Phil Bainbridge is not a famous cricketer, but he is a competent one. Keith Fletcher once described him as a 'good player in a strong side'. Perhaps the reason he is not better known is because he has never played in one. The quality is there, though. Predominantly a back-foot player, he feeds on balls outside off stump which he creams relentlessly past cover. Woe

[150]

betide the spinner who drops fractionally short. He doesn't seem to hit the ball hard, but it still rifles into the boards once past the field.

It is Bainbridge the-partnership-breaker in whom Graveney, his long-time captain, has most faith. Time and again he will lope in off an angled run and dismiss unsuspecting batsmen with a nifty little cutter. The sheer predictability of this eventuality is baffling. It must be down to the fact he appears to be negotiating a force-nine gale as he runs in, and that no-one, not even the purveyor himself, is quite sure what he bowls. Gentle out-wobblers with the odd inswinger and a spinning slower ball, might be the gist of it. The sheer variety of his bowling makes it difficult to tame and represents the personification of Durham's 'sneaky mentality'.

It has been a tricky summer for the imports like Bainbridge and Graveney. Both family men, they have commuted from Bristol much of the season which only adds to the pressures of public expectation. But in spite of long drives after dark, both arrive at the ground the following day grinning cheerfully and are quickly out on to the paddock. Bainbridge is usually the last to leave the bar in the evening too – he always bumps into some old friend or a client from his corporate hospitality business. But can't one of them tell him not to wear those white polo-necks? He won't listen to me.

Chapter 9

The season winds down

The last Sunday League game of the summer, and a capacity crowd expected because of the local nature of the opposition – Darlington is almost in Yorkshire. As I drove across the Pennines from a wedding in southern Scotland, I knew they were going to be disappointed. Masses of angry, black clouds surged over the hills from the south-west as if fed by a conveyor belt, and the rain fell in torrents. As I passed by the little Durham villages smelling of wood smoke, and the farmhouses on the high moor, I wondered how many of their inhabitants would be following the progress of their new team, and, even, how many would be sufficiently interested to buy this book!

All they will read in tomorrow's paper will be 'Darlington – Durham v Yorkshire. No play, rain. 2 points each'. Therein lies a story, however. At 12.45 pm it looked like the end of the world was approaching, and a minute later the heavens opened. By one o'clock the ground was awash, the covers were in danger of floating away and the ignition key to the water-hog was elsewhere. Umpires White and Burgess called the game off with commendable speed and the players happily retired to the marquee. But there was no more rain and by 5 pm we could have played a 15-over match. The local groundsman was most upset at the lost opportunity, a rarity in itself due to the fact that such men are usually neurotic about their beloved turf.

*   *   *

[152]

Geoff Cook, well ahead with ideas for next year, took me aside to find out my plans. This was our conversation:

Cook: Have you come to any decision yet?

Me: I've very much enjoyed this season – maybe more than any other I've ever played, but I'm worried my knee and ankle might not stand up to another year with this many overs. Is there any chance of getting another bowler?

Cook: Fifty-fifty.

Me: What would you feel about a part-time contract, say one-day games only, or a salary for the first two months and then fees on a match to match basis afterwards?

Cook: Look, I can't contemplate these part-time arrangements. It's not the commitment I'm looking for. You've been our most consistent if not penetrative bowler, setting standards others don't even aspire to. It'll take the younger element another year or two to develop, therefore your presence in the immediate future is important to us.

Me: I've been commuting from London most of the summer, trying to fit other things in. Have you been happy with that arrangement?

Cook: Yeah, fine. I realise at your stage of life you've got other demands. It's up to you.

He's a persuasive man, and they say you're a long time retired. Maybe I'll give it one more year. It's not a good economic climate in which to be out of work either. Which brings me on to two people who will be. Steve Wright, our dressing-room attendant, and our scorer, Brian Hunt.

Ian Mackintosh can earn his winter-keep painting the interior of the Lord's pavilion, having supplied towels, biros and Lucozade to the Middlesex lads all summer. Those other stalwarts of the cricketing infrastructure – the Rons, Barrys, Teds and Cliffs – will be returning to the place they regularly attended in March; the dole office. Maybe our Steve will be able to dine out for a while on his experiences as Ian Botham's head waiter, but the number of county cricket employees collecting Giros in the close season looks set to break all records this year.

Monday 31 August – President's XI v. Old Latymerians CC (Whitton)

There's never any harm popping back into the company of club cricketers for an afternoon, I always find I learn something. On this occasion the experience only underlined my suspicion that the reason the new ball doesn't swing in county cricket is due to the lacquer encasing it, and not because of the deterioration in bowlers' actions. I bowled with a grade of shiny, unlacquered ball today, and it swung all over the place, out of control. Still didn't help me get any wickets, of course. I think I prefer no swing to too much.

Tuesday–Friday, 1–4 September

Frittered away time and money in various West London drinking establishments, as you do. The schools have gone back so the roads are chocka. Agreed to meet some friends in a very crickety pub, The Pavilion End, near St Paul's. They were late but I was confident someone would soon recognise me and strike up a conversation as they seem to in Durham pubs. Immediately a couple approached me in a knowing sort of way and I smiled. The bloke scrutinized me then said, 'You're not the strippergram are you by any chance?' Friends didn't turn up so left after an hour feeling thoroughly let down. Cheered up by sight of billboard advertising recycled loo paper. Beneath photo of roll were the words – 'In my previous life I was an *Eldorado* script'.

Meanwhile Essex have wrapped up the championship with two games to spare. This has happened for three reasons: 1. They have so much variety – batsmen and bowlers for every eventuality. 2. It never rains in Essex (it must be in the rain shadow of Hampstead Heath). 3. There are no really comfortable hotels in Chelmsford so the opposition is always knackered.

Saturday 5 September

Attended NatWest final at Lord's which Northants won easily against Leicestershire. Inhabitants of hospitality boxes more intriguing than match. Met one man whose company manufactured artificial limbs; another who was a police dog-handler; and a third who, loudly dressed and smoking a fat cigar, said, 'By the way, do they still have sixes in cricket?'

Monday 7 September – Somerset v. Durham
Championship match, four days, at Taunton

All the major trophies have been decided now so the remaining matches have a rather anti-climactic atmosphere. Unless Ian Botham is involved. Returning to his original stamping ground, he grabbed the new ball when Graveney inserted the hosts, and marked out his run. 'What, have they just cut this from the outfield?' he said, surveying a lush-looking wicket. Seventy-five minutes later Somerset were 80 for no wicket. Mark Lathwell, just announced in the England 'A' squad to Australia, had whipped up a quick fifty without looking wholly convincing. He didn't impress his legendary opponent anyway, who comically posted a long-stop when the batsman top-edged two attempted hooks over the 'keeper. 'You better sort that one out, Sonny,' Botham said glaring, 'or the Aussies'll have you for breakfast.' And with that he retired to the pavilion with a recurrence of his shoulder injury.

You have to admire the man. He still bowls with the same vigour and aggression at thirty-six as he did at twenty-three, without the same pace, naturally. He attempts bouncers, jags deliveries about off the seam, and bowls what is termed in the trade 'a heavy ball'. He makes confident young batsmen jittery with bounce and bristle. He sets imaginative, predatory fields. Unfortunately he does sometimes concede rather too many runs early on which, with our threadbare attack, we cannot afford.

On this occasion the Somerset middle order cashed in on a healthy start and it became a batting bonanza. Smith and

Larkins stood stoically at slip but the ball never looked as if it would go their way and they began playing word games with the advertising hoardings around the ground. We did make slight inroads after tea, but with the home side in sight of 400 by the close, Graveney returned to the pavilion in dejection. He had put the opposition in to bat, seen only five wickets fall all day, and his own bowling treated with scant respect.

Mind you, his disappointment was nothing in relation to how David Gower must have felt when he learned he had failed to make the England tour party. This is astonishing news. Recalled to blunt the rampaging Pakistanis at Old Trafford, he tamed them there, piloted England to victory at Headingley, and is as keen as mustard. Plus the fact that he is less likely to come unstuck on Indian wickets than on English ones, and is very much at ease in the sub-continent, unlike the Knott or Boycott types who can't exist without special supplies of their own home comforts. Presumably the all-powerful Gooch feels Gower's attitude on tour is divisive, further evidence that our game is run by automatons. Gower himself offered a typical summary – 'it seems runs round the block are more important than runs in the middle,' he said. The fact that Frank Woolley was omitted from the 1928–29 tour of Australia after scoring 3,300 first-class runs that summer, is no consolation; the huge public outcry over this latest selectorial blunder probably is.

Tuesday, Wednesday 8, 9 September – Somerset v. Durham Second and third days

Trench warfare the rest of the match as Somerset's quintet of fast bowlers made the ball zing about. I'm afraid their attack versus ours resembles the proverbial Cannons v. Peashooters. We failed to save the follow-on by some distance, and Bainbridge suffered the indignity of a pair in a day. After a tremendous display in the previous match, he only managed to last a total of five balls in two innings in this one. I suppose I put the mockers on him singing his praises.

At least he could enjoy a quite breathtaking assault by Ian

Smith. A compulsive hooker – both his weakness and his strength – he was fed a liberal diet of head-high deliveries, about twenty of which he swatted to the boundary. With a quick wicket and small boundaries, Taunton is a fast scoring ground, perfect for a short-ball bully like Smith, and he soon had a hundred. This cameo inspired Larkins to a painstaking second innings century against some fearsome stuff, particularly from Caddick. He was black and blue by the end, and a bruise on the back of his hamstring became so swollen, he had to call for a runner. Never having batted with one before, he soon nudged the ball into a gap and set off for the single as usual. He only remembered his predicament half-way down and scuttled back in agony and embarrassment.

Most of the other batsmen took a rising delivery or two on the body, Scott had to retire hurt with a chipped thumb, and the Somerset captain, Tavaré, was so worried about the fate of Graveney's fingers he lent him a pair of specially reinforced batting gloves. The cheery rural scene of a wicker basket containing rosy apples and one ragged cricket ball on the front of the Taunton telephone directory hardly reflects the hostility of the reception once you have taken guard there these days. Or indeed in the town car parks. Three sponsored cars were broken into on consecutive nights, and all Geoff Cook's gear stolen. The thieves would have encountered some unpleasant resistance if they had returned a third time as Botham and Larkins waited for them in the bushes till 3 am, but they obviously thought better of it.

Back on the green battleground, the unlikely figure of Jimmy Daley ensured Somerset had to bat again to win. There can have been few innings of this quality and courage played before on a first-class debut. Aged eighteen, and coming in at 29-3, he made 88 with secure defence and positive strokes particularly off the back foot. Daley has been a patient achiever in the second team all season, but seemed instantly able to raise his game – the hallmark of someone with real ability. Some of his shots reminded me of a less flamboyant Mark Ramprakash, and he has the same reserved nature and dark good looks, too. Definitely one to watch.

[157]

Thursday 10 September

A sad day. Worcester have won their match, so Durham are confirmed as 1992 wooden spoonists, unless somebody in the lower echelons is docked 25 points next week for a dodgy pitch. This is straw-clutching in the extreme.

Friday 11 September – Durham CCC Golf Day, Newton Aycliffe

Not as relaxing as it should have been. County cricketers never particularly enjoy playing as 'celebrities' in foursomes with businessmen who have never heard of them. Added to that my golf was atrocious, though at least it gave everyone more of a laugh than the dour comedian who rambled on after dinner.

Saturday 12 September – Durham v. Lancashire
Championship match, four days, at Gateshead Fell

So we finish the season the way we began it, with a home match against Lancashire. The personnel on both sides is much the same but their reputations have changed – the summer has either enhanced or tarnished them. With Allott and Fowler now on the transfer list, Lancashire have a youthful look about them.

Poor crowd, but it wasn't surprising. Newcastle United had a home match (the tannoy gave regular score updates) and Botham was due in hospital for an exploration of his sore shoulder. His walk across the south coast on behalf of Leukemia Research begins in a week and he has got to be fit for that. Gusty winds also forecast but weather stable enough for Dickie Bird, arriving from freezing Seaton Carew, to exclaim – 'Cor, it feels like t'desert art 'ere in comparison'.

For counties not in contention for prize money, the last match of the year is there to be enjoyed – a chance to sweeten the taste of earlier less palatable memories. It is also a time when teams indulge in all night card-sessions, wear silly hats and spend six month's bonuses at some salubrious restaurant. The opposition didn't join in the spirit of the occasion. After a tasty starter with Larkins and Parker at the wicket, things turned rather sour and we finished the day with a nasty dose of indigestion at 216-7.

Sunday 13 September – Durham v. Lancashire
Second day

This soon became 217-8 and with the ghastly early start of 10.30am in September, we were in danger of being all out before the time a mid-season game would have even begun. For no apparent reason I suddenly took on the Lancashire bowling, pulling and driving with rare gusto, egged on by the umpires. ''Ere, with shots like thart, you want to put in for't pay rise,' Bird advised. In partnership with a pugnacious Glendenen we raised the 300, the first time Durham had secured maximum batting points since 28 June – on this same ground as it happens.

Ian Smith then claimed three wickets in a sustained spell. Once a tearaway quickie with Glamorgan, his pace has diminished due to a back injury and an almost insatiable appetite for pints of lager. Without much use of the front arm he has learnt to swing the ball away, however, and with a little more purpose could become a valuable all rounder. He is one of those happy-go-lucky team members whose overall contributions are often ignored because they don't look particularly impressive on paper. But at the business end of contests he's a trusty servant and a reassuring influence.

With Lancashire 100 behind and six wickets down we could go off to Botham's Bungee Jumping Jamboree with a sniff of satisfaction, for once. You might think it is sheer madness to part with £37 to be hauled up into the night by a 200-foot crane, then pitch off a platform attached only by an elasticated rope which abruptly arrests your progress twenty feet from the ground. Well, you're right, it is. But 160 people, some jumping in pairs, took the plunge, unperturbed by the G-force or the serious nip in the North Yorkshire air. Paul Parker, abandoning his Homer refresher course for an evening (he takes up a Latin & Greek teaching post at Tonbridge on Friday), plummeted landwards bound to Sheila the physio, Bainbridge and Glendenen also had a turn, but Botham's shoulder surgeon had declared him unfit to take part. In a way I can see the fascination for this burgeoning pastime. Every time I climb up a high building I have this urge to throw myself off which has nothing to do with a failed marriage or a receding hairline.

Monday 14 September – Durham v. Lancashire
Third day

I have to admit I was too casual this morning. I imagined we might take about an hour to polish off Lancashire on a pitch that was bouncing rather unreliably, leaving us with a lead of about 50 and me all afternoon to write my last *Independent* column of the season. Therefore I didn't do the pre-match looseners with usual vigour, or worry unduly when a couple of early morning half volleys shot to the boundary.

At 4.55pm we were still fielding. This was a disastrous state of affairs, and everyone knew it. Our season has been a bit like a novice's round of golf – some fair drives, the odd good hole and plenty of double bogeys. At least when you get to the 18th tee you expect a firm strike, and a chip and putt for par. But on a brisk Monday at Gateshead Fell we had suddenly found ourselves in the trees with no clear view of the green.

Everything Lancashire tried came off. Running down the wicket to the seamers, hooking, slogging, massive straight hitting. That was just the night watchman, Martin. At the other end Atherton progressed sedately towards 200. Perhaps the field settings and bowling changes were a touch unimaginative, perhaps the wicket had eased up, but the truth is the Durham attack looked a spent force, and when it finally claimed the tenth wicket, Lancashire had amassed 562. It was all utterly depressing – the atmosphere in the dressing-room was like that of a morgue. Graveney was so dejected he went off for a drive, returning to announce that he had just resumed smoking. It was one of those days when bowlers attempt to hide their final analyses, but the announcer read them out at about 90 decibels, so that virtually the whole of Newcastle could hear.

Met Dickie Bird having a cold shower afterwards. 'Closes t'pores,' he explained. Just as well there's no team bath here, otherwise the supporters might have drowned some of us tonight.

Tuesday 15 September – Durham v. Lancashire
Fourth and final day

The players are in a state of limbo on the final day of the county season, feeling a mixture of relief and sadness. What they will miss most is the team cameraderie – northerners call it 'the crack' – the shared suffering, being in each other's pockets for days on end. Meeting colleagues socially in the winter is never the same. What they will miss least is another day in the field and the travelling.

Commuting from London to Durham most of the time, I have covered 11,800 miles, much of it on British Rail, never mind sent down somewhere near 800 overs. Tired knees have had their fill of jarring on compacted wickets, ankles enough of worn footholds and sliding encounters with boundary hoardings. Adrenalin and pride sustain the energy levels through August and September; once the air of competition expires, the body goes into voluntary hibernation.

The way we batted on the final afternoon suggested that condition had developed a day early. With one notable exception. Jimmy Daley surpassed his efforts at Taunton with a polished unbeaten 80. What a pity no-one could stay with him for long. At least the loyal home supporters could witness for themselves a local product climbing the ladder to success. They stayed till the end, at 3.45, when Atherton hooked Parker for four. Then many of them came on to the field and shook us individually by the hand. 'Thanks for a greet season,' they said as one. 'It's been proper champion.' A moving moment.

The season finished as it had started, sixteen players crammed into a tiny dressing-room jovially drinking cans of McEwan's lager, besieged by piles of kit and television crews. Parker got out his guitar and everyone joined in with the Beach Boys 'Sloop John B'. You can't fault the spirit of this squad. Just think what we'd be like if we won something!

David Graveney must have pondered on that as he thanked everybody personally for their wholehearted efforts, then slowly repacked his case for the last time. In it he put:

1 well used bat, held together with white tape
2 pairs batting gloves, extra protection on forefingers
1 frayed armguard
1 pair pads, rather torn
1 helmet (dented)
Box and thigh pad
1 chest pad
3 pairs dirty flannels – stained with green
1 sleeveless sweater, size 46
3 clean shirts
2 jockstraps
1 sock
1 worn pair rubber-soled fielding shoes
1 pair full-spiked boots (hardly used)
1 tube Factor 34 sunblock
1 can ozone-friendly Deep Heat spray
1 sponge bag

The team hit the bright lights of Newcastle later with every intention of making it a night to remember, but individual desires varied as people drifted off in different directions and the last evening petered out. As it usually does.

Wednesday 16 September

Paul Parker was named 'Player of the Season' tonight at a Newcastle Building Society reception. He deserves it. The sheer effort he puts in is extraordinary. Even in lost causes he throws himself about the field as if it would be embarrassing to return to the pavilion with clean whites. He is annoyed by other's excuses or lack of devotion, but never shows it, remaining the captain's perfect lieutenant – totally reliable and committed, ready with ideas, but quite happy to take a back seat if his views are not sought.

Well equipped technically, he yo-yoed about the batting order as we sought to find the best formula, but never complained or gave up his wicket tamely. A better player when attacking, he regularly dented bowlers' figures in a blaze of classical drives and hooks, or flimsy dressing-room doors if out to an indifferent shot. The partnership he established with Dean Jones became an electrifying mix of muscular batting, fearless running and booming calls. Their presence in the field evoked memories of Randall and Gower in their pomp.

Demoted as captain of Sussex because his attitude was at variance with that of the coach, Norman Gifford, Parker nevertheless led Durham well in Graveney's absence, in spite of a bristling presence that could be unnerving, and was perpetually good company whether leading sing-songs or discussing ethics. It is well rounded, charismatic people like this that the game under-utilises, but cricket's eventual loss will be teaching's gain.

Thursday 17 September

The event every cricketer dreads has occurred, and I'm not talking about a sudden alarming rise in bank base rates. The complete first-class averages have been published, even before players have managed to slip away on holiday. Its galling enough to discover oneself below Peter Such in the batting averages, without being reminded about it every time someone rings up. Irritatingly only the county championship averages, in which I come 126th, are ever listed, the combined limited-over ones where I'm probably lying about fourth, never are. Yet this year we've played 24 first-class matches, 26 one-dayers. I'll have to try and rectify this situation.

[163]

Chapter 10

Looking back with pride

The Prime Minister John Major has always advocated a classless society, so he would have been pleased that, for a considerable part of the season, this new Durham outfit contained a Jones, a Smith and a Brown, and was managed by a Cook. Players came from the Ridings, the Potteries, Wales, and from southern public schools. Oh, and from the north-east, of course. There lies a clue to the eventual deterioration of the team's performances, however. There was no West Indian disposal expert to blow away flimsy opposition batting, no Asian master to take up the cudgels with a flashing blade. Jones' expertise and panache was sorely missed once he departed for Australia in late July.

As injuries took their toll, the youthful Durham aspirants were cruelly exposed, and at times it was too much for them. As Cook himself observes in his book *The Narrow Line*: 'Nothing in cricket even begins to compare with the intense psychological rupture involved in moving from a county 2nd XI to the 1st XI'. The gulf in standards is far wider than anything they have had to cross in the past, or will in the future; even the climb to Test cricket is less precipitous.

So Mark Briers and Stewart Hutton, after promising beginnings, faded as the burden of responsibility grew too onerous; similarly Simon Brown's mind and body could not sustain the general expectation he initially promoted. John Wood and Paul Henderson would not yet have played any first-team cricket in more established squads. All are well ahead of schedule in the wider aspect of their own careers. Whether each will make it through the obstacle course of the next few seasons is another matter.

The loyal Durham supporters can take heart from many memories. The first match at the Racecourse, two championship wins – one a complete rout – ninth place in the Sunday League, the quarter-finals of the NatWest, the emergence of Jimmy Daley whom the clairvoyant Cook cleverly introduced for the last two matches. Overall they will remember enterprising batting, spirited outcricket and a team with which they could mingle and exchange frank views. Humour and imagination were never left on the back burner.

There are question marks for the future. Can Graveney's body and resolve withstand another summer; can Brown rediscover his brisk inswinger; will we locate an overseas player with any credentials; will Chris Scott ever utter a sound behind the stumps? All these queries may be answered in time. Right now the team's immediate needs must be reviewed. Another bowler, preferably 6ft 6in. and capable of speeds up to 95 mph and a reputable opening batsman to take some of the pressure off Larkins are the most pressing requirements. And a luxury coach – of the six-wheeled variety. This would ease some of the travel problems, although those members of staff who actually live in the north are flung all round the region – it is a good hour's drive from Hutton's home in Guisborough to Smith's in the suburbs of Newcastle.

In April cynics described the senior players as 'imported mercenaries' but their contributions were immense. Larkins made over 1500 runs without ever compromising his positive inclinations, even during courageous rearguard actions; Bainbridge soon rediscovered his talents after a year out of the first-class game, Parker revelled in fresh surroundings, batting with great conviction and worth two men in the field. Jones was an inspiration, of course, and so was Botham to a lesser extent, though he found it harder to motivate himself once injuries materialised.

And then there was Graveney. He would never have encountered such a catalogue of imponderables before, and I bet he never will again. Merely making sure everyone got from A via XYZ to B was a full-time job. Perhaps the biggest problem was identifying each individual's mentality, then correctly responding to it. Roping in players of varying experience from all corners of the country is one thing, deciphering what makes them tick quite another. Establishing a player's pain threshold or extent of self-belief takes time and understanding. When, eventually he could turn his mind to actually bowling, he had either injury or dead wickets or short boundaries to contend with, sometimes all three at once. But he confirmed he is still a fine spinner, and comfortably won £10 off me for scoring more runs, although he went through the wars to get there.

It was he and Cook who instigated the compulsory morning warm-ups and the permanent physiotherapist. The latter was a sensible step, the former sometimes seemed mundane, but it at least got everyone together so the captain could address them. There is a danger that the army square-bashing type of mentality is encroaching into English cricket and stifling flair. It did not happen at Durham.

There were a lot of injuries, but these mainly involved contact with the ball. Despite fearing the worst, I managed to remain the only first-teamer who never missed a match through knocks or tweaks. I didn't take as many wickets as I'd hoped, though, which partly contributed to some lengthy sessions in the field. But we still recorded more bowling bonus points than batting and no batsman managed a double-hundred against us. These facts mask the vulnerability of the bowling which bestowed extra confidence in the minds of the opposition, and landed us on the receiving end of torrid spells by fielding sides who knew we hadn't the firepower to retaliate.

Geoff Cook surveyed the whole from a distance at times, leading the second eleven but keeping in constant touch with the first eleven by phone. Occasionally he waded into the front line, organising vigorous practices and even taking part in a couple of important one-day games when reserves were depleted. He and Graveney had their differences, but it never showed except occasionally at the end of a bad day. Then, while Graveney sat dejectedly contemplating where things had gone

[166]

wrong, Cook considered the future, thinking of his five-year-plan like Mao Tse-Tung.

His hardest task was to inform Gary Brown that he was no longer required. Gary, a most personable and dedicated opening bat, had been contracted to Durham for several years and developed an almost impenetrable defence. It wasn't staying in he found the problem, but scoring runs. He earned only three first-team opportunities this year, two of them, against Allan Donald and a marauding Martin McCague, hardly to be relished. Yet he acquitted himself competently and in his third outing, against Hampshire, scored 39 before suffering an ill-judged LBW verdict. It was a decision that effectively ended his career and placed his whole life into turmoil. Devoted to cricket since his late teens he leaves the profession with no other skill, and no redundancy pay or benefit to help support his family. He has been sucked in, chewed up and spat out by the system, with nothing to show for it but some happy memories.

The trouble is, there is still a certain feudalism within the fabric of English cricket, dominated as it is by committees of predominantly older gentlemen. 'A committee,' said the late Warwickshire secretary Leslie Deakins, 'is a body of the unfit elected by the unwilling to do the unnecessary.' For Durham there was a chance to learn from the mistakes of old and avoid the hazardous road of fiefdom. They achieved it in a way. A chairman and various directors were allocated responsibilities and went about them in a businesslike sort of fashion, though it looked as if most were answerable to one. But there's nothing wrong with that, you need chiefs as well as Indians. So small club grounds were transformed into well appointed arenas with portable toilets, fast food and drink bars, temporary stands and the inevitable tannoy. Throngs of businessmen were lured to entertain their customers with lavish lunches served in marquees alongside the players. On the surface everything seemed to run smoothly, though I dare say beneath it things were frenetic.

But that is what it is all about – appearances. And the public lapped it up. No praise would be too high for the people of the north-east, who monitored the progress of our travelling entourage with unbridled enthusiasm, as local newspapers and radio stations relayed the news. Home grounds were packed on Sundays, and well attended in midweek even in September when we had not won a match for a month. Men in flat caps, university lecturers, vicars, ladies with blue rinses, left-wing girls in flares, energetic little boys and disabled adults, they were all there to support *their* team, many wearing *their* club tie. They smiled and cheered and asked for autographs: 'It's not for me, it's for my son, y'know.' They looked content even in times of adversity.

The same could be said for the team. After demoralising defeats there was no sulking or flouncing around, but an invigorating purpose – looking forward to the next match. The quick-witted banter survived even the most abysmal days, delivered in a host of largely indecipherable accents. No player felt really neglected or inferior, each one's suggestions were welcomed from the corner of the dressing-room or a cluster in the bar.

In its review of the first-class season, *The Times* put this whole new venture in good perspective: 'Most hospitable county 1992 – Durham.'

Appendixes

A. The Durham staff
B. Scorecards of the 1992 season
C. Durham 1st XI Averages

Appendix A

The Durham staff

GEOFF COOK, 41 (Director of Cricket). Former Northants captain and opening bat. Seven Test appearances.

DAVID GRAVENEY, 39 (Captain). Slow left-arm bowler and former captain of Gloucestershire. One season with Somerset.

PAUL PARKER, 36 (Vice-captain). Legendary fielder and middle-order bat. Seventeen seasons with Sussex. Captain 1988–91. One Test.

PHIL BAINBRIDGE, 34. Canny all-rounder of fluent strokes and reliable medium pace. Gloucester 1977–90.

PHIL BERRY, 25. Off-spinner and sound no. 7 bat, formerly with Yorkshire.

DARREN BLENKIRON, 18. Punchy left-hand bat. No 1st XI experience.

IAN BOTHAM, 37. Still a batsman to be reckoned with, and crafty bowler despite loss of hostility. Over 100 Tests.

MARK BRIERS, 24. Middle-order batsman and improving leg-spin bowler, signed from Worcestershire.

GARY BROWN, 28. Solid opening bat, brother of Middlesex's Keith.

SIMON BROWN, 23. Bowls fiery left-arm-over, in sustained spells. Much improved after three disappointing seasons at Northants.

JIMMY DALEY, 18. Highly promising batsman from Sunderland. Made 88 on first-class debut v. Somerset.

ANDY FOTHERGILL, 30. Locally born wicket-keeper-batsman who first kept for Durham in 1984.

JOHN GLENDENEN, 27. Powerful batsman with Yorkshire pedigree. Made 200* for Durham v. Victoria, 1991.

SIMON HUGHES, 32. Right-arm fast-medium bowler, Middlesex 1980–91.

STEWART HUTTON, 23. Positive left-handed opener with good temperament. Holds various records for Guisborough CC.

DEAN JONES, 31. The finest one-day batsman in the world, scored two centuries in the match v. Pakistan before returning to Australia.

WAYNE LARKINS, 39. Gifted opening bat who assaults fast bowling. Northants 1973–91. Should have appeared in more than ten Tests.

STEVE McEWAN, 30. Hard-working seamer who contributed much to Worcester's Championship title in 1989.

CHRIS SCOTT, 28. Spent ten years in the shadow of Bruce French at Notts. Underestimated wicket-keeper and batsman.

IAN SMITH, 25. Originally bowled fast for Glamorgan, now converted to aggressive batsman, medium-pacer, and safe slip.

GARY WIGHAM, 20. Tall seamer. One Sunday appearance 1992.

JOHN WOOD, 22. Strapping pace bowler and hard-hitting tailender from Wakefield. Took five wickets on county debut v. Hants.

BRIAN HUNT (scorer). Durham's stats man since 1975.

SHEILA JOB (physiotherapist). Formerly with the British athletics team. Travels to all Durham matches.

Appendix B

Scorecards of the 1992 season

OXFORD UNIVERSITY v DURHAM

Friendly first-class match
The Parks, Oxford, 14, 15 & 16 April 1992
Toss: Oxford. Match drawn

Durham

P.W.G. Parker b Gallian	103
J.D. Glendenen b Gallian	117
D.M. Jones not out	36
P. Bainbridge not out	24
G.K. Brown	
I. Smith	
C.W. Scott†	
P.J. Berry	
D.A. Graveney*	
S.M. McEwan	
J. Wood	
Extras (B 2, LB 4)	6
TOTAL (68 overs, 2 wkt dec.)	**286**

1/222, 2/235

Bowling: Jeh 20-4-74-0; Wood 12.3-0-39-0; Anderson 5-0-25-0; Gallian 15-1-64-2; Davies 13.3-2-62-0; Gupte 2-0-16-0.

Oxford University

R.R. Montgomerie c Parker b Bainbridge	17
J.E.R. Gallian c Scott b Wood	53
A.C. Storie not out	23
C.M. Gupte not out	8
G.B.T. Lovell*	
S.N. Warley	
R.D. Oliphant-Callum†	
M.P. Jeh	
H.R. Davies	
D.J. Anderson	
B.S. Wood	
Extras (NB 4)	4
TOTAL (65 overs, 2 wkt)	**105**

1/45, 2/89

Bowling: Wood 14-5-24-1; McEwan 11-4-26-0; Bainbridge 11-3-14-1; Smith 8-3-11-0; Berry 17-5-25-0; Graveney 4-1-5-0.

Umpires: J.C. Balderstone and G. Sharp

No play after lunch on the first day and no play on the second day. Durham CCC's initial first-class match.

DURHAM v LANCASHIRE

Sunday League match
The Racecourse, Durham, 19 April 1992
Toss: Lancashire. Durham won by 9 runs

Durham

I.T. Botham st Hegg b Allott	14
W. Larkins c Austin b Atherton	59
D.M. Jones c Morrison b DeFreitas	114
P. Bainbridge c Fairbrother b Morrison	35
P.W.G. Parker not out	11
J.D. Glendenen	
A.R. Fothergill†	
D.A. Graveney*	
S.P. Hughes	
S.M. McEwan	
S.J.E. Brown	
Extras (LB 10, W 1, NB 2)	13
TOTAL (40 overs, 4 wkt)	**246**

1/33, 2/120, 3/192, 4/246

Bowling: Allott 8-0-30-1; Morrison 8-0-43-1; DeFreitas 8-0-53-1; Watkinson 5-0-34-0; Austin 7-0-46-0; Atherton 4-0-30-1.

Lancashire

G. Fowler c & b Hughes	27
M.A. Atherton c Hughes b McEwan	11
G.D. Lloyd c Brown b McEwan	4
N.H. Fairbrother* c Botham b McEwan	2
N.J. Speak b Hughes	58
M. Watkinson b Botham	37
I.D. Austin lbw b Brown	27
P.A.J. DeFreitas b Brown	33
W.K. Hegg† run out	22
P.J.W. Allott c Parker b Brown	2
D.K. Morrison not out	0
Extras (B 1, LB 8, W4, NB 1)	14
TOTAL (39.1 overs, 10 wkt)	**237**

1/38, 2/48, 3/52, 4/52, 5/123, 6/168, 7/200, 8/213, 9/237

Bowling: McEwan 8-0-35-3; Brown 8-0-32-3; Hughes 7.1-0-31-2; Botham 8-0-57-1; Bainbridge 6-0-60-0; Graveney 2-0-13-0.

Umpires: N.T. Plews and A.G.T. Whitehead

DURHAM v GLAMORGAN

Benson & Hedges Cup, Group D
The Racecourse, Durham, 21 April 1992
Toss: Glamorgan. Glamorgan won by 4 wickets.
Gold Award: I.T. Botham

Durham

W. Larkins c Croft b Frost	0
J.D. Glendenen c Richards b Watkin	7
D.M. Jones lbw b Watkin	6
P.W.G. Parker c and b Croft	22
I.T. Botham c Richards b Frost	86
P. Bainbridge lbw b Dale	22
C.W. Scott† lbw b Dale	3
D.A. Graveney* b Frost	13
S.P. Hughes b Frost	3
S.M. McEwan not out	12
S.J.E. Brown not out	4
Extras (B 4, LB 7, W 7)	18
TOTAL (55 overs, 9 wkt)	196

1/1, 2/17, 3/18, 4/80, 5/124, 6/154, 7/166, 8/173, 9/176

Bowling: Watkin 11-6-20-2; Frost 11-4-26-4; Barwick 11-0-32-0; Croft 9-0-28-1; Dale 6-0-40-2; Cowdrey 7-0-39-0.

Glamorgan

A. Dale c Larkins b Hughes	30
H. Morris c Jones b Brown	0
M.P. Maynard* lbw b Botham	1
I.V.A. Richards c and b Botham	1
C.S. Cowdrey c Graveney b Hughes	78
P.A. Cottey c Larkins b Brown	38
R.D.B. Croft not out	30
C.P. Metson† not out	6
S.L. Watkin	
S.R. Barwick	
M. Frost	
Extras (LB 5, W 5, NB 3)	13
TOTAL (54.2 overs, 6 wkt)	197

1/1, 2/3, 3/8, 4/52, 5/137, 6/183

Bowling: Brown 10-0-36-2; Botham 11-2-21-2; Hughes 10.2-2-32-2; Graveney 11-1-41-0; McEwan 7-0-32-0; Bainbridge 5-0-30-0.

Umpires: J.D. Bond and B. Leadbeater

DURHAM v LEICESTERSHIRE

Championship match
The Racecourse, Durham, 25, 27, 28 & 29 April 1992
Toss: Durham. Leicestershire won by 7 wickets

Durham

W. Larkins c Hepworth b Mullally	5	b Mullally	9
J.D. Glendenen c Mullally b Wells	16	lbw b Wells	18
D.M. Jones c Briers b Millns	2	c Briers b Potter	32
P.W.G. Parker lbw b Wells	77	c and b Millns	117
P. Bainbridge lbw b Millns	19	c Briers b Wells	9
I.T. Botham c Whitticase b Wells	12	c sub b Millns	105
P.J. Berry c Briers b Potter	9	c Whitticase b Millns	2
C.W. Scott* lbw b Potter	0	lbw b Millns	1
D.A. Graveney* c Whitaker b Mullally	12	b Wells	5
S.P. Hughes not out	3	c sub b Millns	1
S.J.E. Brown c Whitticase b Mullally	0	not out	2
Extras (B 6, W 1, NB 2)	9	(B 2, LB 14, NB 1)	17
TOTAL	164		318

1/12, 2/18, 3/33, 4/82, 5/96, 6/132, 7/134, 8/156, 9/164

1/24, 2/30, 3/91, 4/112, 5/290, 6/292, 7/304, 8/315, 9/315

Bowling: First innings—Mullally 21.1-10-29-3; Millns 14-1-31-0; Potter 12-3-23-2. Second innings—Millns 21.3-4-69-5; Mullally 24-9-53-1; Wells 29-13-57-3; Parsons 12-3-28-0; Potter 26-10-50-1; Hepworth 8-0-45-0.

Leicestershire

T.J. Boon c Glendenen b Berry	110	c Jones b Botham	6
N.E. Briers* c and b Botham	10	c Parker b Graveney	43
J.J. Whitaker b Botham	2	c Hughes b Berry	35
L. Potter c Jones b Graveney	31	not out	38
B.F. Smith not out	100		
P.N. Hepworth lbw b Berry	8		
V.J. Wells lbw b Brown	42	(5) not out	9
P. Whitticase† b Hughes	11		
G.J. Parsons c Scott b Brown	10		
D.J. Millns b Brown	6		
A.D. Mullally b Hughes	1		
Extras (LB 8, NB 3)	11	(B 2, LB 5, W 4)	11
TOTAL	342	(3 wkt)	142

1/22, 2/28, 3/101, 4/197, 5/215, 6/287, 7/304, 8/327, 9/335

1/6, 2/63, 3/114

Bowling: First innings—Botham 25-10-51-2; Brown 26-2-80-3; Hughes 25-9-63-2; Berry 26-7-60-2; Graveney 28-6-80-1. Second innings—Botham 5-2-7-1; Hughes 9-3-17-0; Berry 12-4-44-1; Jones 7-0-20-0; Brown 3-0-10-0; Graveney 12.2-2-37-1.

Umpires: B. Dudleston and J.H. Harris

DURHAM v LEICESTERSHIRE

Sunday League match

Eastwood Gardens, Gateshead Fell CC, 26 April 1992

Toss: Leicestershire.   Durham won by 8 runs

Durham

I.T. Botham b Mullally	67
W. Larkins b Wells	17
D.M. Jones c Benson b Parsons	21
P.W.G. Parker lbw b Millns	16
P. Bainbridge c Millns b Benson	3
J.D. Glendenen c Whiticase b Benson	38
A.R. Fothergill† not out	42
D.A. Graveney* c Briers b Mullally	11
S.M. McEwan not out	7
S.P. Hughes	
S.J.E. Brown	
Extras (LB 5, W 5)	10
TOTAL (40 overs, 7 wkt)	**232**

1/44, 2/75, 3/122, 4/129, 5/135, 6/193, 7/214

Bowling: Mullally 8-0-42-2; Millns 8-0-45-1; Parsons 8-1-32-1; Wells 8-0-45-1; Benson 8-0-64-2.

Leicestershire

J.D.R. Benson c Bainbridge b Hughes	45
N.E. Briers* c Hughes b Bainbridge	36
J.J. Whitaker c and b Botham	0
L. Potter c Glendenen b Bainbridge	21
B.F. Smith lbw b Graveney	31
T.J. Boon run out	49
V.J. Wells c McEwan b Hughes	4
P. Whiticase† b Botham	7
G.J. Parsons c Botham b Hughes	11
D.J. Millns not out	1
A.D. Mullally not out	10
Extras (B 1, LB 5, W 2, NB 1)	9
TOTAL (40 overs, 9 wkt)	**224**

1/61, 2/61, 3/101, 4/116, 5/147, 6/164, 7/176, 8/205, 9/210

Bowling: McEwan 4-0-31-0; Brown 4-0-29-0; Hughes 8-0-46-3; Botham 8-0-30-2; Bainbridge 8-0-41-2; Graveney 8-0-41-1.

Umpires: B. Dudleston and J.H. Harris

WORCESTERSHIRE v DURHAM

Benson & Hedges Cup, Group D

County Ground, New Road, Worcester, 30 April 1992

Toss: Durham.   Durham won by 3 wickets.   Gold Award: P. Bainbridge

Worcestershire

T.S. Curtis* c and b Bainbridge	60
A.C.H. Seymour c Larkins b McEwan	17
G.A. Hick c Botham b Bainbridge	26
T.M. Moody b Bainbridge	8
D.A. Leatherdale lbw b Botham	14
S.J. Rhodes† lbw b Bainbridge	0
S.R. Lampitt c Parker b Brown	4
N.V. Radford c Hughes b McEwan	5
G.R. Haynes c Glendenen b McEwan	14
P.J. Newport c Jones b Hughes	9
R.K. Illingworth not out	5
Extras (B 2, LB 4, W 5)	11
TOTAL (52.4 overs)	**173**

1/51, 2/101, 3/115, 4/128, 5/128, 6/138, 7/138, 8/149, 9/162

Bowling: Botham 10-2-27-1; Brown 11-1-27-1; McEwan 11-2-45-3; Bainbridge 11-0-38-4; Hughes 9.4-1-30-1.

Durham

W. Larkins c Haynes b Illingworth	19
J.D. Glendenen c Haynes b Lampitt	45
D.M. Jones run out	13
P.W.G. Parker* st Rhodes b Illingworth	9
I.T. Botham c Rhodes b Newport	2
P. Bainbridge c Rhodes b Newport	5
I. Smith not out	29
A.R. Fothergill† lbw b Haynes	17
S.M. McEwan not out	29
S.P. Hughes	
S.J.E. Brown	
Extras (LB 4, W 2, NB 3)	9
TOTAL (51.5 overs, 7 wkt)	**177**

1/31, 2/56, 3/85, 4/89, 5/92, 6/108, 7/142

Bowling: Newport 10.5-0-45-2; Radford 10-0-37-0; Haynes 9-1-33-1; Illingworth 11-4-22-2; Lampitt 9-1-28-1; Hick 2-0-8-0.

Umpires: J.W. Holder and K.E. Palmer

COMBINED UNIVERSITIES v DURHAM

Benson & Hedges Cup, Group D
Fenner's, Cambridge, 2 May 1992   Gold Award: W. Larkins

Toss: Durham.   Durham won by 51 runs.

Durham

W. Larkins c Storie b Pearson	73
J.D. Glendenen c sub b Pearson	60
D.M. Jones b Snape	6
P.W.G. Parker* b Snape	22
I.T. Botham c Snape b Gallian	72
P. Bainbridge c and b Bovill	16
A.R. Fothergill† not out	12
S.M. McEwan not out	1
P.J. Berry	
S.P. Hughes	
S.J.E. Brown	
Extras (LB 3, W 5, NB 1)	9
TOTAL (55 overs, 6 wkt)	271

1/125, 2/140, 3/143, 4/196, 5/226, 6/268

Bowling: Hallett 5-2-21-0; Bovill 10-0-67-1; Usher 11-1-66-0; Pearson 11-2-31-2; Snape 11-0-44-2; Gallian 7-0-39-1.

Combined Universities

R.R. Montgomerie c and b Hughes	45
J.E.R. Gallian c Fothergill b Hughes	50
J.P. Crawley* st Fothergill b Jones	42
J.N. Snape run out	26
A.C. Storie lbw b Jones	5
A.M. Hooper not out	25
S.F. Shephard† not out	11
R.M. Pearson	
B.C. Usher	
J.C. Hallett	
J.N.B. Bovill	
Extras (LB 8, W 8)	16
TOTAL (55 overs, 5 wkt)	220

1/103, 2/114, 3/165, 4/178, 5/183

Bowling: Brown 5-2-14-0; Botham 7-2-20-0; Bainbridge 10-0-41-0; McEwan 7-0-23-0; Berry 11-0-49-0; Hughes 8-0-31-2; Jones 7-0-34-2.

Umpires: G.I. Burgess and B.J. Meyer

DURHAM v DERBYSHIRE

Benson & Hedges Cup, Group D
County Ground, Jesmond, 5 May 1992
Derbyshire won by 80 runs.   Gold Award: J.E. Morris

Toss: Durham.

Derbyshire

K.J. Barnett* b Bainbridge	28
P.D. Bowler lbw b Botham	8
J.E. Morris c Larkins b Brown	121
T.J.G. O'Gorman c Glendenen b McEwan	37
C.J. Adams c Fothergill b McEwan	1
I.R. Bishop c Parker b Hughes	42
A.E. Warner run out	13
K.M. Krikken† run out	5
D.G. Cork not out	5
D.E. Malcolm c Parker b Hughes	2
O.H. Mortensen	
Extras (B 4, LB 9, W 5, NB 1)	19
TOTAL (55 overs, 9 wkt)	281

1/13, 2/57, 3/145, 4/156, 5/249, 6/261, 7/272, 8/279, 9/281

Bowling: Botham 11-1-46-1; Brown 11-1-52-1; McEwan 11-1-54-2; Bainbridge 10-1-51-1; Hughes 11-0-52-2; Graveney 1-0-13-0.

Durham

W. Larkins lbw b Cork	58
J.D. Glendenen llbw b Mortensen	20
D.M. Jones c Krikken b Mortensen	0
P.W.G. Parker run out	22
I.T. Botham c Krikken b Warner	6
P. Bainbridge c Krikken b Mortensen	27
A.R. Fothergill† lbw b Cork	3
D.A. Graveney* c Krikken b Cork	21
S.M. McEwan c Barnett b Cork	9
S.P. Hughes run out	0
S.J.E. Brown not out	2
Extras (LB 12, W 14, NB 7)	33
TOTAL (46.2 overs, 10 wkt)	201

1/44, 2/44, 3/116, 4/117, 5/123, 6/134, 7/182, 8/195, 9/195

Bowling: Bishop 9-1-44-0; Mortensen 10-1-39-3; Malcolm 9-0-46-0; Warner 9-0-34-1; Cork 9.2-0-26-4.

Umpires: V. A. Holder and D. O. Oslear

KENT v DURHAM

Championship match

St Lawrence Ground, Canterbury, 7, 8, 9 (no play), 11 May 1992
Toss: Kent.   Match drawn

Kent

T.R. Ward c Fothergill b Botham	32	lbw b Botham	9
M.R. Benson* c Parker b Brown	75	b Brown	27
N.R. Taylor lbw b Brown	57	(4) not out	78
C.L. Hooper lbw b Brown	1	(5) not out	115
J.I. Longley c Botham b Brown	5		
M.V. Fleming c Glendenen b Brown	14		
S.A. Marsh† c Parker b Graveney	20		
M.A. Ealham c Parker b Brown	32		
R.M. Ellison c and b Graveney	0		
R.P. Davis not out	0	(3) c Graveney b Brown	9
M.J. McCague b Brown	0		
Extras (B 4, LB 4)	8	(B 4, LB 9, W 1, NB 1)	15
TOTAL	**244**	(3 wkt dec.)	**253**

1/57, 2/166, 3/168, 4/174, 5/185, 6/196, 7/240, 8/240, 9/244

1/32, 2/47, 3/56

Bowling: *First innings*—Botham 12-3-40-1; Brown 27-4-105-7; Hughes 19-4-39-0; Bainbridge 13-3-40-0; Berry 2-0-4-0. *Second innings*—Hughes 14-0-63-0; Brown 19.2-2-94-2; Botham 7-3-5-1; Graveney 16-6-43-0; Bainbridge 3-0-35-0.

Durham

W. Larkins lbw b McCague	40	c Longley b Ellison	4
J.D. Glendenen lbw b Ellison	28	not out	57
D.M. Jones lbw b McCague	34	c Ward b Ellison	1
P.W.G. Parker b Ealham	17	b Hooper	14
P. Bainbridge lbw b McCague	8	not out	61
I.T. Botham c Benson b Ellison	23		
A.R. Fothergill† c Hooper b Ellison	0		
P.J. Berry lbw b Ellison	28		
D.A. Graveney* c Marsh b Ealham	18		
S.P. Hughes b Ellison	5		
S.J.E. Brown not out	27		
Extras (B 1, LB 22, NB 4)	27	(B 4, LB 3, NB 1)	8
TOTAL	**239**	(3 wkt)	**145**

1/68, 2/84, 3/118, 4/137, 5/152, 6/158, 7/159, 8/184, 9/233

1/5, 2/7, 3/37

Bowling: *First innings*—McCague 26-8-75-3; Ealham 26-16-28-2; Ellison 34.4-6-77-5; Hooper 10-5-15-0; Fleming 13-6-21-0. *Second innings*—McCague 10-2-35-0; Ellison 5-2-7-2; Hooper 20-2-59-1; Davis 14-6-33-0; Fleming 1-0-4-0.

Umpires: G.I. Burgess and B. Leadbeater

KENT v DURHAM

Sunday League match

St Lawrence Ground, Canterbury, 10 May 1992
Toss: Durham. No result – match abandoned (rain)

Kent

T.R. Ward c Parker b Botham	45
M.R. Benson* c Fothergill b Brown	0
N.R. Taylor not out	30
C.L. Hooper not out	13
G.R. Cowdrey	
M.V. Fleming	
S.A. Marsh†	
M.A. Ealham	
R.M. Ellison	
R.P. Davis	
M.J. McCague	
Extras (LB 5, W 1)	6
TOTAL (20 overs, 2 wkt)	**94**

1/10, 2/64

Bowling: McEwan 5-1-27-0; Brown 3-0-21-1; Botham 6-0-12-1; Graveney 5-0-19-0; Bainbridge 1-0-10-0.

Durham

I.T. Botham
W. Larkins
D.M. Jones
P.W.G. Parker
P. Bainbridge
J.D. Glendenen
A.R. Fothergill†
D.A. Graveney
S.M. McEwan
S.P. Hughes
S.J.E. Brown

Umpires: G.I. Burgess and B. Leadbeater

GLAMORGAN v DURHAM

Championship match
Sophia Gardens, Cardiff, 14, 15, 16 & 17 May 1992
Toss: Glamorgan. Durham won by an innings and 104 runs

Glamorgan

S.P. James	c Fothergill b Brown	2	c Parker b Botham	5
H. Morris	c Jones b Henderson	46	lbw b Botham	0
A. Dale	c Jones b Brown	29	c Botham b Brown	3
M.P. Maynard*	c Larkins b Henderson	88	c Larkins b Brown	15
I.V.A. Richards	c Jones b Henderson	1	c Botham b Brown	7
P.A. Cottey	lbw b Brown	24	not out	112
R.D.B. Croft	lbw b Hughes	14	b Brown	3
C.P. Metson†	run out	1	c Fothergill b Hughes	30
S.L. Watkin	c Fothergill b Hughes	1	c Fothergill b Botham	12
S.R. Barwick	b Hughes	7	c Brown b Graveney	0
S. Bastien	not out	0	b Brown	0
Extras	(B 3, LB 4, NB 3)	10	(B 1, LB5)	6
TOTAL		224		193

1/3, 2/58, 3/121, 4/125, 5/184,
6/208, 7/210, 8/214, 9/221

1/1, 2/8, 3/14, 4/29, 5/32,
6/40, 7/117, 8/170, 9/189

Bowling: *First innings*—Botham 8-0-35-0; Brown 22-6-70-3; Hughes 22.5-5-51-3; Henderson 17-4-61-3; Graveney 2-2-0-0. *Second innings*—Botham 22-7-47-3; Brown 26.1-8-66-5; Hughes 18-4-41-1; Graveney 16-5-20-1; Jones 3-0-13-0.

Durham

W. Larkins	c Maynard b Croft	143
J.D. Glendenen	c Metson b Watkin	15
D.M. Jones	c Barwick b Watkin	94
P.W.G. Parker	c Metson b Watkin	124
I.T. Bainbridge	c James b Bastien	11
A.R. Fothergill†	b Croft	40
P.W. Henderson	c Metson b Croft	8
S.P. Hughes	c Dale b Croft	46
D.A. Graveney*	not out	1
S.J.E. Brown		8
Extras	(B 13, LB 9, W 3, NB 6)	31
TOTAL	(9 wkt dec.)	521

1/44, 2/250, 3/301, 4/317, 5/371,
6/416, 7/481, 8/484, 9/521

Bowling: *First innings*—Watkin 42-11-115-2; Bastien 30-5-113-2; Barwick 30-7-86-0; Dale 23-8-54-0; Croft 32.5-8-105-5; Richards 9-1-26-0.

Umpires: B. Dudleston and A.A. Jones

DURHAM v NORTHAMPTONSHIRE

Championship match
Grangefield Road, Stockton-on-Tees, 23, 25, 26 May 1992
Toss: Northamptonshire. Northamptonshire won by 8 wickets
(off last ball)

Northamptonshire

A. Fordham	c Jones b Brown	18	c Jones b Botham	39
N.A. Felton	c Hughes b Brown	20		
R.J. Bailey	lbw b Botham	34		
A.J. Lamb*	c Jones b Hughes	58	not out	8
D.J. Capel	c Parker b Brown	36	c Bainbridge b Brown	30
M.B. Loye	lbw b Graveney	46	(2) not out	7
K.M. Curran	c Bainbridge b Hughes	82		
D. Ripley†	lbw b Brown	104	(4)	
A.R. Roberts	c Graveney b Brown	16		
C.E.L. Ambrose	not out	16		
J.P. Taylor				
Extras	(LB 4, W 2)	6	(B 5, LB 6)	11
TOTAL	(9 wkt dec.)	420	(2 wkt)	95

1/30, 2/45, 3/118, 4/140, 5/214,
6/218, 7/379, 8/379, 9/420

1/78, 2/79

Bowling: *First innings*—Brown 27-3-124-5; Hughes 25-4-93-2; McEwan 16-2-65-0; Botham 18-2-59-1; Bainbridge 16-3-54-0; Graveney 8-2-21-1. *Second innings*—Botham 5-0-41-1; Hughes 3-0-38-0; Brown 1-0-5-1.

Durham

W. Larkins	c Jones b Capel	46	b Taylor	14
J.D. Glendenen	c Ripley b Taylor	5	c Loye b Ambrose	0
D.M. Jones	lbw b Taylor	5	c Bailey b Capel	157
P.W.G. Parker	c Taylor b Ambrose	35	c Ripley b Curran	5
P. Bainbridge	not out	92	c Ripley b Curran	5
I.T. Botham	run out	1	c Ripley b Curran	3
A.R. Fothergill†	c Ripley b Taylor	18	lbw b Capel	15
S.M. McEwan	c Fordham b Roberts	22	c Lamb b Ambrose	0
D.A. Graveney*	c Lamb b Ambrose	5	c Ripley b Curran	5
S.P. Hughes	c Ripley b Ambrose	0	b Capel	20
S.J.E. Brown	c Ripley b Curran	19	not out	5
Extras	(B 4, LB 6, W 2, NB 1)	13	(B 4, LB 11, W 4, NB 3)	24
TOTAL		258		253

1/10, 2/20, 3/80, 4/112, 5/143,
6/144, 7/185, 8/197, 9/240

1/2, 2/37, 3/47, 4/57, 5/75,
6/111, 7/112, 8/153, 9/240

Bowling: *First innings*—Ambrose 24-7-59-3; Taylor 17-2-48-3; Curran 12.3-2-58-1; Capel 16-0-44-1; Roberts 16-2-39-1. *Second innings*—Ambrose 28-13-44-2; Taylor 24-4-90-2; Curran 17-4-41-3; Capel 17-3-45-3; Bailey 3-0-6-0; Roberts 7-1-12-0.

Umpires: B.J. Meyer and D.R. Shepherd

HAMPSHIRE v DURHAM

Championship match

County Ground, Southampton, 29, 30 May, 1 June 1992

Toss: Hampshire. Match drawn. No play on third day (rain)

Durham

W. Larkins c Nicholas b Shine	45		lbw b Ayling	26
P.W.G. Parker lbw b Connor	41		not out	20
D.M. Jones b Connor	4			
P. Bainbridge c Smith b James	6			
J.D. Glendenen c Gower b Connor	64		(2) c and b Connor	38
I.T. Botham c Aymes b Connor	51			
C.W. Scott† b Ayling	3			
J. Wood c Connor b James	1			
D.A. Graveney* lbw b Connor	33			
S.P. Hughes b Shine	40		(4) not out	0
S.J.E. Brown not out	0			
Extras (LB 16, W 1, NB 1)	18		(NB 3)	3
TOTAL	**306**		**(2 wkt)**	**87**

1/84, 2/94, 3/94, 4/107, 5/206, 6/226, 7/230, 8/236, 9/299

1/50, 2/82

Bowling: *First innings*—Connor 27-10-58-5; Shine 24.4-3-99-2; Udal 12-2-38-0; Ayling 13-2-50-1; James 18-7-45-2. *Second innings*—Connor 12-1-34-1; Shine 5-1-18-0; Ayling 2-0-17-1; Udal 4-0-18-0.

Hampshire

T.C. Middleton c Scott b Wood	0
K.D. James c Botham b Graveney	62
D.I. Gower c Larkins b Wood	0
R.A. Smith c Bainbridge b Wood	25
M.C.J. Nicholas* lbw b Botham	27
J.R. Wood lbw b Brown	57
J.R. Ayling c Scott b Brown	6
A.N. Aymes† c Bainbridge b Wood	7
S.D. Udal not out	14
C.A. Connor b Graveney	5
K.J. Shine b Wood	7
Extras (LB 6, W 1)	7
TOTAL	**210**

1/0, 2/0, 3/28, 4/62, 5/145, 6/165, 7/193, 8/203, 9/203

Bowling: *First innings*—Wood 15.4-2-68-5; Brown 13-2-59-2; Hughes 13-2-25-0; Botham 8-2-14-1; Graveney 17-3-38-2.

Umpires: D.J. Constant and R. Julian

DURHAM v NORTHAMPTONSHIRE

Sunday League match

Grangefield Road, Stockton-on-Tees, 24 May 1992

Toss: Durham. Northamptonshire won by 6 wickets

Durham

I.T. Botham b Walker	8
W. Larkins c Ripley b Taylor	4
D.M. Jones b Curran	26
P. Bainbridge run out	2
P.W.G. Parker b Curran	2
J.D. Glendenen c Ripley b Capel	35
A.R. Fothergill† c Ripley b Capel	4
S.M. McEwan b Capel	18
D.A. Graveney* not out	11
S.P. Hughes b Capel	0
S.J.E. Brown c Fordham b Taylor	1
Extras (LB 12, W 1)	13
TOTAL (35.3 overs)	**124**

1/10, 2/14, 3/18, 4/37, 5/70, 6/75, 7/105, 8/114, 9/116

Bowling: Walker 6-0-17-1; Taylor 7.3-1-15-2; Ambrose 6-1-10-0; Curran 8-0-29-2; Capel 8-1-41-4.

Northamptonshire

A. Fordham lbw b Botham	5
N.A. Felton c Brown b Bainbridge	27
A.J. Lamb* c Bainbridge b Graveney	42
D.J. Capel st Fothergill b Graveney	16
R.J. Bailey not out	33
K.M. Curran not out	0
D. Ripley†	
A.R. Roberts	
C.E.L. Ambrose	
J.P. Taylor	
A. Walker	
Extras (W 4)	4
TOTAL (30.3 overs, 4 wkt)	**127**

1/8, 2/58, 3/87, 4/118

Bowling: Botham 5-0-19-1; Hughes 8-0-22-0; Brown 5-0-25-0; Bainbridge 7-1-32-1; Graveney 5.3-0-29-2.

Umpires: B.J. Meyer and D.R. Shepherd

HAMPSHIRE v DURHAM

Sunday League match
County Ground, Southampton, 31 May 1992
Toss: Hampshire. Hampshire won by 2 wickets

Durham

I.T. Botham c Middleton b Udal	64
W. Larkins c Aymes b James	8
D.M. Jones c Middleton b Bakker	55
P. Bainbridge c and b Udal	5
P.W.G. Parker not out	42
J.D. Glendenen b Udal	2
I. Smith b Connor	19
A.R. Fothergill† c Gower b Udal	8
S.P. Hughes not out	1
D.A. Graveney*	
S.J.E. Brown	
Extras (LB 3, W 2)	5
TOTAL (40 overs, 7 wkt)	**209**

1/24, 2/109, 3/117, 4/162, 5/166, 6/193, 7/205

Bowling: Connor 8-0-26-1; James 8-0-32-1; Maru 8-0-43-0; Bakker 8-0-41-1; Udal 8-0-64-4.

Hampshire

R.A. Smith lbw b Botham	78
T.C. Middleton c Parker b Brown	7
D.I. Gower c Parker b Botham	56
M.C.J. Nicholas* c Jones b Hughes	20
K.D. James c Jones b Graveney	6
J.R. Wood c Parker b Bainbridge	12
A.N. Aymes† not out	3
S.D. Udal run out	9
C.A. Connor run out	2
R.J. Maru not out	8
P.J. Bakker	
Extras (LB 6, W 5)	11
TOTAL (40 overs, 8 wkt)	**212**

1/11, 2/146, 3/151, 4/166, 5/187, 6/190, 7/200, 8/204

Bowling: Brown 7-0-36-1; Hughes 8-0-37-1; Bainbridge 7-0-53-1; Botham 8-0-30-2; Smith 2-0-17-0; Graveney 8-0-33-1.

Umpires: D.J. Constant and R. Julian

DURHAM v SOMERSET

Championship match
Feethams, Darlington, 2, 3, 4 June 1992
Toss: Somerset. Durham won by 8 wickets

Somerset

A.N. Hayhurst b Henderson	76	c Graveney b Hughes	7
M.N. Lathwell lbw b Bainbridge	53	b Henderson	50
R.J. Harden b Brown	24	lbw b Brown	35
C.J. Tavaré* c Hughes b Henderson	2	b Briers	10
R.J. Bartlett c Scott b Henderson	21	lbw b Briers	4
G.D. Rose c Briers b Brown	47	lbw b Hughes	36
N.D. Burns† c Scott b Bainbridge	9	not out	26
R.P. Snell lbw b Brown	5	not out	10
N.A. Mallender lbw b Brown	7		
A.R. Caddick not out	1		
H.R.J. Trump c Scott b Hughes	4		
Extras (LB15, W 4, NB 2)	21	(B 1, LB 1, W 1, NB 11)	14
TOTAL	**270**	(6 wkt dec.)	**192**

1/96, 2/150, 3/153, 4/177, 5/198, 6/221, 7/236, 8/254, 9/265
1/25, 2/74, 3/94, 4/108, 5/125, 6/175

Bowling: *First innings*—Brown 19-3-71-4; Hughes 20.5-2-50-1; Henderson 19-1-59-3; Graveney 15-4-30-0; Bainbridge 20-4-45-2. *Second innings*—Brown 15-3-45-1; Hughes 13.3-4-27-2; Bainbridge 9-3-15-0; Henderson 8-1-39-1; Briers 10-2-43-2; Graveney 15-7-21-0.

Durham

W. Larkins c Trump b Caddick	21	c Bartlett b Caddick	92
P.W.G. Parker b Hayhurst	42	not out	16
D.M. Jones c Harden b Mallender	21	(3) lbw b Caddick	78
P. Bainbridge c Burns b Mallender	45	(2) lbw b Caddick	14
M.P. Briers lbw b Mallender	12	not out	14
P.W. Henderson c Tavaré b Caddick	8		
C.W. Scott† not out	57		
D.A. Graveney* c Rose b Snell	13		
S.P. Hughes c Snell b Trump	6		
S.J.E. Brown not out	5		
J.D. Glendenen			
Extras (B 4, LB 6, NB 10)	20	(B 1, LB 11, W 1)	13
TOTAL (8 wkt dec.)	**250**	(2 wkt)	**213**

1/27, 2/73, 3/123, 4/146, 5/159, 6/160, 7/206, 8/230
1/175, 2/182

Bowling: *First innings*—Snell 17-3-61-1; Caddick 24-6-52-2; Trump 9.2-1-34-1; Mallender 15-3-42-3; Rose 12-4-25-0; Hayhurst 7-0-26-1. *Second innings*—Mallender 5-0-27-0; Caddick 10-0-54-2; Snell 8-1-51-0; Rose 5-0-19-0; Hayhurst 5-0-24-0; Trump 6-0-26-0.

Umpires: H.D. Bird and N.T. Plews

DERBYSHIRE v DURHAM

Championship match
Queen's Park, Chesterfield, 5, 6, 8 June 1992
Toss: Derbyshire. Match drawn – abandoned (rain), no play on first two days

Durham

W. Larkins c O'Gorman b Mortensen 5
J.D. Glendenen c Krikken b Malcolm 5
D.M. Jones not out 93
P.W.G. Parker c Mortensen b Adams 75
P. Bainbridge not out 48
M.P. Briers
I. Smith
C.W. Scott*
D.A. Graveney*
S.P. Hughes
J. Wood
Extras (LB 13, NB 2) 15
TOTAL (45 overs, 3 wkt dec.) **241**
1/6, 2/22, 3/159
Bowling: Bishop 6-1-17-0; Malcolm 6-1-29-1; Warner 4-1-11-0; Mortensen 8-0-29-1; Goldsmith 13-1-82-0; Adams 8-0-60-1.

Derbyshire

K.J. Barnett* not out 16
P.D. Bowler not out 15
S.C. Goldsmith
T.J.G. O'Gorman
C.J. Adams
A.M. Brown
I.R. Bishop
K.M. Krikken†
A.E. Warner
D.E. Malcolm
O.H. Mortensen
Extras 0
TOTAL (11 overs, 0 wkt) **31**
Bowling: Hughes 6-0-8-0; Wood 5-0-23-0.
Umpires: J.W. Holder and B. Leadbeater

DERBYSHIRE v DURHAM

Sunday League match
Queen's Park, Chesterfield, 7 June 1992
Toss: Derbyshire. Derbyshire won by 7 wickets

Durham

W. Larkins lbw b Mortensen 3
D.M. Jones c Adams b Bishop 67
P.W.G. Parker b Malcolm 17
P. Bainbridge c Warner b Malcolm 57
J.D. Glendenen b Bishop 14
I. Smith c Goldsmith b Malcolm 8
A.R. Fothergill† not out 11
P.W. Henderson not out 3
D.A. Graveney*
S.P. Hughes
S.J.E. Brown
Extras (B 11, W 6) 17
TOTAL (40 overs, 6 wkt) **197**
1/6, 2/59, 3/150, 4/165, 5/176, 6/182
Bowling: Mortensen 8-2-37-1; Bishop 8-0-25-2; Warner 8-0-24-0; Malcolm 8-0-52-3; Goldsmith 8-0-48-0.

Derbyshire

K.J. Barnett* c Glendenen b Bainbridge 53
P.D. Bowler not out 77
S.C. Goldsmith st Fothergill b Smith 20
T.J.G. O'Gorman c and b Graveney 15
C.J. Adams not out 20
A.M. Brown
I.R. Bishop
K.M. Krikken†
A.E. Warner
D.E. Malcolm
O.H. Mortensen
Extras (LB 7, W 8, NB 1) 16
TOTAL (37.1 overs, 3 wkt) **201**
1/97, 2/148, 3/168
Bowling: Hughes 7-0-35-0; Brown 7-0-23-0; Henderson 5-0-30-0; Bainbridge 8-0-41-1; Graveney 8-0-44-1; Smith 2-0-17-1; Jones 0.1-0-1-0.
Umpires: J.W. Holder and B. Leadbeater

DURHAM v SUSSEX

Tilcon Trophy semi-final

St George's Road Ground, Harrogate, 9 June 1992

Toss: Durham. Sussex won by 37 runs.

Man of the Match: M.P. Speight

Sussex

D.M. Smith st Scott b Graveney	28
J.W. Hall c Lenham b Hughes	10
N.J. Lenham c Hughes b Graveney	9
F.D. Stephenson b Smith	0
M.P. Speight c Parker b Hughes	71
P. Moores† c Briers b Smith	3
A.P. Wells* lbw b Smith	43
B.T.P. Donelan run out	0
I.D.K. Salisbury not out	22
A.N. Jones not out	10
A.G. Robson	
Extras (B 5, LB 6, W 5, NB 2)	18
TOTAL (55 overs, 8 wkt)	214

1/36, 2/50, 3/53, 4/53, 5/57, 6/153, 7/154, 8/189

Bowling: Hughes 8-2-21-2; Wood 10-0-48-0; Smith 11-2-34-3; Graveney 11-2-41-2; Bainbridge 8-0-25-0; Jones 7-0-34-0.

Durham

W. Larkins c Jones b Donelan	20
S. Hutton c Robson b Lenham	41
D.M. Jones c Moores b Jones	8
P.W.G. Parker c Jones b Wells	31
P. Bainbridge c Stephenson b Lenham	2
M.P. Briers lbw b Lenham	17
I. Smith not out	35
J. Wood st Moores b Lenham	3
C.W. Scott† c Moores b Stephenson	0
S.P. Hughes c Smith b Stephenson	5
D.A. Graveney* c Smith b Stephenson	2
Extras (B 1, LB 9, W 3)	13
TOTAL (48.3 overs)	177

1/36, 2/54, 3/106, 4/109, 5/118, 6/139, 7/162, 8/163, 9/171

Bowling: Stephenson 9.3-3-20-3; Robson 3-0-19-0; Donelan 10-1-24-1; Jones 6-0-34-1; Lenham 11-0-32-4; Wells 9-0-38-1.

Umpires: R. Julian and N.T. Plews

DURHAM v ESSEX

Championship match

Park Drive, Hartlepool, 12, 13, 15 June 1992

Toss: Essex. Essex won by 190 runs

Essex

G.A. Gooch* c Scott b Wood	113	c Scott b Berry	86
J.P. Stephenson c Glendenen b Brown	23	c sub b Brown	81
P.J. Prichard c Jones b Brown	19	c sub b Graveney	66
M.E. Waugh c and b Graveney	75	c sub b Graveney	7
N.V. Knight c Jones b Wood	21	(6) not out	32
M.A. Garnham† c and b Bainbridge	17	c Scott b Graveney	16
D.R. Pringle run out	18	(8) not out	14
N.A. Foster c Scott b Graveney	54	(5) lbw b Bainbridge	0
M.C. Ilott run out	7		
P.M. Such not out	2		
J.H. Childs c Jones b Berry	4		
Extras (LB 6, NB1)	7	(B 4, LB 3)	7
TOTAL	360	(6 wkt dec.)	309

1/55, 2/79, 3/236, 4/236, 5/267, 6/280, 7/307, 8/325, 9/355

1/152, 2/210, 3/229, 4/235, 5/251, 6/277

Bowling: First innings—Wood 22-2-86-2; Brown 9-0-51-2; Botham 14-2-67-0; Bainbridge 24-7-46-1; Berry 5-0-39-1; Graveney 19-3-65-2. Second innings—Wood 5-0-28-0; Bainbridge 22-8-87-2; Berry 12-0-99-1; Graveney 13-0-88-3.

Durham

J.D. Glendenen lbw b Ilott	1	c Gooch b Foster	10
S. Hutton c Waugh b Ilott	43	c Such b Foster	40
D.M. Jones c Stephenson b Childs	57	c Foster b Waugh	22
P.W.G. Parker c Knight b Childs	55	(6) c Gooch b Ilott	0
P. Bainbridge c Foster b Childs	60	(4) retired hurt	6
I.T. Botham not out	55	(5) c Garnham b Foster	22
C.W. Scott† b Childs	0	c Stephenson b Foster	2
P.J. Berry b Stephenson	6	c Garnham b Pringle	30
D.A. Graveney* not out	5	not out	25
J. Wood		c Prichard b Pringle	8
S.J.E. Brown		c Childs b Pringle	10
Extras (B 1, LB 8, W 1, NB 8)	18	(LB 1, NB 3)	4
TOTAL (7 wkt dec.)	300		179

1/2, 2/107, 3/108, 4/226, 5/231, 6/231, 7/277

1/14, 2/15, 3/82, 4/83, 5/98, 6/106, 7/143, 8/151, 9/179

Bowling: First innings—Foster 20-4-52-0; Ilott 17-3-72-2; Childs 20-6-85-4; Pringle 15-5-31-0; Stephenson 5.4-0-35-1; Such 6-2-16-0. Second innings—Foster 20-8-49-4; Ilott 11-2-43-1; Childs 3-0-9-0; Pringle 10.2-1-50-3; Waugh 6-0-27-1.

Umpires: J.H. Hampshire and M.J. Kitchen

DURHAM v ESSEX

Sunday League match
Park Drive, Hartlepool, 14 June 1992
Toss: Durham.   Essex won by 15 runs

Essex

G.A. Gooch* lbw b Hughes	0
J.P. Stephenson c Fothergill b Wigham	23
M.E. Waugh run out	22
P.J. Prichard c Larkins b Hughes	83
N.V. Knight run out	28
N. Shahid c Smith b Graveney	10
M.A. Garnham† c Larkins b McEwan	4
D.R. Pringle c Botham b McEwan	37
T.D. Topley not out	6
M.C. Ilott	
P.M. Such	
Extras (LB 4, W 2, NB 1)	7
TOTAL (40 overs, 8 wkt)	**220**

1/0, 2/46, 3/46, 4/108, 5/129, 6/139, 7/207, 8/220

Bowling: Hughes 8-1-34-2; Wigham 8-1-43-1; McEwan 7-0-44-2; Bainbridge 8-1-39-0; Smith 5-0-37-0; Graveney 4-0-19-1.

Durham

I.T. Botham b Stephenson	27
W. Larkins lbw b Topley	3
D.M. Jones c Knight b Ilott	100
P.W.G. Parker c Shahid b Waugh	10
P. Bainbridge c Gooch b Ilott	41
I. Smith c Topley b Pringle	3
A.R. Fothergill† c Topley b Ilott	4
S.M. McEwan c Such b Pringle	0
S.P. Hughes not out	5
D.A. Graveney* not out	2
G. Wigham	
Extras (LB 4, W 5, NB 1)	10
TOTAL (40 overs, 8 wkt)	**205**

1/7, 2/48, 3/80, 4/163, 5/169, 6/191, 7/195, 8/198

Bowling: Topley 6-1-31-1; Ilott 8-0-40-3; Stephenson 6-0-23-1; Pringle 8-0-37-2; Such 6-0-30-0; Waugh 6-0-40-1.

Umpires: J. H. Hampshire and M.J. Kitchen

SUSSEX v DURHAM

Championship match
Cricketfield Road, Horsham, 19, 20, 22 June 1992
Toss: Durham.   Sussex won by 4 wickets (off last ball)

Durham

W. Larkins lbw b Pigott	53	c Wells b Jones	15
S. Hutton c Pigott b Stephenson	78	c Moores b Pigott	5
D.M. Jones c Moores b Stephenson	5	not out	89
P.W.G. Parker b Pigott	44	b Pigott	11
M.P. Briers lbw b Stephenson	2	not out	62
I. Smith c Speight b Stephenson	17		
C.W. Scott† c Moores b Pigott	48		
D.A. Graveney* not out	27		
S.P. Hughes c Stephenson b Donelan	9		
S.M. McEwan not out	0		
J. Wood			
Extras (LB 16, NB 1)	17	(B 1, LB 3, NB 4)	8
TOTAL (8 wkt dec.)	**300**	(3 wkt dec.)	**190**

1/20, 2/108, 3/119, 4/125, 5/149, 6/247, 7/272, 8/299
1/13, 2/32, 3/51

Bowling: *First innings*—Stephenson 25-8-65-4; Robson 10-1-20-0; Pigott 15-3-34-3; Jones 13-0-63-0; Donelan 32.4-4-102-1. *Second innings*—Stephenson 1-1-0-0; Jones 9-0-72-1; Pigott 11-2-38-2; Robson 6-0-29-0; Donelan 8-0-47-0.

Sussex

D.M. Smith c McEwan b Wood	3	b Graveney	67
J.W. Hall not out	82	b Hughes	0
N.J. Lenham c McEwan b Wood	1	c Hughes b McEwan	118
A.P. Wells* c McEwan b Wood	1	(5) c Larkins b Wood	65
M.P. Speight run out	28	(4) c Larkins b Wood	49
P. Moores† not out	26	(7) c McEwan b Hughes	1
B.T.P. Donelan		(6) not out	30
A.C.S. Pigott		(6) not out	0
A.N. Jones			
A.G. Robson			
Extras (LB 6, W 1, NB 3)	10	(B 2, LB 8)	10
TOTAL (4 wkt dec.)	**151**	(6 wkt)	**340**

1/7, 2/9, 3/32, 4/85
1/2, 2/159, 3/231, 4/247, 5/322, 6/338

Bowling: *First innings*—Wood 11-0-47-3; McEwan 10-3-24-0; Hughes 8-0-30-0; Briers 7-2-29-0; Graveney 3.1-0-15-0. *Second innings*—Wood 9-1-46-2; Hughes 15-3-57-2; McEwan 12-1-72-1; Briers 11-4-34-0; Graveney 18-2-121-1.

Umpires: J.C. Balderstone and D.R. Shepherd

SUSSEX v DURHAM

Sunday League match

Cricketfield Road, Horsham, 21 June 1992

Toss: Sussex.   Durham won by 5 runs

Durham

W. Larkins c Hall b Lenham	86
J.D. Glendenen lbw b Greenfield	64
D.M. Jones not out	74
P.W.G. Parker run out	19
M.P. Briers c Wells b Pigott	16
A.R. Fothergill† not out	0
P.W. Henderson	
S.M. McEwan	
D.A. Graveney*	
S.P. Hughes	
J. Wood	
Extras (LB 10, W6)	16
TOTAL (40 overs, 4 wkt)	**275**

1/107, 2/185, 3/246, 4/271

Bowling: Stephenson 8-0-43-0; Robson 6-0-34-0; Pigott 8-0-65-1; Greenfield 7-0-39-1; Hansford 6-0-50-0; North 1-0-13-0; Lenham 4-0-21-1.

Sussex

K. Greenfield b Wood	1
J.W. Hall c Fothergill b Hughes	19
M.P. Speight run out	38
A.P. Wells* c Fothergill b Graveney	36
F.D. Stephenson c Henderson b Graveney	10
N.J. Lenham c Graveney b Wood	43
P. Moores† c Hughes b Graveney	42
J.A. North c Fothergill b Hughes	56
A.C.S. Pigott run out	6
A.R. Hansford not out	5
A.G. Robson not out	1
Extras (B 4, LB 7, W 2)	13
TOTAL (40 overs, 9 wkt)	**270**

1/10, 2/26, 3/100, 4/100, 5/111, 6/180, 7/222, 8/257, 9/267

Bowling: Wood 8-0-58-2; Hughes 8-0-51-2; Henderson 8-0-60-0; McEwan 8-0-50-0; Graveney 8-1-40-3.

Umpires: J.C. Balderstone and D.R. Shepherd

IRELAND v DURHAM

NatWest Bank Trophy, First Round

Castle Avenue, Clontarf, Dublin, 24 June 1992

Toss: Durham.   Durham won by 189 runs

Man of the Match: S. M. McEwan

Durham

W. Larkins c Warke b Dunlop	113
J.D. Glendenen c Warke b P. McCrum	18
D.M. Jones b Hoey	46
P.W.G. Parker c P. McCrum b Dunlop	10
M.P. Briers not out	54
I. Smith b McBrine	3
A.R. Fothergill† b Dunlop	4
S.M. McEwan not out	34
J. Wood	
D.A. Graveney*	
S.P. Hughes	
Extras (LB 9, W 14)	23
TOTAL (60 overs, 6 wkt)	**305**

1/24, 2/186, 3/203, 4/210, 5/217, 6/230

Bowling: McCrum 10-2-47-1; Nelson 10-0-45-0; Lewis 8-0-44-0; Hoey 12-1-52-1; McBrine 12-0-63-1; Dunlop 8-0-45-3.

Ireland

S.J.S. Warke* c Fothergill b Wood	10
M.P. Rea b Hughes	20
S. Graham lbw b McEwan	7
D.A. Lewis lbw b Smith	2
A.R. Dunlop lbw b Smith	8
C. McCrum c Jones b McEwan	6
A. McBrine b McEwan	30
P.B. Jackson† c Fothergill b McEwan	0
C.J. Hoey c sub b Briers	12
P. McCrum c Fothergill b Wood	5
A.N. Nelson not out	0
Extras (LB 4, W 11, NB 1)	16
TOTAL (37.2 overs, 10 wkt)	**116**

1/24, 2/32, 3/44, 4/44, 5/59, 6/62, 7/63, 8/105, 9/115

Bowling: Wood 7-1-22-2; Hughes 6-1-9-1; Smith 12-1-40-2; McEwan 12-1-41-4; Briers 0.2-0-0-1.

Umpires: J.C. Balderstone and D. R. Shepherd

DURHAM v KENT

Championship match

Eastwood Gardens, Gateshead Fell CC, 27, 28, 29 June 1992

Toss: Durham.   Match drawn

Kent

M.A. Ealham b S.J.E. Brown	0	c Larkins b S.J.E. Brown	2
M.R. Benson* c Scott b Hughes	46	c Scott b S.J.E. Brown	5
N.J. Llong c Scott b Wood	2	c Wood b Hughes	92
C.L. Hooper st Scott b Graveney	87	c Larkins b Briers	8
G.R. Cowdrey c G.K. Brown b Graveney	115	run out	46
N.R. Taylor b Wood	29	not out	50
M.V. Fleming c Briers b Hughes	49	c Briers b S.J.E. Brown	24
S.A. Marsh† c S.J.E. Brown b Graveney	24	not out	0
R.M. Ellison not out	4		
R.P. Davis c Parker b Wood	1		
M.J. McCague c G.K. Brown b Wood	9		
Extras (B 2, LB 15, W 2, NB 7)	26	(LB 6, W 1, NB 1)	8
TOTAL	**392**	(6 wkt dec.)	**235**

1/2, 2/15, 3/78, 4/186, 5/237, 6/323, 7/359, 8/374, 9/382

1/3, 2/8, 3/52, 4/144, 5/205 6/234

Bowling: *First innings*—Wood 24.4-3-92-4; S.J.E. Brown 23-4-76-1; Hughes 30-6-114-2; Graveney 22-2-93-3. *Second innings*—Wood 9-1-46-0; S.J.E. Brown 14-4-59-3; Hughes 5-2-13-1; Briers 12.3-5-50-1; G.K. Brown 4-0-25-0; Graveney 3.3-0-36-0.

Durham

W. Larkins c Cowdrey b Davis	90	lbw b Ellison	41
S. Hutton c McCague b Davis	76	c Marsh b Ellison	37
D.M. Jones retired hurt	6		
P.W.G. Parker not out	72	(3) c Ellison b Davis	22
M.P. Briers c Llong b Hooper	16	(4) not out	56
G.K. Brown lbw b Davis	15	(5) c Ellison b Hooper	48
J. Wood c and b Davis	0	(6) b McCague	3
C.W. Scott† c Benson b Davis	11	(7) not out	3
D.A. Graveney* c Fleming b Davis	11		
S.P. Hughes lbw b Davis	1		
S.J.E. Brown			
Extras (B 7, LB 10, W 2, NB 7)	26	(LB 6)	6
TOTAL	(8 wkt dec.) **329**	(5 wkt)	**216**

1/169, 2/197, 3/217, 4/281, 5/302, 6/304, 7/320, 8/329

1/70, 2/99, 3/107, 4/197, 5/205

Bowling: *First innings*—McCague 22-8-50-0; Ealham 17-4-58-0; Davis 24.1-7-64-7; Ellison 14-3-47-0; Hooper 20-4-53-1; Fleming 9-0-40-0. *Second innings*—McCague 13.4-0-46-1; Ealham 4-0-13-0; Davis 13-0-62-1; Ellison 9-2-27-2; Hooper 11-2-49-1; Fleming 2-0-13-0.

Umpires: B.J. Meyer and G.A. Stickley

DURHAM v GLOUCESTERSHIRE

Championship match

Grangefield Road, Stockton-on-Tees, 3, 4, 6 July 1992

Toss: Durham.   Match drawn

Gloucestershire

G.D. Hodgson c Fothergill b Briers	35
C.W.J. Athey c Jones b Briers	56
S.G. Hinks b Smith	10
A.J. Wright* not out	83
M.W. Alleyne b Briers	11
R.J. Scott not out	51
R.C. Williams	
R.C.J. Williams†	
A.M. Smith	
M. Davies	
A.M. Babington	
Extras (B 4, LB 6, NB 3)	13
TOTAL	(4 wkt dec.) **259**

1/95, 2/96, 3/109, 4/132

Bowling: Wood 5-0-21-0; Brown 7-0-14-0; Hughes 6-3-8-0; Botham 7-3-28-0; Briers 23-3-109-3; Smith 10-2-35-1; Jones 6.3-1-34-0.

Durham

W. Larkins c Scott b Alleyne	74
J.D. Glendenen lbw b Smith	4
D.M. Jones c R.C.J. Williams b Davies	18
P.W.G. Parker* lbw b Alleyne	43
I.T. Botham st R.C.J. Williams b Davies	11
M.P. Briers st R.C.J. Williams b Davies	15
I. Smith c R.C.J. Williams b Davies	12
J. Wood not out	25
A.R. Fothergill† not out	11
S.P. Hughes	
S.J.E. Brown	
Extras (B 1, LB 6, W 1, NB 6)	14
TOTAL	(7 wkt) **227**

1/11, 2/59, 3/131, 4/157, 5/163, 6/185, 7/210

Bowling: Smith 9-0-43-1; Babington 13-0-64-0; R.C. Williams 3-1-4-0; Davies 14-0-73-4; Alleyne 5-0-28-2; Athey 2-0-8-0.

Umpires: A.A. Jones and G.A. Stickley

MIDDLESEX v DURHAM

NatWest Bank Trophy, second round
Park Road, Uxbridge, 9 July 1992

Toss: Durham. Durham won by 6 wickets.
Man of the Match: P.W.G. Parker

Middlesex

D.L. Haynes c Fothergill b Hughes	20
M.A. Roseberry c Parker b Brown	14
M.W. Gatting* run out	57
M.R. Ramprakash c Parker b McEwan	46
J.D. Carr c Parker b Hughes	45
K.R. Brown† not out	44
P.N. Weekes c Fothergill b Botham	0
J.E. Emburey c Fothergill b Hughes	4
N.F. Williams b Hughes	4
A.R.C. Fraser not out	1
C.W. Taylor	
Extras (B 5, LB 6, W 13)	24
TOTAL (60 overs, 8 wkt)	**259**

1/39, 2/51, 3/137, 4/184, 5/212, 6/213, 7/240, 8/258

Bowling: McEwan 12-1-45-1; Brown 12-2-43-1; Hughes 12-3-41-4; Botham 12-0-53-1; Smith 10-0-50-0; Jones 2-0-16-0.

Durham

W. Larkins c Carr b Taylor	0
J.D. Glendenen b Weekes	57
D.M. Jones lbw b Fraser	25
P.W.G. Parker* lbw b Williams	69
I.T. Botham not out	63
I. Smith not out	12
A.R. Fothergill†	
S.M. McEwan	
S.P. Hughes	
S.J.E. Brown	
J. Wood	
Extras (LB 12, W 17, NB 5)	34
TOTAL (58.3 overs, 4 wkt)	**260**

1/0, 2/52, 3/116, 4/239

Bowling: Taylor 11-1-54-1; Williams 10-0-55-1; Fraser 12-1-45-1; Carr 5-1-11-0; Emburey 10.3-1-36-0; Weekes 10-0-47-1.

Umpires: H.D. Bird and B. Dudleston

DURHAM v GLOUCESTERSHIRE

Sunday League match
Grangefield Road, Stockton-on-Tees, 5 July 1992

Toss: Durham. Durham won by 6 wickets

Gloucestershire

G.D. Hodgson run out	12
M.W. Alleyne c Fothergill b Botham	32
C.W.J. Athey lbw b Jones	38
A.J. Wright* c Jones b Hughes	93
R.J. Scott not out	39
S.G. Hinks c Larkins b Botham	4
R.I. Dawson not out	0
R.C.J. Williams†	
R.C. Williams	
A.M. Smith	
A.M. Babington	
Extras (LB 6, W 1, NB 1)	8
TOTAL (40 overs, 5 wkt)	**226**

1/31, 2/59, 3/117, 4/210, 5/218

Bowling: Hughes 8-0-47-1; Brown 8-0-56-0; McEwan 5-2-13-0; Botham 8-1-34-2; Smith 5-0-33-0; Jones 6-0-37-1.

Durham

I.T. Botham c and b Smith	23
W. Larkins c R.C.J. Williams b Scott	20
D.M. Jones not out	81
P.W.G. Parker c Hinks b Alleyne	19
J.D. Glendenen run out	52
I. Smith not out	23
A.R. Fothergill†	
D.A. Graveney*	
S.M. McEwan	
S.P. Hughes	
S.J.E. Brown	
Extras (B 1, LB 6, W 1, NB 2)	10
TOTAL (39.1 overs, 4 wkt)	**228**

1/41, 2/46, 3/85, 4/182

Bowling: Babington 6.1-0-40-0; Smith 8-0-42-1; Scott 7-0-44-1; Williams 6-0-32-0; Alleyne 8-0-40-1; Athey 4-0-23-0.

Umpires: A.A. Jones and G.A. Stickley

SOMERSET v DURHAM

Sunday League match
County Ground, Taunton, 12 July 1992
Toss: Durham. Durham won by 11 runs

Durham

Batsman		Runs
I.T. Botham	b MacLeay	27
W. Larkins	b LeFebvre	52
D.M. Jones	c Mallender b Rose	83
P.W.G. Parker*	c Harden b Rose	82
J.D. Glendenen	not out	4
I. Smith	not out	0
M.P. Briers		
A.R. Fothergill†		
S.M. McEwan		
S.P. Hughes		
S.J.E. Brown		
Extras	(B 1, LB 10, W 3, NB 4)	15
TOTAL	(40 overs, 4 wkt)	**263**

1/67, 2/98, 3/239, 4/262

Bowling: Caddick 8-0-40-0; Rose 8-1-63-2; Mallender 8-0-33-0; Snell 2-0-17-0; MacLeay 6-0-44-1; LeFebvre 6-0-44-1; Hayhurst 2-0-11-0.

Somerset

Batsman		Runs
A.N. Hayhurst	c Larkins b Brown	73
M.N. Lathwell	c Jones b Hughes	33
C.J. Tavaré*	b McEwan	41
R.J. Harden	c Larkins b Brown	28
G.D. Rose	c and b Botham	26
N.D. Burns†	not out	14
K.H. MacLeay	c Fothergill b Botham	3
R.P. Snell	run out	6
R.P. LeFebvre	lbw b Botham	0
N.A. Mallender	not out	12
A.R. Caddick		
Extras	(B 1, LB 9, W 6)	16
TOTAL	(40 overs, 8 wkt)	**252**

1/58, 2/130, 3/180, 4/193, 5/219, 6/226, 7/237, 8/237

Bowling: Brown 8-0-61-2; McEwan 8-0-47-1; Hughes 8-0-49-1; Briers 8-0-48-0; Botham 8-0-37-3.

Umpires: B. Dudleston and V.A. Holder

DURHAM v PAKISTAN

Tour match
Ropery Lane, Chester-le-Street, 14, 15, 16 July 1992
Toss: Pakistan. Pakistan won by 107 runs

Pakistan

Batsman	First innings	Runs	Second innings	Runs
Aamir Sohail	c Parker b Botham	53	lbw b Brown	90
Ramiz Raja	c Hughes b Brown	14	c Parker b Briers	59
Asif Mujtaba	b Berry	79	b McEwan	8
Salim Malik	c Fothergill b McEwan	23	c Glendenen b McEwan	40
Javed Miandad*	c Fothergill b Botham	25	(6) c Parker b Jones	67
Wasim Akram	c Fothergill b McEwan	21	(5) c Brown b Berry	27
Moin Khan†	c Larkins b McEwan	53	not out	29
Waqar Younis	not out	23		
Mushtaq Ahmed	not out	10		
Aqib Javed				
Ata-ur-Rehman				
Extras	(LB 2, W 1, NB 4)	7	(LB 13, W 2, NB 3)	18
TOTAL	(7 wkt dec.)	**308**	(6 wkt dec.)	**338**

1/58, 2/78, 3/135, 4/198, 5/204, 6/273, 7/278

1/139, 2/160, 3/194, 4/214, 5/247, 6/339

Bowling: First innings— McEwan 23-8-52-3; Brown 17-2-67-1; Botham 19-2-73-2; Hughes 14-2-37-0; Berry 8-0-40-1; Briers 9-0-37-0. Second innings— McEwan 15-2-65-2; Brown 16-3-59-1; Hughes 15-2-41-0; Briers 14-0-99-1; Berry 12-2-57-1; Jones 1.4-0-4-1.

Durham

Batsman	First innings	Runs	Second innings	Runs
W. Larkins	c Ata-ur-Rehman b Salim Malik	118	b Waqar Younis	1
J.D. Glendenen	c Mushtaq Ahmed b Aqib Javed	33	lbw b Waqar Younis	36
D.M. Jones	not out	134	c Wasim Akram	105
P.W.G. Parker*	c Waqar Younis b Rehman	0	c Mushtaq b Waqar Younis	10
M.P. Briers	c sub b Wasim Akram	13	lbw b Waqar Younis	0
P.J. Berry	not out	13	c Moin Khan b Ata-ur-Rehman	8
A.R. Fothergill†			lbw b Wasim Akram	13
S.M. McEwan			b Wasim Akram	1
S.P. Hughes			not out	2
S.J.E. Brown			c Waqar Younis	2
I.T. Botham			absent hurt	
Extras	(B 6, LB 11, W 1, NB 12)	30	(B 1, LB 8, NB 11)	20
TOTAL	(4 wkt dec.)	**341**	(9 wkt)	**198**

1/96, 2/258, 3/260, 4/304

1/1, 2/159, 3/159, 4/159, 5/171, 6/187, 7/188, 8/193, 9/198

Bowling: First innings—Wasim Akram 17-4-67-1; Aqib Javed 6.1-0-35-1; Mushtaq Ahmed 8.5-1-59-0; Waqar Younis 14-2-48-0; Ata-ur-Rehman 15-2-65-1; Asif Mujtaba 4-0-28-0; Salim Malik 4-0-15-1; Second innings—Wasim Akram 17-2-65-3; Waqar Younis 17.1-5-22-5; Ata-ur-Rehman 8-2-39-1; Mushtaq Ahmed 6-1-35-0; Salim Malik 7-0-28-0.

Umpires: H.D. Bird and M.J. Harris

NOTTINGHAMSHIRE v DURHAM

Championship match
Trent Bridge, Nottingham, 17, 18, 20 July 1992
Toss: Durham. Match drawn

Nottinghamshire

M.A. Crawley lbw b Botham ... 21
P.R. Pollard lbw b Botham ... 23
R.T. Robinson* not out ... 164
P. Johnson c Briers b Brown ... 20
D.W. Randall c Scott b McEwan ... 22
C.C. Lewis c Scott b Briers ... 107
C.L. Cairns c McEwan b Botham ... 42
K.P. Evans not out ... 0
B.N. French†
M.G. Field-Buss
D.B. Pennett
Extras (B 6, LB 14, W 12) ... 32
TOTAL (6 wkt dec.) **431**
1/49, 2/52, 3/92, 4/140, 5/325, 6/427

Bowling: *First innings*— McEwan 19-4-60-1; Brown 18-3-57-1; Henderson 14-2-68-0; Botham 27-4-104-3; Hughes 16-0-61-0; Briers 16-2-61-1.

Durham

W. Larkins c Robinson b Cairns ... 5	c Robinson b Cairns ... 57	
P.W.G. Parker* b Cairns ... 6	(4) b Cairns ... 7	
D.M. Jones b Pennett ... 15	not out ... 154	
M.P. Briers c Crawley b Cairns ... 53	(5) not out ... 30	
I.T. Botham b Evans ... 7		
P.W. Henderson c and b Lewis ... 7		
J.D. Glendenen c Evans b Cairns ... 13	(2) b Cairns ... 0	
C.W. Scott† c Evans b Pennett ... 10		
S.P. Hughes lbw b Evans ... 2		
S.M. McEwan c Evans b Lewis ... 3		
S.J.E. Brown not out ... 6		
Extras (LB 7, NB 13) ... 20	(B 1, LB 11, NB 5) ... 17	
TOTAL **147**	(3 wkt) **265**	

1/11, 2/18, 3/60, 4/69, 5/90, 6/111, 7/132, 8/132, 9/139

1/9, 2/178, 3/194

Bowling: *First innings*—Lewis 14-4-27-2; Cairns 14-2-41-4; Evans 15.5-4-31-2; Pennett 16-5-41-2.
Second innings—Cairns 20-3-93-3; Lewis 15-2-40-0; Pennett 5-1-21-0; Evans 15-2-63-0; Field-Buss 11-0-34-0; Crawley 4-2-2-0.

Umpires: B.J. Meyer and P.B. Wight

NOTTINGHAMSHIRE v DURHAM

Sunday League match
Trent Bridge, Nottingham, 19 July 1992
Toss: Nottinghamshire. Durham won by 21 runs

Durham

I.T. Botham c Pollard b Pennett ... 19
W. Larkins c Crawley b Pennett ... 47
D.M. Jones b Cairns ... 35
P.W.G. Parker* b Cairns ... 23
J.D. Glendenen not out ... 33
M.P. Briers c Bramhall b Mike ... 8
A.R. Fothergill† b Evans ... 27
S.M. McEwan c Bramhall b Evans ... 0
P.W. Henderson not out ... 10
S.P. Hughes
S.J.E. Brown
Extras (LB 2, W 5, NB 2) ... 9
TOTAL (40 overs, 7 wkt) **211**
1/72, 2/72, 3/132, 4/135, 5/155, 6/196, 7/196

Bowling: Cairns 8-0-53-2; Pennett 8-0-28-2; Evans 8-0-53-2; Mike 8-0-37-1; Field-Buss 8-0-38-0.

Nottinghamshire

P.R. Pollard c and b McEwan ... 9
M.A. Crawley c Fothergill b Brown ... 1
R.T. Robinson* c Glendenen b Henderson ... 51
P. Johnson b Hughes ... 11
G.F. Archer b Henderson ... 9
C.L. Cairns b Hughes ... 26
K.P. Evans b Henderson ... 18
G.W. Mike not out ... 26
M.G. Field-Buss b Botham ... 7
S. Bramhall† run out ... 1
D.B. Pennett not out ... 12
Extras (B 2, LB 10, W 7) ... 19
TOTAL (40 overs, 9 wkt) **190**
1/6, 2/23, 3/37, 4/71, 5/96, 6/140, 7/142, 8/153, 9/155

Bowling: McEwan 8-1-26-1; Brown 8-0-27-1; Hughes 8-0-37-2; Botham 8-0-41-1; Henderson 8-0-47-3.

Umpires: B.J. Meyer and P.B. Wight

LEICESTERSHIRE v DURHAM

Championship match
Grace Road, Leicester, 21, 22, 23 July 1992
Toss: Leicestershire. Leicestershire won by 10 wickets

Durham

W. Larkins c Nixon b Millns	8	c Benson b Millns		8
S. Hutton c Nixon b Millns	13	c Benson b Millns		5
M.P. Briers lbw b Millns	0	(4) c Nixon b Benjamin		1
P.W.G. Parker c Boon b Benjamin	22	(5) b Millns		10
J.D. Glendenen c Nixon b Millns	6	(6) lbw b Benjamin		5
P.W. Henderson c Benson b Mullally	31	(7) c Whitaker b Benjamin		27
C.W. Scott† not out	35	(8) c Nixon b Millns		33
S.M. McEwan c Benson b Mullally	4	(9) c Potter b Benjamin		0
S.P. Hughes b Mullally	3	(3) lbw b Millns		2
D.A. Graveney* c Whitaker b Mullally	16	retired hurt		8
S.J.E. Brown c Benson b Millns	0	not out		4
Extras (LB 5, NB 2)	7	(LB 10, NB 3)		13
TOTAL	**145**	**(9 wkts)**		**116**

1/16, 2/16, 3/31, 4/39, 5/82, 6/82, 7/86, 8/100, 9/134
1/13, 2/14, 3/15, 4/25, 5/27, 6/49, 7/74, 8/78, 9/116

Bowling: *First innings*—Millns 16.1-2-41-5; Benjamin 18.1-5-46-5; Mullally 18-5-34-4; Wells 5-1-15-0. *Second innings*—Millns 14-3-39-4; Benjamin 18-5-34-4; Mullally 5-2-11-0; Wells 5-1-15-0.

Leicestershire

T.J. Boon c Parker b Brown	33	not out		5
N.E. Briers* lbw b Graveney	93	not out		1
J.J. Whitaker c Scott b McEwan	40			
B.F. Smith lbw b Hughes	3			
J.D.R. Benson c Glendenen b Brown	33			
L. Potter c Graveney b Henderson	8			
V.J. Wells c Graveney b Henderson	0			
P.A. Nixon† c Larkins b Graveney	0			
W.K.M. Benjamin b Hughes	22			
D.J. Millns not out	8			
A.D. Mullally b Graveney	11			
Extras (LB 9, W 2)	11			0
TOTAL	**256**	**(0 wkt)**		**6**

1/55, 2/114, 3/119, 4/196, 5/220, 6/222, 7/222, 8/236, 9/249

Bowling: *First innings*—Brown 20-2-84-2; Hughes 20.5-41-2; Henderson 13-1-56-2; McEwan 34.5-83-5; Graveney 15.2-6-22-3. *Second innings*—Larkins 2-1-4-0; Parker 1.1-0-2-0.

Umpires: J.C. Balderstone and B.J. Meyer

MIDDLESEX v DURHAM

Championship match
Lord's, 24, 25, 27 July 1992
Toss: Middlesex. Middlesex won by 175 runs

Middlesex

D.L. Haynes st Scott b Berry	26	c Larkins b Berry		18
M.A. Roseberry b Berry	173	b Berry		81
M.W. Gatting* c Botham b Berry	90	c Hutton b Berry		37
J.D. Carr c Briers b Berry	1			
K.R. Brown† c Hutton b Berry	17	(4) not out		18
P.N. Weekes c Briers b Berry	5			
J.E. Emburey run out	0			
N.F. Williams b Berry	3			
A.R.C. Fraser b Briers	4			
C.W. Taylor c Parker b Briers	14			
P.C.R. Tufnell not out	11			
Extras (B 7, LB 15)	22	(LB 5)		5
TOTAL	**366**	**(3 wkt dec.)**		**159**

1/72, 2/239, 3/247, 4/285, 5/299, 6/312, 7/325, 8/330, 9/346
1/25, 2/97, 3/159

Bowling: *First innings*—Brown 17-3-48-0; Botham 16-4-41-0; Berry 40-5-113-7; Hughes 23-6-64-0; Briers 18-2-78-2. *Second innings*—Brown 13-2-44-0; Berry 18.3-1-78-3; Briers 1-0-2-0; Hughes 5-0-30-0.

Durham

W. Larkins c Weekes b Tufnell	30	c Williams b Taylor		11
S. Hutton c Brown b Tufnell	33	c Brown b Taylor		1
I.T. Botham c Roseberry b Emburey	16	st Brown b Tufnell		20
P.W.G. Parker c Carr b Emburey	0	c Emburey b Tufnell		42
M.P. Briers c Brown b Tufnell	9	c Carr b Emburey		4
J.D. Glendenen c Weekes b Emburey	3	c Carr b Emburey		0
C.W. Scott† c Roseberry b Tufnell	76	lbw b Emburey		2
P.J. Berry c Carr b Emburey	33	not out		14
S.P. Hughes lbw b Fraser	7	c Williams b Emburey		2
S.J.E. Brown lbw b Tufnell	4	c Gatting b Tufnell		4
D.A. Graveney* not out	4	c Carr b Emburey		1
Extras (B 2, LB 9, W 1, NB 5)	17	(B 2, LB 6, NB 9)		17
TOTAL	**232**			**118**

1/61, 2/72, 3/79, 4/82, 5/88, 6/101, 7/101, 8/190, 9/217
1/3, 2/40, 3/50, 4/57, 5/59, 6/61, 7/101, 8/106, 9/114

Bowling: *First innings*—Taylor 6-4-3-0; Williams 8-1-16-0; Emburey 44.2-12-94-4; Tufnell 34-5-83-5; Weekes 2-0-5-0; Fraser 10-1-20-1. *Second innings*—Taylor 7-2-16-2; Williams 5-0-20-0; Fraser 4-3-5-0; Tufnell 14-1-26-3; Emburey 12.3-2-43-5.

Umpires: R. Palmer and G.A. Stickley

LEICESTERSHIRE v DURHAM

NatWest Bank Trophy, quarter-final
Grace Road, Leicester, 29 July 1992
Toss: Durham.   Leicestershire won by 45 runs
Man of the Match: J.D.R. Benson

Leicestershire

T.J. Boon st Fothergill b Bainbridge		25
N.E. Briers* c Fothergill b Botham		7
J.J. Whitaker b Hughes		63
P.E. Robinson lbw b Hughes		31
J.D.R. Benson c Cook b Brown		42
L. Potter run out		31
W.K.M. Benjamin not out		24
P.A. Nixon† b Hughes		10
V.J. Wells run out		0
G.J. Parsons run out		3
A.D. Mullally run out		0
Extras (LB 7, W 6)		13
TOTAL	(59.3 overs)	**249**

1/15, 2/57, 3/131, 4/142, 5/204,
6/222, 7/239, 8/239, 9/249

Bowling: Botham 12-2-54-1; Brown 11.3-1-53-1; Bainbridge 8-0-29-1; Hughes 12-2-34-3; Smith 5-0-24-0; Berry 11-0-48-0.

Durham

W. Larkins c Boon b Benson		41
J.D. Glendenen c Benson b Wells		39
G. Cook st Nixon b Benson		16
P.W.G. Parker* run out		54
I.T. Botham run out		5
P. Bainbridge c and b Mullally		6
I. Smith c Potter b Mullally		2
P.J. Berry b Benjamin		9
A.R. Fothergill† c Benjamin b Wells		7
S.P. Hughes c Mullally b Wells		2
S.J.E. Brown not out		3
Extras (B 1, LB 9, W 10)		20
TOTAL	(55.4 overs)	**204**

1/66, 2/99, 3/106, 4/130, 5/147,
6/153, 7/175, 8/198, 9/198

Bowling: Benjamin 10-3-18-1; Mullally 10-2-33-2; Wells 8.5-2-38-3; Parsons 3-0-24-0; Potter 12-0-37-0; Benson 12-1-44-2.

Umpires: H.D. Bird and B. Leadbeater

191

MIDDLESEX v DURHAM

Sunday League match
Lords, 26 July 1992
Toss: Middlesex. Middlesex won by 7 wickets

Durham

I.T. Botham b Headley		48
W. Larkins b Williams		9
G. Cook run out		49
P.W.G. Parker* c Brown b Headley		1
J.D. Glendenen c Williams b Weekes		28
I. Smith c Emburey b Fraser		23
A.R. Fothergill† not out		20
P.J. Berry b Headley		6
S.M. McEwan not out		1
S.P. Hughes		
S.J.E. Brown		
Extras (LB 4, W 8, NB 1)		13
TOTAL	(40 overs, 7 wkt)	**198**

1/27, 2/74, 3/78, 4/132, 5/155,
6/176, 7/197

Bowling: Fraser 7-0-35-1; Williams 4-0-27-1; Carr 7-0-30-0; Headley 6-0-21-3; Emburey 8-0-44-0; Weekes 8-0-37-1.

Middlesex

D.L. Haynes c Parker b McEwan		70
M.A. Roseberry st Fothergill b Berry		44
M.W. Gatting* c McEwan b Hughes		48
J.D. Carr not out		20
K.R. Brown† not out		10
P.N. Weekes		
R.J. Sims		
J.E. Emburey		
D.W. Headley		
A.R.C. Fraser		
N.F. Williams		
Extras (B 3, LB 4, W 3)		10
TOTAL	(38.5 overs, 3 wkt)	**202**

1/102, 2/154, 3/174

Bowling: Brown 7-0-40-0; McEwan 8-0-40-1; Botham 7.5-0-49-0; Hughes 8-0-31-1; Berry 8-0-35-1.

Umpires: R. Palmer and G.A. Stickley

DURHAM v SURREY

Championship match
The Racecourse, Durham, 31 July, 1, 3 August 1992
Toss: Surrey.   Surrey won by 7 wickets

Durham

			Second innings	
W. Larkins c Stewart b M.P. Bicknell	15		lbw b Benjamin	9
S. Hutton b Bryson	0		lbw b M.P. Bicknell	42
I.T. Botham c Bainbridge b Boiling	36		(6) c Lynch b M.P. Bicknell	48
P. Bainbridge c Lynch b Benjamin	39		(3) c Sargeant b M.P. Bicknell	9
M.P. Briers c Sargeant b Bryson	29		(4) c sub b Boiling	4
I. Smith b Benjamin	29		(5) c Sargeant b M.P. Bicknell	74
C.W. Scott† c Sargeant b Benjamin	9		(8) c D.J. Bicknell b M.P. Bicknell	35
P.J. Berry b Benjamin	0		(7) c Sargeant b Benjamin	0
S.M. McEwan c Thorpe b Benjamin	0		c Stewart b Boiling	8
D.A. Graveney* c Brown b Benjamin	0		c Boiling b Benjamin	36
S.J.E. Brown not out	4		not out	47
Extras (LB 16, NB 12)	28		(B 5, LB 11, W 4, NB 25)	45
TOTAL	**189**			**357**

1/2, 2/42, 3/80, 4/125, 5/141, 6/155, 7/177, 8/178, 9/182
1/26, 2/49, 3/58, 4/127, 5/216, 6/217, 7/224, 8/242, 9/287

Bowling: *First innings*—M.P. Bicknell 15-4-39-1; Bryson 11-0-80-2; Benjamin 15.3-9-30-6. *Second innings*—M.P. Bicknell 34-3-120-5; Benjamin 32.1-3-98-3; Bryson 6-1-17-0; Boiling 36-9-72-2; Thorpe 8-3-32-0; Stewart 2-1-1-0; Brown 1-0-1-0.

Surrey

			Second innings	
D.J. Bicknell c Larkins b Brown	8		run out	49
P.D. Atkins b McEwan	60		b McEwan	2
A.J. Stewart*† lbw b McEwan	42		c Scott b McEwan	60
G.P. Thorpe lbw b Botham	11		not out	1
M.A. Lynch c Scott b McEwan	175		not out	1
A.D. Brown lbw b Botham	21			
M.P. Bicknell c Larkins b Botham	48			
R.E. Bryson b Graveney	30			
N.F. Sargeant† c Scott b Graveney	18			
J. Boiling run out	6			
J.E. Benjamin not out	8			
Extras (B 1, LB 5, W 2)	8		(B 1, LB 2)	3
TOTAL	**431**		(3 wkt)	**116**

1/14, 2/82, 3/87, 4/104, 5/223, 6/293, 7/376, 8/376, 9/416
1/9, 2/11, 3/110

Bowling: *First innings*—Brown 16-3-77-1; Botham 40-6-135-3; McEwan 20-3-107-3; Bainbridge 6-0-41-0; Graveney 21.2-5-57-2; Briers 1-0-8-0. *Second innings*—McEwan 9-1-40-2; Brown 7-0-31-0; Berry 9-1-15-0; Graveney 4-0-20-0; Briers 1-0-3-0; Hutton 0.1-0-4-0.

Umpires: M.J. Kitchen and D.O. Oslear

DURHAM v SURREY

Sunday League match
The Racecourse, Durham, 2 August 1992
Toss: Durham.   Surrey won by 100 runs

Surrey

D.J. Bicknell c Briers b Hughes	125
A.D. Brown c Smith b Botham	75
D.M. Ward b Graveney	45
A.J. Stewart*† c and b Graveney	9
A.J. Hollioake b Hughes	22
M.A. Lynch c Smith b Briers	16
G.P. Thorpe not out	3
J.D. Robinson not out	3
M.A. Feltham	
M.P. Bicknell	
J. Boiling	
Extras (B 4, LB 16, W 11, NB1)	32
TOTAL (39 overs, 6 wkt)	**330**

1/117, 2/210, 3/251, 4/298, 5/315, 6/325

Bowling: McEwan 6-0-57-0; Wood 5-0-26-0; Graveney 8-0-51-2; Botham 5-0-39-1; Hughes 8-0-72-2; Smith 2-0-18-0; Briers 5-0-47-1.

Durham

I.T. Botham run out	52
W. Larkins c Stewart b M.P. Bicknell	14
G. Cook c Stewart b Robinson	3
I. Smith c Thorpe b Hollioake	28
J.D. Glendenen c Brown b Boiling	69
M.P. Briers c and b Boiling	39
A.R. Fothergill† c Ward b Boiling	4
J. Wood not out	
S.M. McEwan	
D.A. Graveney*	
S.P. Hughes	
Extras (LB 6, W 5, NB 1)	12
TOTAL (39 overs, 7 wkt)	**230**

1/32, 2/78, 3/83, 4/89, 5/146, 6/217, 7/230

Bowling: M.P. Bicknell 8-0-48-1; Feltham 8-0-45-0; Hollioake 8-0-37-1; Robinson 7-0-46-1; Boiling 8-0-48-3.

Umpires: M.J. Kitchen and D.O. Oslear

DURHAM v YORKSHIRE

Championship match
The Racecourse, Durham, 4, 5, 6 August 1992
Toss: Durham.   Yorkshire won by 5 wickets

Durham

W. Larkins c Tendulkar b Robinson	67	b Jarvis	0
S. Hutton c Byas b Carrick	31	c Blakey b Jarvis	0
P. Bainbridge c Blakey b Robinson	14	run out	21
M.P. Briers b Jarvis	15	lbw b Hartley	7
I. Smith b Robinson	6	b Robinson	8
I.T. Botham b Jarvis	29	c Kellett b Jarvis	13
P.J. Berry lbw b Jarvis	1	lbw b Robinson	10
C.W. Scott† not out	25	c Kellett b Jarvis	54
S.M. McEwan c Batty b Robinson	12	c Batty b Robinson	0
D.A. Graveney* c Blakey b Robinson	0	not out	32
S.P. Hughes c Blakey b Robinson	1	b Robinson	1
Extras (LB 4, NB 9)	13	(LB 2, NB 7)	9
TOTAL	**214**		**155**

1/72, 2/114, 3/121, 4/130, 5/163, 6/173, 7/174, 8/199, 9/199

1/1, 2/3, 3/22, 4/41, 5/42, 6/60, 7/68, 8/68, 9/154

Bowling: First innings—Jarvis 19-3-49-3; Hartley 13-3-62-0; Robinson 21.1-4-57-6; Carrick 12-5-26-1; Batty 12-5-16-0. Second innings—Jarvis 15-4-43-4; Robinson 20.1-5-44-4; Hartley 11-0-51-1; Tendulkar 3-0-6-0; Moxon 3-0-7-0; Carrick 1-0-2-0.

Yorkshire

M.D. Moxon* c Bainbridge b McEwan	25	c and b Graveney	44
S.A. Kellett b Hughes	6	c Scott b McEwan	30
D. Byas lbw b Botham	37	c sub b Botham	11
S.R. Tendulkar c Scott b Hughes	21	(5) c Hutton b Botham	100
R.J. Blakey† c Smith b Botham	5	(6) not out	26
C. White lbw b Botham	0	(7) not out	5
P.W. Jarvis c Bainbridge b Hughes	0		
P. Carrick c McEwan b Hughes	3	(4) lbw b Botham	46
P.J. Hartley c Scott b Botham	0		
J.D. Batty b Hughes	5		
M.A. Robinson not out	4		
Extras (LB 1, W 1)	2	(B 1)	1
TOTAL	**108**	(5 wkt)	**263**

1/16, 2/45, 3/86, 4/87, 5/94, 6/95, 7/95, 8/96, 9/101

1/70, 2/79, 3/87, 4/217, 5/242

Bowling: First innings—Botham 21-2-72-4; Hughes 15.4-8-25-5; McEwan 5-2-10-1. Second innings—Botham 26-5-92-3; Hughes 23.1-6-77-0; McEwan 16-2-60-1; Graveney 9-3-33-1.

Umpires: M.J. Kitchen and D.O. Oslear

WARWICKSHIRE v DURHAM

Championship match
Edgbaston, 7, 8, 10 August 1992
Toss: Warwickshire.   Match drawn

Durham

W. Larkins c Reeve b Donald	0	c Smith b Twose	77
J.D. Glendenen b Donald	0	c Piper b Donald	8
G.K. Brown b Donald	7	lbw b Reeve	16
M.P. Briers c Piper b Donald	13	c sub b Reeve	11
P. Bainbridge c Munton b Small	11	not out	71
I.T. Botham c Penney b Donald	44	not out	28
I. Smith c Munton b Small	4		
C.W. Scott† b Donald	29		
D.A. Graveney* c Lloyd b Munton	2		
S.J.E. Brown b Donald	7		
S.P. Hughes not out	12		
Extras (LB 7)	7	(B 14, LB 8, W 2, NB 3)	27
TOTAL	**136**	(4 wkt)	**238**

1/0, 2/5, 3/21, 4/28, 5/49, 6/59, 7/98, 8/109, 9/121

1/11, 2/65, 3/81, 4/170

Bowling: First innings—Donald 16.1-6-37-7; Small 13-3-41-2; Munton 22-7-45-1; Smith 3-1-6-0. Second innings—Donald 18-6-59-1; Small 16-4-25-0; Smith 10-2-38-0; Munton 19-6-43-0; Reeve 16-7-30-2; Twose 8-2-21-1.

Warwickshire

A.J. Moles b Graveney	51
R.G. Twose b Hughes	65
T.A. Lloyd† c Botham b S.J.E. Brown	60
D.P. Ostler c and b Graveney	45
D.A. Reeve not out	44
T.L. Penney not out	37
P.A. Smith	
K.J. Piper†	
G.C. Small	
A.A. Donald	
T.A. Munton	
Extras (B 2, LB 9, W 2, NB 1)	14
TOTAL (4 wkt dec.)	**316**

1/85, 2/175, 3/200, 4/256

Bowling: First innings—Botham 15-2-61-0; S.J.E. Brown 16-1-77-1; Hughes 22-0-88-1; Graveney 18-3-79-2.

Umpires: N.T. Plews and P.B. Wight

WARWICKSHIRE v DURHAM

Sunday League match

Edgbaston, 9 August 1992

Toss: Warwickshire.   Durham won by 17 runs

Durham

I.T. Botham run out	10
W. Larkins c Holloway b P.A. Smith	29
J.D. Glendenen b Reeve	78
I. Smith c Ostler b Twose	26
A.R. Fothergill† c N.M.K. Smith b Reeve	5
M.P. Briers b Munton	22
S. Hutton not out	8
S.M. McEwan not out	1
D.A. Graveney*	
S.J.E. Brown	
S.P. Hughes	
Extras (B 1, LB 7, W 3)	11
TOTAL (39 overs, 6 wkt)	**190**

1/13, 2/89, 3/130, 4/151, 5/160, 6/188

Bowling: Munton 8-0-26-1; Welch 8-0-22-0; Reeve 8-0-40-2; P.A. Smith 7-0-39-1; N.M.K. Smith, 3-0-21-0; Twose 5-0-34-1.

Warwickshire

A.J. Moles c Fothergill b Hughes	4
R.G. Twose c Fothergill b Hughes	1
D.P. Ostler c Fothergill b Brown	8
D.A. Reeve* c Hutton b McEwan	25
T.L. Penney c Fothergill b Brown	14
M. Burns c Larkins b McEwan	44
N.M.K. Smith c Hughes b McEwan	20
P.A. Smith st Fothergill b Graveney	20
P.C.L. Holloway† not out	23
G. Welch c Hutton b Brown	
T.A. Munton b Hughes	
Extras (LB 7, W 5)	12
TOTAL (38.1 overs)	**173**

1/5, 2/13, 3/23, 4/39, 5/46, 6/66, 7/126, 8/126, 9/170

Bowling: Brown 8-0-43-3; Hughes 7.1-0-26-3; Botham 4-0-17-0; McEwan 8-0-27-3; Graveney 8-0-36-1; Smith 3-0-17-0.

Umpires: N.T. Plews and P.B. Wight

YORKSHIRE v DURHAM

Floodlit match

Don Valley Stadium, Sheffield, 11 August 1992

Toss: Yorkshire.   Yorkshire won by 8 wickets

Durham

W. Larkins c Batty b Jarvis	16
J.D. Glendenen c Pickles b Robinson	3
S. Hutton c Blakey b Jarvis	2
P. Bainbridge b Batty	53
I. Smith c Metcalfe b Jarvis	2
M.P. Briers c and b Batty	16
A.R. Fothergill† b Tendulkar	10
S.M. McEwan c Robinson b Tendulkar	0
S.P. Hughes c Batty b Gough	9
D.A. Graveney* c Blakey b Pickles	9
S.J.E. Brown not out	0
Extras (B 1, LB 7, W 13, NB 3)	24
TOTAL (36.4 overs)	**144**

1/21, 2/23, 3/24, 4/30, 5/99, 6/112, 7/113, 8/125, 9/139

Bowling: Robinson 5-1-14-1; Jarvis 5-2-14-3; Pickles 6-2-10-1; Gough 6.4-0-38-1; Batty 7-0-32-2; Tendulkar 7-0-28-2.

Yorkshire

M.D. Moxon* c Briers b Graveney	34
S.A. Kellett c Glendenen b Brown	59
A.A. Metcalfe not out	25
S.R. Tendulkar not out	21
R.J. Blakey†	
C. White	
C.S. Pickles	
P.W. Jarvis	
D. Gough	
J.D. Batty	
M.A. Robinson	
Extras (LB 2, W 3, NB 1)	6
TOTAL (28.1 overs, 2 wkt)	**145**

1/61, 2/120

Bowling: McEwan 7-0-26-0; Hughes 7-0-22-0; Brown 7-0-33-1; Bainbridge 1-0-11-0; Graveney 6.3-0-51-1.

Umpires: A. Birkenshaw and S.B. Hassan

194

DURHAM v GLAMORGAN

Championship match
Park Drive, Hartlepool, 14, 15, 17 August 1992
Toss: Glamorgan.   Match drawn

Glamorgan

S.P. James b Brown	10
H. Morris c Briers b Graveney	126
A. Dale c Scott b Hughes	68
M.P. Maynard* c Scott b Hughes	22
I.V.A. Richards lbw b Brown	31
P.A. Cottey c Hughes b Brown	91
R.D.B. Croft not out	29
C.P. Metson†	
S.L. Watkin	
D.J. Foster	
S.R. Barwick	
Extras (B 10, LB 8, W 1)	19
TOTAL (6 wkt dec.)	**396**

1/10, 2/156, 3/190, 4/232, 5/315, 6/396

Bowling: *First innings*—Brown 17.1-2-54-3; Hughes 26-2-84-2; Botham 16-1-66-0; Graveney 27-2-99-1; Berry 17-2-75-0.

Durham

W. Larkins c James b Watkin	9	c Metson b Barwick	140
J.D. Glendenen c Maynard b Foster	0	c James b Watkin	0
P.J. Berry b Barwick	26	(8) not out	1
P. Bainbridge c Metson b Watkin	3	(3) lbw b Dale	56
M.P. Briers lbw b Dale	25	(4) b Maynard	52
I. Smith b Dale	23	(5) c Metson b Croft	0
I.T. Botham c Richards b Foster	54	(6) lbw b Croft	7
C.W. Scott† c Richards b Foster	16	(7) c Dale b Croft	33
D.A. Graveney* c Maynard b Foster	6	not out	1
S.P. Hughes not out	4		
S.J.E. Brown c Richards b Foster	16		
Extras (B4, LB 7, W 1, NB 7)	19	(B 7, LB 11, W 1, NB 4)	23
TOTAL	**201**	(7 wkt)	**313**

1/0, 2/22, 3/30, 4/48, 5/86, 6/120, 7/171, 8/173, 9/179

1/1, 2/166, 3/230, 4/231, 5/241, 6/302, 7/309

Bowling: *First innings*—Watkin 13-4-35-2; Foster 22.4-2-87-5; Barwick 19-5-46-1; Dale 6-2-22-2. *Second innings*—Watkin 27-8-75-1; Dale 22-5-56-1; Barwick 24-4-91-1; Croft 23-6-37-3; Foster 6-1-33-0; Maynard 2-0-3-1.

Umpires: D.J. Constant and R.C. Tolchard

DURHAM v GLAMORGAN

Sunday League match
Park Drive, Hartlepool, 16 August 1992
Toss: Durham.   Glamorgan won by 16 runs

Glamorgan

S.P. James st Fothergill b Graveney	63
H. Morris c Botham b Wood	26
M.P. Maynard* c Smith b Graveney	65
I.V.A. Richards lbw b Smith	2
A. Dale c and b Smith	6
D.L. Hemp c and b Smith	4
R.D.B. Croft not out	26
C.P. Metson† c McEwan b Hughes	6
D.J. Foster not out	2
S. Bastien	
S.D. Thomas	
Extras (B 1, LB 9, W 5, NB 1)	16
TOTAL (40 overs, 7 wkt)	**216**

1/39, 2/153, 3/156, 4/168, 5/170, 6/176, 7/191

Bowling: Wood 6-0-33-1; Hughes 7-1-27-1; McEwan 5-0-38-0; Botham 6-0-36-0; Graveney 8-0-40-2; Smith 8-1-32-3.

Durham

I.T. Botham c Foster b Bastien	9
W. Larkins c Metson b Thomas	9
J.D. Glendenen c Croft b Dale	15
M.P. Briers run out	32
S. Hutton b Richards	70
I. Smith c Morris b Foster	18
A.R. Fothergill† b Foster	0
J. Wood st Metson b Richards	4
S.M. McEwan not out	13
D.A. Graveney* b Richards	2
S.P. Hughes not out	10
Extras (LB 7, W 6, NB 5)	18
TOTAL (40 overs, 9 wkt)	**200**

1/20, 2/22, 3/66, 4/95, 5/128, 6/139, 7/159, 8/178, 9/186

Bowling: Thomas 8-1-34-1; Bastien 8-0-24-1; Dale 8-0-55-1; Foster 8-1-37-2; Richards 8-0-43-3.

Umpires: D.J. Constant and R.C. Tolchard

WORCESTERSHIRE v DURHAM

Championship match
New Road, Worcester, 21, 22, 24 August 1992
Toss: Durham. Match drawn

Durham

W. Larkins b Lampitt	40	lbw b Radford	13
P.W.G. Parker c Tolley b Radford	1	lbw b D'Oliveira	94
P. Bainbridge c Rhodes b Radford	20	not out	20
M.P. Briers c Rhodes b Radford	0	not out	11
S. Hutton c Weston b Tolley	2		
I. Smith b Lampitt	44		
C.W. Scott† c Curtis b Radford	30		
D.A. Graveney* c D'Oliveira b Radford	9		
J. Wood run out	28		
S.M. McEwan c Rhodes b Newport	7		
S.J.E. Brown not out	0		
Extras (LB 2, NB 16)	18	(B 8, LB 3, NB 5)	16
TOTAL	**199**	(2 wkt)	**199**

1/2, 2/29, 3/29, 4/32, 5/104, 6/126, 7/152, 8/169, 9/198   1/15, 2/160

Bowling: *First innings*— Radford 21-3-60-5; Tolley 12-4-26-1; Newport 15-1-62-1; Lampitt 9.3-2-35-2; Stemp 9-6-14-0. *Second innings*— Radford 7-0-21-1; Newport 12-4-41-0; Tolley 4-1-16-0; Lampitt 6.3-0-38-0; Stemp 4-1-36-0; Weston 6-1-17-0; D'Oliveira 7-2-19-1.

Worcestershire

T.S. Curtis* b Graveney	50
W.P.C. Weston b Graveney	34
D.A. Leatherdale c Graveney b Brown	20
D.B. D'Oliveira b Smith	81
G.R. Haynes c Scott b Smith	41
S.J. Rhodes† not out	24
S.R. Lampitt c Smith b Bainbridge	4
P.J. Newport not out	25
C.M. Tolley	
N.V. Radford	
R.D. Stemp	
Extras (B 1, LB 7, W 2, NB 5)	15
TOTAL (6 wkt dec.)	**294**

1/82, 2/87, 3/147, 4/236, 5/237, 6/246

Bowling: Wood 14-3-53-0; Brown 15.2-1-69-1; McEwan 21-1-70-0; Graveney 30-16-49-2; Briers 1-0-7-0; Smith 8-2-26-2; Bainbridge 7-2-12-1.

Umpires: J.H. Harris and J.W. Holder

WORCESTERSHIRE v DURHAM

Sunday League match
New Road, Worcester, 23 August 1992
Toss: Worcestershire.   No result – match abandoned (rain)

Durham

W. Larkins c Rhodes b Weston	2
J.D. Glendenen lbw b Radford	33
P. Bainbridge c Rhodes b Weston	5
S. Hutton not out	29
M.P. Briers lbw b Radford	0
I. Smith c Tolley b Radford	3
C.W. Scott† not out	8
J. Wood	
D.A. Graveney*	
S.M. McEwan	
S.P. Hughes	
Extras (LB 5, W 9)	14
TOTAL (23 overs, 5 wkt)	**94**

1/19, 2/35, 3/53, 4/53, 5/72
Bowling: Haynes 2-0-15-0; Weston 8-0-27-2; Radford 8-0-27-3; Stemp 3-0-13-0; Newport 2-0-7-0.

Worcestershire

T.S. Curtis*
D.B. D'Oliveira
D.A. Leatherdale
G.R. Haynes
M.J. Weston
S.J. Rhodes†
P.J. Newport
S.R. Lampitt
N.V. Radford
C.M. Tolley
R.D. Stemp

Umpires: J.H. Harris and J.W. Holder

196

DURHAM v HAMPSHIRE

Feethams, Darlington, 26, 27, 28, 29 August 1992
Toss: Hampshire. Match drawn

Hampshire

First innings		Second innings	
T.C. Middleton not out	127	c. McEwan b S.J.E. Brown	12
K.D. James c Larkins b S.J.E. Brown	3	c Larkins b Briers	57
D.I. Gower b Bainbridge	28	c Bainbridge b Hughes	39
R.A. Smith b McEwan	1	c G.K. Brown b Hughes	3
M.C.J. Nicholas* lbw b McEwan	0	not out	95
J.R. Ayling c Graveney b Hughes	90	lbw b Briers	0
A.N. Aymes† lbw b S.J.E. Brown	0	not out	4
R.J. Maru not out	23		
I.J. Turner			
C.A. Connor			
K.J. Shine			
Extras (B1, LB 7, W 11, NB 2)	21	(B 9, LB 8, W 2)	19
TOTAL (6 wkt dec.)	303	(5 wkt dec.)	229

1/7, 2/70, 3/71, 4/71, 5/266, 6/268

1/20, 2/87, 3/97, 4/198, 5/210

Bowling: *First innings*—Hughes 28.3-7-80-1; S.J.E. Brown 20-4-72-2; Bainbridge 14-4-46-1; McEwan 27-6-75-2; Graveney 5-1-13-0; Smith 3-0-9-0. *Second innings*—S.J.E. Brown 12-1-40-1; Hughes 16-1-45-2; Bainbridge 2-1-3-0; McEwan 8-1-30-0; Briers 8-0-30-2; G.K. Brown 5-1-39-0; Parker 2-0-25-0.

Durham

First innings		Second innings	
W. Larkins b Connor	0	b Shine	11
G.K. Brown b Ayling	10	lbw b Ayling	39
P.W.G. Parker c Smith b James	68	lbw b Shine	6
M.P. Briers c Turner b Ayling	5	c Aymes b Shine	2
P. Bainbridge not out	84	c Aymes b Shine	83
I. Smith not out	68	b Maru	4
C.W. Scott†		lbw b Shine	18
S.M. McEwan		b Maru	0
S.J.E. Brown		b Shine	3
D.A. Graveney*		not out	3
S.P. Hughes		not out	9
Extras (LB 6, W 3, NB 6)	15	(LB 10, W 1, NB 8)	19
TOTAL (4 wkt dec.)	250	(8 wkt)	194

1/0, 2/38, 3/44, 4/136

1/21, 2/34, 3/36, 4/102, 5/169, 6/178, 7/178, 8/178

Bowling: *First innings*—Connor 16.2-2-55-1; Shine 12-3-48-0; Ayling 10-3-24-2; Turner 13-2-46-0; James 8-3-29-1; Maru 20-4-42-0. *Second innings*—Connor 12-1-55-0; Shine 17-2-68-6; Turner 6-2-17-0; Ayling 11-3-35-1; Maru 5-2-9-1.

Umpires: G.I. Burgess and R.A. White

DURHAM v PAKISTAN

International Floodlit match
International Stadium, Gateshead, 25 August 1992
Toss: Pakistan. Pakistan won by 58 runs

Pakistan

Aamir Sohail c Bainbridge b McEwan	22
Shoaib Mohammed* run out	34
Zahid Fazal lbw b McEwan	3
Inzamam-ul-Haq run out	15
Asif Mujtaba c McEwan b Smith	1
Naved Anjum c and b Berry	38
Moin Khan† c McEwan b Berry	2
Waqar Younis c Scott b Berry	23
Mushtaq Ahmed c McEwan b Berry	37
Aqib Javed c Larkins b Smith	28
Ata-ur-Rehman not out	2
Extras (B4, LB 5, W 3)	12
TOTAL (38.3 overs)	217

1/25, 2/31, 3/56, 4/61, 5/116, 6/119, 7/122, 8/166, 9/215

Bowling: Brown 6-0-32-0; McEwan 6-0-27-2; Bainbridge 6-0-40-0; Smith 7-1-26-2; Berry 7.3-0-39-4; Graveney 6-0-44-0.

Durham

W. Larkins c Naved Anjum b Waqar Younis	11
G.K. Brown c Asif Mujtaba b Mushtaq Ahmed	26
P.W.G. Parker b Mushtaq Ahmed	44
M.P. Briers lbw b Naved Anjum	17
P. Bainbridge b Ata-ur-Rehman	21
I. Smith c Aqib Javed b Ata-ur-Rehman	8
C.W. Scott† c Mushtaq Ahmed b Waqar Younis	12
P.J. Berry b Waqar Younis	0
S.M. McEwan lbw b Waqar Younis	3
S.J.E. Brown not out	1
D.A. Graveney* b Waqar Younis	16
Extras (B 2, LB 8, W 6)	16
TOTAL (35.5 overs)	159

1/23, 2/95, 3/96, 4/96, 5/127, 6/137, 7/149, 8/150, 9/157

Bowling: Waqar Younis 5.5-0-13-5; Aqib Javed 6-0-18-0; Ata-ur-Rehman 8-0-33-2; Naved Anjum 8-0-31-1; Mushtaq Ahmed 8-1-54-2.

Umpires: S.B. Hassan and R. Nevin

DURHAM v YORKSHIRE

Sunday League match

Feethams, Darlington, 30 August 1992

No result: match abandoned without a ball bowled

Durham (from)
I.T. Botham
W. Larkins
P. Bainbridge
P.W.G. Parker
I. Smith
J.D. Glendenen
S. Hutton
A.R. Fothergill†
D.A. Graveney*
S.M. McEwan
S.P. Hughes
S.J.E. Brown

Yorkshire (from)
M.D. Moxon*
S.A. Kellett
R.J. Blakey†
A.A. Metcalfe
D. Byas
C. White
P.W. Jarvis
C.S. Pickles
P.J. Hartley
J.D. Batty
A.P. Grayson
M.A. Robinson

Umpires: G.I. Burgess and R.A. White

YORKSHIRE v DURHAM

Joshua Tetley Trophy match

North Marine Road, Scarborough, 5 September 1992

Toss: Durham.   Yorkshire won by 9 wickets

Durham
W. Larkins c Hartley b Jarvis 103
P.W.G. Parker b Pickles 40
I. Smith b Carrick 30
P. Bainbridge b Jarvis 16
I.T. Botham not out 25
J.A. Daley c Hartley b Jarvis 8
C.W. Scott† run out 5
P.W. Henderson
P.J. Berry
D.A. Graveney*
S.J.E. Brown
Extras ((LB 9, W8) 17
TOTAL   (50 overs, 6 wkt) **244**
1/90, 2/173, 3/198, 4/206, 5/228 6/224

Bowling: Robinson 10-1-25-0; Hartley 10-0-45-0; Pickles 10-0-62-1; Jarvis 10-0-52-3; Carrick 10-0-51-1.

Yorkshire
M.D. Moxon* c Graveney b Brown 108
S.A. Kellett not out 109
D. Byas not out 19
A.A. Matcalfe
R.J. Blakey†
C. White
P.W. Jarvis
C.S. Pickles
P. Carrick
P.J. Hartley
M.A. Robinson
Extras (B 3, LB 3, W 6) 12
TOTAL   (1 wkt) (48.1 overs, 1 wkt) **248**
1/217

Bowling: Botham 10-2-29-0; Brown 10-0-62-1; Henderson 8-0-39-0; Graveney 10-0-42-0; Berry 4-0-27-0; Bainbridge 3-0-21-0; Smith 3-0-18-0; Parker 0-1-0-4-0.
Umpires: J.H. Hampshire and B. Leadbeater

SOMERSET v DURHAM

Championship match

County Ground, Taunton, 7, 8, 9, 10 September 1992

Toss: Durham. Somerset won by 8 wickets

Somerset

		First innings		Second innings	
A.N. Hayhurst	c Scott b Hughes	102			
M.N. Lathwell	c Daley b Henderson	50	c. Graveney b Brown	8	
R.J. Harden	c Henderson b Smith	126	c Parker b Brown		
C.J. Tavaré*	c Parker b Brown	124			
R.J. Turner†	c Parker b Hughes	0			
N.D. Burns	c Graveney b Bainbridge	54			
G.D. Rose	c Daley b Smith	33	(3) not out	8	
R.P. Snell	c Smith b Hughes	1	(4) not out	1	
N.A. Mallender	b Hughes	33			
A.R. Caddick	c Sub b Brown	33			
A.P. Van Troost	not out	9		0	
Extras	(LB 5, W 4)	9			
TOTAL		**534**	(2 wkt)	**25**	

1/96, 2/285, 3/285, 4/287, 5/375, 6/450, 7/450, 8/454, 9/514

1/16, 2/17

Bowling: First innings—Botham 11-2-45-0; Brown 22.1-3-115-2; Henderson 23-5-110-1; Hughes 32-5-112-4; Graveney 12-1-46-0; Bainbridge 14-5-31-1; Smith 21-6-70-2. Second innings—Brown 3-0-13-2; Henderson 2-0-12-0.

Durham

		First innings		Second innings	
W. Larkins	c Burns b Mallender	0	lbw b Lathwell	117	
P.W.G. Parker	c Snell b Caddick	16	c Mallender b Caddick	10	
I. Smith	c Rose b Snell	110	c Burns b Snell	7	
P. Bainbridge	c Burns b Caddick	0	c Tavaré b Snell	0	
J.A. Daley	lbw b Mallender	5	c Harden b Caddick	88	
C.W. Scott†	not out	10	absent hurt	—	
P.W. Henderson	c and b Mallender	0	c Burns b Caddick	0	
I.T. Botham	b Mallender	4	(6) c Lathwell b Mallender	74	
D.A. Graveney*	c Burns b Caddick	29	(8) c Tavaré b Caddick	3	
S.P. Hughes	c Snell b Mallender	24	(9) hit wicket b Snell	4	
S.J.E. Brown	lbw b Caddick	8	(10) not out	19	
Extras	(B 4, LB 2, NB 7)	13	(LB 10, NB 7)	17	
TOTAL		**219**	(9 wkts)	**339**	

1/0, 2/23, 3/23, 4/44, 5/61, 6/69, 7/175, 8/185, 9/197

1/12, 2/29, 3/29, 4/230, 5/234, 6/255, 7/279, 8/309, 9/339

Bowling: First innings—Mallender 13.4-2-65-5; Caddick 14-1-62-4; Snell 9-2-39-1; Van Troost 4-0-31-0; Rose 4-1-16-0. Second innings—Caddick 24-9-53-4; Snell 22-3-81-3; Rose 19-2-75-0; Van Troost 4-0-22-0; Lathwell 12-2-41-1; Mallender 13.1-3-26-1; Hayhurst 8-0-31-0.

Umpires: R. Julian and G. Sharp

DURHAM v LANCASHIRE

Championship match

Eastwood gardens, Gateshead Fell, 12, 13, 14, 15 September 1992

Toss: Durham. Lancashire won by 10 wickets

Durham

		First innings		Second innings	
W. Larkins	c Fairbrother b DeFreitas	53	lbw b Martin	24	
P.W.G. Parker	lbw b Watkinson	70	b DeFreitas	52	
I. Smith	lbw b DeFreitas	0	lbw b DeFreitas	15	
P. Bainbridge	c Watkinson b DeFreitas	18	c Hegg b DeFreitas	18	
J.A. Daley	run out	17	not out	80	
J.D. Glendenen	c Speak b Watkinson	76	lbw b Austin	43	
M.P. Briers	lbw b Watkinson	15	b Austin	7	
A.R. Fothergill†	lbw b Watkinson	0	c Hegg b DeFreitas	0	
D.A. Graveney*	b Austin	0	c Hegg b Austin	0	
S.P. Hughes	c Hegg b Watkinson	42	b De Freitas	0	
S.J.E. Brown	not out	6	c Hegg b DeFreitas	18	
Extras	(B 1, LB 10, NB 4)	15	(10) (B 7, LB 3, NB 4)	14	
TOTAL		**312**		**271**	

1/104, 2/104, 3/156, 4/148, 5/172, 6/206, 7/210, 8/217, 9/293

1/57, 2/88, 3/102, 4/121, 5/222, 6/238, 7/239, 8/243, 9/244

Bowling: First innings—DeFreitas 26-7-94-3; Martin 19-5-62-0; Watkinson 24.1-7-63-5; Austin 22-11-52-1; Barnett 11-1-30-0. Second innings—DeFreitas 26.3-6-94-6; Martin 16-4-49-1; Watkinson 14-3-56-0; Austin 15-4-44-3; Barnett 7-3-18-0.

Lancashire

		First innings		Second innings	
G.D. Mendis	st Fothergill b Bainbridge	45	not out	2	
M.A. Atherton	c Fothergill b Bainbridge	199	not out	22	
N.J. Speak	b Smith	20			
N.H. Fairbrother*	lbw b Hughes	46			
M. Watkinson	c Larkins b Bainbridge	2			
G.D. Lloyd	lbw b Smith	16			
W.K. Hegg†	b Smith	133			
P.J. Martin	c Smith b Brown	22			
P.A.J. DeFreitas	c Brown b Bainbridge	58			
I.D. Austin	c Larkins b Bainbridge	7			
A.A. Barnett	not out	14			
Extras	(B 2, LB 9, W 2, NB 1)				
TOTAL		**562**	(0 wkt)	**24**	

1/71, 2/108, 3/113, 4/175, 5/188, 6/220, 7/463, 8/485, 9/546

Bowling: First innings—Brown 28-4-137-1; Hughes 36-2-136-1; Bainbridge 27.1-4-100-5; Briers 12-2-31-0; Smith 38-7-85-3; Graveney 20-3-62-0. Second innings—Hughes 3-1-14-0; Smith 2-0-6-0; Parker 0.1-0-4-0.

Umpires: H.D. Bird and J.H. Hampshire

Appendix C

Durham 1st XI Averages

DURHAM COUNTY CRICKET CLUB

1st XI First-Class Averages, 1992

Batting (Qualification 10 innings)

	Matches	Inns	NO	Runs	H/S	Avge	50's	100's
D.M. Jones	14	23	7	**1179**	157	73.68	5	4
P. Bainbridge	17	30	9	**923**	92*	43.95	8	–
P.W.G. Parker	20	35	2	**1331**	124	40.33	8	3
W. Larkins	22	41	0	**1536**	143	37.46	8	4
I.T. Botham	15	23	2	**705**	105	33.57	4	1
I. Smith	12	16	1	**435**	110	29.00	2	1
S. Hutton	8	15	0	**406**	78	27.06	2	–
C.W. Scott†	18	24	5	**433**	57*	22.78	2	–
J.D. Glendenen	17	28	1	**607**	117	22.48	3	1
M.P. Briers	16	28	4	**460**	62*	19.16	4	–
S.J.E. Brown	20	24	13	**197**	47*	17.90	–	–
P.J. Berry	9	15	3	**205**	76	17.08	1	–
D.A. Graveney	21	29	9	**333**	36	16.65	–	–
S.P. Hughes	20	25	5	**229**	42	11.45	–	–
S.M. McEwan	10	13	1	**59**	22	4.91	–	–

Also batted:

	Matches	Inns	NO	Runs	H/S	Avge	50's	100's
J.A. Daley	2	4	1	**190**	88	63.33	2	–
G.K. Brown	4	6	0	**136**	48	22.66	–	–
P.W. Henderson	5	7	0	**119**	46	17.00	–	–
J. Wood	8	6	1	**60**	28	16.00	–	–
A.R. Fothergill†	6	8	1	**71**	23	10.14	–	–

Bowling (Qualification 8 wickets)

	Overs	Mdns	Runs	Wkts	Avge	B/B	5wi
I. Smith	90	20	242	**8**	30.25	3-85	–
J. Wood	134.2	17	534	**17**	31.41	5-68	1
S.J.E. Brown	509.1	75	1973	**58**	34.01	7-105	3
P.J. Berry	178.3	27	649	**17**	38.17	7-113	1
P.W. Henderson	96	14	405	**10**	40.50	3-59	–
P. Bainbridge	188.1	39	569	**14**	40.64	5-100	1
I.T. Botham	322	62	1083	**26**	41.65	4-72	–
D.A. Graveney	380.4	87	1201	**28**	42.89	3-22	–
S.M. McEwan	229	44	800	**17**	47.05	3-52	–
S.P. Hughes	548.3	98	1672	**34**	49.17	5-25	–
M.P. Briers	144.3	22	621	**12**	51.75	3-109	–

Also bowled: G.K. Brown 9-1-64-0; S. Hutton 0.1-0-4-0; D.M. Jones 18.1-1-71-1; W. Larkins 2-1-4-0; P.W.G. Parker 3.2-0-31-0.

* Denotes Not Out

Sunday League Averages, 1992

Batting (Qualification 4 innings)

	Matches	Inns	NO	Runs	H/S	Avge	50's	100's
D.M. Jones	11	10	2	**656**	114	82.00	5	2
J.D. Glendenen	15	13	2	**424**	78	38.54	3	–
I.T. Botham	13	12	0	**368**	67	30.66	3	–
P.W.G. Parker	12	11	2	**242**	82	26.88	1	–
M.P. Briers	7	6	0	**147**	69	24.50	1	–
W. Larkins	16	15	0	**357**	86	23.80	3	–
A.R. Fothergill†	15	11	4	**160**	42*	22.85	–	–
P. Bainbridge	8	7	0	**148**	57	21.14	1	–
S.P. Hughes	16	4	3	**16**	10*	16.00	–	–
I. Smith	10	10	2	**126**	26	15.75	–	–
S.M. McEwan	14	7	4	**40**	18	13.33	–	–
D.A. Graveney	13	4	2	**26**	11*	13.00	–	–

Also batted: S. Hutton 107 runs from 3 innings, 2 not out; G. Cook, 64 runs from 2 innings.

Bowling (Qualification 5 wickets)

	Overs	Mdns	Runs	Wkts	Avge	B/B
S.P. Hughes	108.2	2	545	**21**	25.95	3-26
D.A. Graveney	72,3	1	365	**14**	26.07	3-40
I.T. Botham	81.5	1	401	**14**	28.64	3-37
S.J.E. Brown	73	0	393	**11**	35.72	3-32
S.M. McEwan	80	4	435	**11**	39.54	3-27
P. Bainbridge	45	2	276	**5**	55.20	2-41

Also bowled: P.J. Berry 8-0-35-1; J. Wood 19-0-117-3; D.M. Jones 6.1-0-41-1; I. Smith 27-1-171-4; P.W. Henderson 21-0-137-3; G. Wigham 8-1-43-1; M.P. Briers 13-0-95-1.

Principal Benson & Hedges Cup Averages, 1992

Batting

	Matches	Inns	NO	Runs	H/S	Avge	50's
S.M. McEwan	4	4	3	**51**	29*	51.00	–
I.T. Botham	4	4	0	**166**	86	41.50	2
W. Larkins	4	4	0	**150**	73	37.50	2
J.D. Glendenen	4	4	0	**132**	60	33.00	1
P.W.G. Parker	4	4	0	**75**	22	18.75	–
P. Bainbridge	4	4	0	**70**	27	17.50	–
A.R. Fothergill†	3	3	1	**32**	17	16.00	–
D.M. Jones	4	4	0	**25**	13	6.25	–

Bowling

	Overs	Mdns	Runs	Wkts	Avge	B/B
S.P. Hughes	39	3	145	**7**	20.71	2-31
I.T. Botham	39	7	114	**4**	28.50	2-21
S.M. McEwan	36	3	154	**5**	30.80	3-45
P. Bainbridge	36	1	160	**5**	32.00	4-38
S.J.E. Brown	37	4	129	**4**	32.25	2-36